Lord Mountcashel: Irish General

Lord Mountcashel: Irish General

Justin MacCarthy in the service of James II and Louis XIV, 1673–1694

D.P. Graham

Pen & Sword
MILITARY

First published in Great Britain in 2018 by
Pen & Sword Military
an imprint of
Pen & Sword Books Ltd
47 Church Street
Barnsley
South Yorkshire
S70 2AS

ISBN 978 1 52672 300 0

A CIP catalogue record for this book is available from the British Library.

Printed and bound in the UK by TJ International Ltd, Padstow, Cornwall

Pen & Sword Books Limited incorporates the imprints of Atlas, Archaeology, Aviation, Discovery, Family History, Fiction, History, Maritime, Military, Military Classics, Politics, Select, Transport, True Crime, Air World, Frontline Publishing, Leo Cooper, Remember When, Seaforth Publishing, The Praetorian Press, Wharncliffe Local History, Wharncliffe Transport, Wharncliffe True Crime and White Owl.

For a complete list of Pen & Sword titles please contact
PEN & SWORD BOOKS LIMITED
47 Church Street, Barnsley, South Yorkshire, S70 2AS, England
E-mail: enquiries@pen-and-sword.co.uk
Website: www.pen-and-sword.co.uk

Contents

A Note on Dates and Places

The period covered in this work relates to a time when the English calendar lagged ten days behind the rest of Europe. Matters were made more complex by the fact that the New Year in England commenced on 25 March.

The reasons behind such a discrepancy are complex; the Gregorian calendar adopted in 1582 by many European countries was not adopted in Britain and Ireland. By the 1680s then, there was a ten-day 'gap' between England and the rest of Europe. The drift had enlarged to eleven days by the mid-eighteenth century when the calendar was finally adopted in Britain and Ireland. Until that time many contemporary writers gave both dates and, in some instances, both years. On other occasions they would distinguish between Old Style dating (O.S.) and New Style European dating (N.S.)

Modern convention tends to stress the importance of 'New Style' dates. I have in this work, however, used both. The reasoning behind this stems from the nature of the original source material and the fact that the battles and strategic manoeuvring outlined in the text hinge so much on the intricacies of dates and times. Rather than change every date, I have kept the original style not only to add a note of authenticity but also to avoid making major changes in the chapters related to Ireland. English and Irish dates will then be old style as per the source material whilst dates related to European sources for Irish troops serving in France will invariably be new style.

Mountcashel's main clash in Ireland, the Battle of Newtownbutler, also raises some questions. The town was called *Newtown* until 1715 when Theophilus Butler was created baron of the area. That said, the battle is popularly and colloquially known as *Newtownbutler* – having been more succinctly analysed and discussed in the following centuries, well after the name change. In order to avoid confusion for those readers who are familiar with other books and publications on the period, where the battle is invariably referred to with the more recent name, I have used *Newtownbutler* throughout.

Introduction

My fascination with the life of Justin MacCarthy, Lord Mountcashel, began a number of years ago whilst carrying out research related to the Battle of Newtownbutler, fought during the Jacobite War in Ireland in 1689. It was at this time that I encountered the commander of the Irish Jacobite forces there. Mountcashel's story is as complex and ironic as that period of Irish and English history within which it is set. His father, a major player in the 1641 conflict that was fought in Ireland alongside the English Civil War, was clever enough to escape Cromwell's wrath and with his lands mostly intact. His sons would see the restoration of the monarchy and Justin would gain military experience in the troubled Europe of the 1670s before witnessing the attempt by James II to gain greater freedoms for his Catholic subjects – an action which the English aristocracy would not forgive.

He also played an important role in the subsequent war in Ireland, especially in its early stages, before taking the first Irish Brigade to France, a group of exiles whose legacy would last until the Napoleonic wars. Indeed, an analysis of French communication at the time would indicate that Justin's destiny always lay on the continent. The French had a particular interest in him and not simply because of his experience and knowledge of French methods (having fought under the famous Turenne). The Irish troops, the last 'Wild Geese' of the seventeenth century needed a strong dependable leader. That leader would prove to be Lord Mountcashel. The journey that Justin takes to reach that position however, in the midst of wars between kings and peaks in religious intolerance, is fascinating. His presence at Newtownbutler is today the most popular reference to the Irish general – perhaps an undeserved legacy. I therefore aim with this work to analyse Mountcashel's life both before and after the fateful battle, in the context of the larger war of the time, Irish and European politics, and his relative success as a soldier and commander.

Justin's story then parallels the troubled history of the British Isles and Europe in the late seventeenth century, which although not a currently 'popular' focus for military history, would plant the political seeds of the fledgling British Empire to follow. This is the story of an Irish general, a man betrayed and defeated, yet able to rise above the odds stacked against him and retain a sense of patriotic duty in a desperate situation where his cause was all but doomed. Admired by the French though at times despised by his enemies, Mountcashel's choices echo the times and the troubled history in the context of the religious war in Ireland, the battleground of Louis XIV's European diversion and the focus of James II's flawed attempts to regain a throne that was all but lost forever. The repercussions of these decisions would form the fate of Lord Mountcashel and so many of his men who went to France to fight for Louis. This is their story as much as it his.

Chapter I

The Early Years

Justin MacCarthy was born in the Irish province of Munster in the early 1640s. This is of course an estimate since no reliable record exists as to his actual birth date, as with so many of his contemporaries. His father was Donough MacCarthy, Lord Muskerry, a powerful man in Munster, the most southerly of Ireland's four provinces. At the time of his birth, Justin's father was embroiled in the complex struggle that was emerging in the Ireland of the 1640s, a time of revolution, where the ostensibly Royalist supporting Catholics sought a resolution of the land question and a debate over their religious freedoms. The ensuing conflict would parallel, and have resounding implications for, the conduct of the English Civil War, fought on the other side of the Irish Sea. The MacCarthy family bore a noble lineage and had been one of the most powerful ancient clans in Ireland. By force of arms they had been kings in ancient Munster. Irish legend speaks of their descent from Heber, son of the legendary Milesius, reputedly one of the founders of the land over 900 years before the arrival of the Normans. Other tales tell of their ancestry having been converted to Christianity by Saint Patrick himself. Despite the legends, however, it is known that Munster was split between the royal houses of Desmond (the MacCarthys) in the southern part of the province and that of Thomond (the O'Briens) in the north, from the third century until the coming of the Normans in the twelfth century.

This split and the inevitable feuding that followed can be traced back to the second century AD. The direct ancestor of the MacCarthy family is Eoghan More, son of Olioll Olum, King of Munster in the second century. King Olioll divided Munster between his two sons Eoghan, whose clan would become the MacCarthys – Princes of Desmond, and Cormac whose clan of Dalcassian Princes of Thomond would become the O'Briens. In theory, the Kingship of Munster would alternate between each clan through the years, though this of course would prove to be a futile romantic notion. Indeed, endless feuding between clans would be the all but inevitable result of such an arrangement. The name *MacCarthy* would be derived from one of the Desmond Kings, Carthach, who ruled just prior to the arrival of the Normans in 1169. His great grandson Diarmuid More (Dermot is the more modern derivation) was known as King of Cork and Prince of Desmond at the time of the Normans' arrival in Ireland. Internal feuding in Munster between the noble houses made the job of conquering the area all the easier for the newly arrived English, and Dermot surrendered Cork to King Henry II in 1172. Pope Adrian IV had encouraged the English incursion, giving Henry the authority to settle certain inconsistencies with the Church in Ireland. After some bloody encounters throughout the country, most of the Irish Chiefs submitted to the English King. Henry would turn Cork into a walled medieval city in true contemporary style. The MacCarthys were to lose substantial amounts of their territory to the English, and Dermot's subsequent attempt to retake Cork in 1185 was to result in his death.

The resultant uneasy peace in Munster, however, would be fleeting, as feuding between the MacCarthys and the Fitzgeralds of Desmond would continue unabated for almost two centuries. The MacCarthys still remained relatively powerful in the region however. By the fourteenth century Cormac More MacCarthy headed the clan. He had two sons. Daniel, the eldest, would become chief after his father and go on to hold land in Killarney and County Kerry. His younger brother Dermot would found the house of Muskerry. By the fifteenth century, the Muskerry branch of the family dwelt in Blarney Castle and controlled a large part of County Cork, their ancestral home.

Blarney Castle is famous today for the good luck associated with the legendary Blarney stone and is still a major Irish tourist attraction. It is believed that a structure existed there as early as the tenth century. Initially a wooden fort or lodge, it later developed into a small stone construction. This was destroyed in the 1440s when the building of a more permanent castle began. Castle building, another of the Normans' favourite pastimes, had become fashionable in Ireland by this time. Blarney Castle was constructed by another Dermot, the King of Munster. Born in 1411, he was known as Dermot Laidir or Dermot the Strong, the fourth Lord of Muskerry, and builder of another castle at Kilcrea. He also appears to have been a generous benefactor as far as the Catholic Church was concerned, constructing a Franciscan abbey at Kilcrea. Even the newly arrived English settlers and colonists looked to his protection in Munster, for which they paid a tribute. This 'Prince of distinguished valour' was laid to rest there in 1494 after having ruled for forty years, in what would become the traditional resting place of the MacCarthys.

For the next century, the family adhered to the traditional Irish clan's way of life at the time, i.e. intermittent cycles of bloody violence conducted with both their neighbours and the English. Cormac Óg Laidir would become the fifth Lord. He suffered at the hands of James, Earl of Desmond, who attacked Muskerry lands in 1521. Cormac defeated James near Mourne Abbey, though the apparently senseless feuding went on unabated. Even by the time of the seventh Lord, Dermot MacCarthy, vicious fighting with the Earl of Desmond was still commonplace, in this case with Sir Maurice of Desmond, his own father-in-law. Irish fighting had little room for sentiment, however, and Dermot's men killed Sir Maurice after capturing him during a feud. Dermot was given the official title of Knight of the Realm by the Earl of Essex in 1558.

By the time of the succession of the eighth Lord of Muskerry, Queen Elizabeth I held power in England, and had little time for petty Irish squabbles, seeing the country as a land of savagery and mindless conflict. She did, however, demand that all Irish chiefs, be they declared lords or knights, should now agree to own their lands under legal tenancy from her. Cormac Teige MacCarthy, the new Lord in Blarney Castle, would not submit to the Queen's demand, but had no intention of admitting this. Cormac, evidently more of a politician and diplomat than his predecessors, answered the Queen's demands with flattery and obsequious compliments, rather than address the content of her demands. Thus began the use of a word that would enter the English language when she described his flattery as mere 'Blarney', perhaps the earliest version of what we would now politely call 'bovine excreta'.

Cormac's power was now considerable in Munster, and he could call on over 3,000 men-at-arms when the situation demanded. With continual border feuding still unchecked, this would be no idle boast but a matter of defensive necessity. Ever adept at political manoeuvring, Cormac stayed on the right side of the English. He fought for them when Spanish troops landed at Kinsale in 1601 in their vain attempt to aid Hugh O'Neill and Hugh O'Donnell. It was a delicate political balancing act and, despite being accused of consorting with the Spanish and thrown into prison, Cormac was later pardoned. He was knighted by the Lords Justices of Ireland and, before his death in 1616, had also earned the title of Baron of Blarney, a nobleman of the finest Irish lineage, who had led the clan for thirty-three years. He left two sons, Cormac, who would become the ninth Lord, and his younger brother Donald. Cormac died in 1640 and was succeeded by his son Donough MacCarthy, Justin MacCarthy's father.[1]

Donough would play a major, if not decisive, role in the 1640s during the civil wars that engulfed Ireland. Beginning with the 1641 rebellion and ending with the Cromwellian invasion of 1649 and its long aftermath, Ireland would see little peace for a decade or more. It is important therefore to provide an analysis, however brief, of the events that shaped the life of Donough MacCarthy while his youngest son was still but an infant. The 1640s would bear witness to political events and an orgy of violence and conflict unparalleled in the British Isles. The war that had its roots in Scotland would move to England and have an effect on the fragile peace in Ireland until a decade of conflict and violent political machinations would result in the death of King Charles I at the hands of the English parliamentarians.

From the Norman invasion until the time of the Tudors the English colonists had been almost imperceptibly absorbed into the Irish population, and had thus become part of the Irish identity rather than distinctly English. This had not been planned, however. In fact, the English crown had tried to impose its customs and society on the Irish, not to mention its language. The Irish in turn showed such implicit resistance to these changes over the years that only force could be used to instil an English identity of sorts. Despite the later moves of Queen Elizabeth I in Ulster and the imposition of English law, many clans remained loyal to their Irish chieftains. Only fear of Elizabeth's continued colonisation policy forced many of the chiefs to swear allegiance to the crown by 1585, and the native Irish were pushed farther and farther to the west. It took the later decades of the century and a number of costly campaigns to complete the conquest. The fruitful lands of choice were given to the new colonists. Despite rebellion (notably the nine-years-war, 1594–1603), by 1603 and the accession of the Stuarts in England, Ireland was essentially an English province. Disarmed and effectively hamstrung, the Irish could only look abroad for aid if they sought to further demonstrate their consternation at English dominance.

The colonial situation had left its mark on the country, however, in the form of the 'old English'. Many of these were original settlers who, in the absence of strict English control, had become a form of Irish elite. By the beginning of the seventeenth century, the mass of the Irish population were committed Catholics, as were most of the old English. The Irish were still frustrated by the eternal debate with England over their religious and political aims. Loyalty to the crown contrasted with religious loyalties on a scale that could not easily be compared with the rest of the British Isles, where there had been no confiscation (or otherwise) of land or colonial plantation. Scotland and England would have different reasons for going to war.

Despite the fomenting of rebellion and the occasional uprising, the situation at the start of the century would remain static for many years. By the 1620s and 30s, the social elite, both native Irish nobles and old English, had common aims in that they understood that their grievances could only be resolved through negotiation with the English crown. In terms of public office and wealth, however, the 'new' English Protestant settlers had supplanted the old English. In Munster the most important Irish Catholic nobles of the time were Viscount Fermoy and Donough MacCarthy, Viscount Muskerry. Gaelic and old English Protestants also held much of the power in the south, namely the Earl of Thomond and Murrough O'Brien, Earl of Inchiquin. The continued strength of the English throne lay not in numbers, however (Catholics outnumbered Protestants by six-to-one in Cork), but in their holding of public office and wealth through land. Imagine then how fragile this situation must have been, established only through loyalty to King Charles I; a situation only marginally held in check, with ongoing stability hanging by a thread.

A contemporary print of Justin MacCarthy (after imprint in O'Callaghan, J.C., *History of the Irish Brigades in the Service of France*), based on Peter de Lily's earlier portrait.

In 1633 Sir Thomas Wentworth was made Lord Lieutenant of Ireland. This would herald a new phase in Anglo-Irish politics as Wentworth made it his aim to enforce religious conformity along the Church of England's lines, and to make the country financially sound. He would also attempt to bring 'civilisation' to Ireland by revitalising the plantation and increasing the number of Protestant settlers. He could only do this by tampering with the already fragile state of landholding title, an act that would unite both Protestant and Catholic nobles and result in Wentworth's downfall by 1640. It is an example, however, of how fragile the entire 'house of cards' remained. Many Englishmen felt as Wentworth did, that the king did not take Ireland seriously enough in terms of its religious and political distance from England. In reality, England lacked the money and resources to do more than govern Ireland from afar. The resulting gap between policy and intent left Ireland in an essentially powerful position should the king be in need of aid during a crisis.

By 1641 around sixty per cent of Ireland was owned by the Catholic noble families that had been settled there for centuries. In the next twenty years, the results of the English Civil War, the Cromwellian expansion and penal laws would reduce this markedly. The war had its roots in Scotland and the first and second 'Bishop's Wars' where Scottish Covenanters rebelled against what they saw as Royalist attacks on their religious liberties. The Scottish element of the conflict is indicative of the war in some respects, where local political and religious grievances would become the focus of rebellion and conflict. The wars in the three kingdoms of England, Scotland and Ireland were unconnected to the savagery of the earlier Thirty Years War in Europe though those warring parties' own combination of interlocking religious conflict and vying of rival groups for power were echoed in the course of the civil wars in the British Isles.

Many commentators point to Charles I being the architect of his own folly due to the general weakness of his monarchy. The King of England after all was the keystone to society, its laws and the governance of its regions, including Ireland. When rebellious forces were unleashed, the weakness of the monarchy would be exploited, and in Ireland there were many powerful lobby groups with a need to express dissatisfaction with their lot. The reactionaries in the regions would find it difficult to control the groundswell of rebellion and conflict that had been unleashed. Indeed, it was the collapse of the king's authority in Scotland and then Ireland that propagated further conflict at home in England. Prior to the rebellion, there had been significant dangers inherent in the Scottish conflict. Charles asked for Irish troops to aid him, but Parliament feared the threat posed by an Irish Catholic army moving anywhere in England. From the Irish point of view, the dangers of an aggressive Parliament were outweighed by the opportunity of having an English king in their debt.

Irish rebellion

On 23 October 1641 the Irish rebellion began. Ulster chiefs led by Phelim O'Neill, seeing the opportunity in addition to the threat caused by the split between king and Parliament, attacked the colonists and settlers with their northern clans. O'Neill had considerable military experience from continental wars, like so many of the exiled Irish who would in the next few years return home to aid the rebellion. It began as a series of popular uprisings but, by the end of 1641 the entire country was consumed by hatred and the need for reprisal against the colonists. The Protestants on all sides were unprepared for the rebellion and thousands were killed, with thousands more being forcibly evicted from their lands and farms. Although the slaughter that took place would later be exaggerated as a propaganda tool, the rebellion was still a very bloody affair whose repercussions would echo down the centuries. Despite the initial surprise, sides were being quickly taken. The colonists would come to regard the Parliamentary Puritans as their sponsors and friends, while the Irish Catholics feared their potential for power. Although Charles I had given the Irish little favour, he was preferable to the Puritanical element that could ultimately crush the Irish lords' power forever.

The rebellion may have come as a surprise but there were several reasons behind it. The long-term causes had been religious (related to the restoration of the Catholic Church) and economic. The plantation and new market forces had created poverty amongst the Catholic populace. Other less strategic factors had also played a part. A series of poor harvests in the 1630s had led many Irish to contemplate action rather than submit to starvation. The relative success of rebellion in Scotland had also created a dangerous precedent and made clear that the king was weak and had a willingness to grant concessions under the right circumstances. Donough MacCarthy, Lord Muskerry, who would later influence the fledgling Irish Parliament, initially disbelieved the reports that he heard from Ulster, laughing at such preposterous notions. The rumours that reached Cork were true, however, and he then had little hesitation in leading the MacCarthy clan against the settlers, driving them as far as Kilkenny, the same garrison town that would become the seat of the Irish Parliament, where Donough would have considerable influence.

In August 1642 the English Civil War began, forcing all factions to take sides, in tandem with their own multifarious interests. By late 1642 the alternative Irish government had emerged as the 'Confederation of Kilkenny'. Its aims included the return of confiscated land, religious freedom and equality for Catholics. Ostensibly loyal to the king, the Confederation was in the position to effectively negotiate the future of Ireland, since Charles would be in desperate need of reinforcements and required the troops under James Butler, Earl of Ormond, that were engaged with the rebels. By September 1645 a truce had been agreed upon and five of Ormond's regiments were able to leave for England. There was a price, however, and Irish leaders were invited to confer with the king at Oxford. They had a number of demands, including a free Irish Parliament, religious freedoms and a repeal of the laws and acts that had hampered the Irish lords. Charles refused, but the Irish were not altogether disappointed, believing that they need only be patient and wait until he became desperate enough to accede to their demands.

By this stage the internal strife and bickering that would so hamper the Irish cause began to emerge. Pope Innocent X had sent the Papal Nuncio, Giovanni Battista Rinuccini, to Ireland in the summer of 1645, and his instructions were clear. He was to ensure that any settlement between the Irish and the king would cater for the restoration of the Catholic Church in Ireland and ensure the appointment of a Catholic Lord Lieutenant. Any other agreement or concession was to be unacceptable. Lord Muskerry, already highly supportive of the Ormond Royalist faction, expressed his concern at the presence and influence of the nuncio, however. His belief was that it would prove disastorous for the country.

Charles had run out of time and, despite secret treaties with the Irish and promises of concessions for Irish troops, the king surrendered to the Scots in 1646, his first civil war at an end. The Irish were still in a relatively strong position, however, and O'Neill was able to defeat Monro's Scottish force at Benburb in 1646, the only real Irish victory of the war. The success would not be followed up or exploited, and internal dispute and wrangling now threatened to split the Supreme Council of the Confederate government. In characteristic style, O'Neill decided to overthrow the Kilkenny administration. Muskerry, who had supported Lord Mountgarret in the Irish Parliament and was thus in O'Neill's way, fled. By 1647 a confused Irish Parliament was in a poor state to resist Michael Jones, the new Parliamentary commander in Ireland. The Scots had delivered the king to the English all too easily, in return for payment for their troops. Ormond left Ireland and those Royalists that remained would have their property and thus their lives assured. In Ulster, Monro, the Scots commander, had recovered from his earlier defeat and reorganised. In Munster, Murtough O'Brien, Lord Inchiquin, who had begun the campaign loyal to the king, had by now sided with Parliament. He captured Cashel, plundering the town and slaughtering the inhabitants. In a bold Parliamentarian move, Jones attempted to link up with Inchiquin and attack the Irish Confederate capital of Kilkenny. O'Neill, in desperation marched across the country to stop them. Despite the apparent stalemate, the supreme council was still deeply split.

By 1648 it appeared that the rift could not be healed. The Confederates would attempt to negotiate with Parliament by first agreeing to a truce with Inchiquin and then isolating O'Neill by declaring him a rebel. In England King Charles I contemplated another civil war with Parliament, while Ormond returned to

Ireland. Ormond used the opportunity to his advantage. The Confederate split meant that he could promise the Irish religious and political freedoms in return for their loyalty to Charles I. Rinuccini was forced to leave, to ensure that Ormond could succeed. He knew that the inevitable split would force most of the Irish to the Royalist side. Amongst these was Muskerry who, amongst other Irish lords, would assist Ormond both in government and war. Inchiquin, perhaps responding to internal pressures, and who had already changed sides once, changed again, a Royalist once more! Only O'Neill remained committed to the original concept of the confederacy, an institution that had now become part of a Royalist alliance against Parliament.

By 30 January 1649, however, circumstances had changed and the war would take a new turn in terms of its conduct, aims and ultimately its repercussions. Charles I was executed at Whitehall. His position was expurgated from the requirements of the new English Republic, which was formally established by May. Oliver Cromwell, the new Lord Lieutenant of Ireland, would not let the remnants of a Royalist alliance remain there for long. He would supplement the 10,000 strong army of Jones with 13,000 more troops. The money for this adventure had to be found first, however, and England was exhausted, her civil war having been long and expensive. To this end Cromwell promised land in Ireland as surety against money put up by 'adventurers' and speculators in England, land which would be made up from the estates confiscated from the Irish lords by the end of the war. The subsequent 'Adventurer's Act' did not permit leniency on the part of the English, since this could potentially harm the speculators' valuable investment. The result was to reinforce the Irish determination to force a settlement and to highlight the fact that they were now dealing with a decisive and thereby merciless Parliament, no longer a weak and potentially flexible king.

By August Cromwell had landed in Ireland and he had little time for parley or debate over the religious and political questions. To him the matter was black and white, and he saw the Irish as the rebels who had perpetrated slaughter against the English, and he would have his terrible revenge at Drogheda and Wexford. By March 1650 Kilkenny had fallen and Cromwell returned to London, leaving his son-in-law Henry Ireton to finish the job. O'Neill had died at the end of the previous year, as it seemed had most of the Irish cause. Over half a million people had died since 1641, amidst massacre, war and disease. The economy remained in ruins and agriculture had been destroyed, mainly due to the scorched earth policy of the armies that had fought over the land, denying their enemies, and thus the indigenous population, from feeding off the land. The implementation of potato crops in Ireland was actually necessary at this time due to the state of the agricultural nation by the end of the war. The land was riven with famine and disease and both hungry wolf packs and bands of Irish guerrillas, roamed the countryside. The institution of Penal Laws worsened the lot of the Catholic population, in stark contrast to the resurgence of religious freedom that the Confederates had hoped for.

By 1652 Galway had surrendered. Pockets of resistance remained all over the country but most were disorganised and ineffective. In Munster and the south, however, the situation had not quite been resolved. Muskerry was still actively resisting in Munster but, by May 1652, the outcome must have been obvious even to the most ardent confederate. Lieutenant General Edmund Ludlow had taken acting command of the English army at the end of 1651, after Ireton's death from plague. He now sought to remove the problem in the south of the country. Muskerry's forces, although several thousand strong, presented little threat to Ludlow in the field, being ill supplied and poorly motivated. Their presence, however, as an occupying force in Munster, potentially threatening the English army nearby, meant that Ludlow had to take action. Muskerry's troops were centred on Ross Castle, a well-positioned fort on a peninsula on the lower lake of Killarney. The approach to the castle required that the attacker move along a raised causeway through a bog (a feature which characterises so much of the Irish countryside and which becomes significant as a battlefield trait for Justin MacCarthy nearly forty years later). Ludlow was aware that he must force Muskerry's surrender if he was to remove the problem of southern resistance. To do this, he had to assault the castle. He opted to command the field force of 4,000 foot and nearly 3,000 horse himself. Realising that the causeway approach would be suicidal for any attacker, he opted to bring boats from Castlemaine, seeing an amphibious assault (of sorts) as the only solution. An assault or siege was still impractical, however, since the castle remained supplied by Tories in the surrounding area. Eager to protect his position, Ludlow forced the surrender of Hugh O'Keefe at nearby Dromagh, attacked Irish troops at Killagh Abbey and scoured the countryside around Ross for Tories. Safe from attack, he was able to commence the assault by the end of June as boats became available. When the boats arrived, Muskerry knew that it was time to submit. Ross was vulnerable and if enough gunpowder could be shipped by sea to a position near the walls they could be breached. He surrendered on 22 June with around 1,000 men. Another 3,000 in the surrounding area also surrendered. Muskerry, in parley with Ludlow, obtained agreement that he could leave Ireland to fight abroad with 3,000 foot and 600 horse. A wise decision since the English troops held many captured officers whom they judged liable for the killing of colonists during 1641.

Ludlow's letters from the siege also give at least some indication as to why Muskerry's discussion and ultimate surrender was so forthcoming;

> From the Campe before Rosse,
> The 24th of June, 1652,

> The Lord of Muskerry's sonne and Lieut Col. Knocher O'Callaghan are hostages with me for the performance of those Articles. God willing I shall hasten northwards with all the force that can be spared hence, least they should stand in need of them.[2]

This hostage would undoubtedly have been Cormac, Muskerry's eldest son who had fought with him and would later lead his own battalion of Munstermen in France. Muskerry had little choice and his initial outward defiance was possibly no more than enough to serve his own honour.

Small pockets of resistance remained. Those Tories that were captured were executed and thousands of Irish were deported to the Americas. Muskerry, however, in common with around 40,000 other surrendering Irish troops would be allowed to leave and fight in Europe under France, Spain or other European states. For Ludlow and the English this arrangement paid real dividends, since the experienced Irish troops would not be able to form bands of Tories and thus further intensify the problem of Irish resistance.[3]

Muskerry left for Spain in 1652 after the surrender at Ross castle. He was, however, to find it difficult to be accepted. His very public disagreement with the arrival and intent of Rinuccini had earned him few friends in Spain amongst the exiled Irish or the clergy. By March 1653 he had returned to Ireland and declared himself to the English.

He was received by Colonel John Jones, who wrote:

> The Lord Muskerry is lately landed at Cork, and says he will cast himself upon the Parliament's mercy, pretending the clergy in Spain had determined to murder him, and that Portugal would not entertain him, of all of which I believe but my share.[4]

By the following February, Muskerry was being held in Marshalsea prison, one of many Irishmen awaiting trial for their activities in 1641 and 1642. Over 100 people had already been officially tried, convicted and executed. Muskerry would have to fight for his life.

The rest of the family had fled to France with the collapse of the Confederate-Royalist pact in Ireland. Muskerry's support of Ormond's cause during the war is not surprising considering his earlier comments regarding the Papal Nuncio. He was, however, also married to Eleanor Butler, Ormond's sister. He had three sons, Cormac, Callaghan and Justin, the youngest. Justin had been born in the midst of the conflict that had shaken Ireland. Now as a young boy he had to live in France, with the exiled remnants of the English monarchy. His father was held in prison by a fledgling English republic, awaiting trial. As far as he could tell, his family could lose their estates and their birthright. It is interesting to speculate how this kind of pressure could have affected Justin and his brothers. It is likely that the events would have left their mark on the boys at least in terms of how their religious and political viewpoints would be formed as they grew older. The young Justin would know of no other life bar that of siege mentality, perhaps moving at short notice, and being somewhat aware of his father rarely being present. Such events at such an age can only contribute to the attitudes and beliefs that govern later decisions.

Justin's brothers must also have had an impact on his life choices. His oldest brother, Cormac, had sought a military career and might well have fought alongside his father. He was a competent officer and would gain an excellent reputation with his regiment of Munstermen in exile in the 1650s. The second brother, Callaghan, began studying for a life in the priesthood in France. There is every indication that the young Justin, impressed by the exploits of his eldest brother Cormac, saw the military as a possible future. The family still had to wait in anticipation, however, for a decision from Ireland and the outcome of Donough's trial.

Muskerry had been influential in his time on the Supreme Council of the Confederate government. He had made powerful friends and was not looked upon by the English with the same contempt as O'Neill. This may help to explain why, unlike many of his fellow prisoners, he was given an indication of how the prosecution would unfold. He was given an opportunity to prepare a defence, where many others were locked up with little idea of what they were accused of until the day of their trial. He could also summon witnesses for his defence. In fact, in the climate of scapegoat mentality, it seemed that Muskerry would get a fair trial.

Muskerry's Trial

By December 1654 the prospect of a trial for Lord Muskerry, one of the leading lights of the Confederate parliament and a leader during the rebellion, lent a popular air to the proceedings in Dublin. Despite this, it must have been clear to him that this was quite literally a matter of life and death. All charges would relate to murders carried out during the summer of 1642.

The trial commenced on 1 December with the charges. Muskerry was charged as an accessory to three separate murders. The first of these involved a group of English colonists, apparently in the wrong place at the wrong time: Mrs Hussey, Mrs Crocker and her daughter, George Miller and his wife, Ellen Colman and her child, Charles Vavasour and his family, and two others unnamed. All had been on Muskerry's estate in August 1642 and had asked to be conveyed to Cork in light of their delicate position on Muskerry's estates. To this end, a convoy or bodyguard was provided. This did not, however, accompany the group for the entire course of the journey and the English were murdered in cold blood by the road. The second charge related to the previous month where Muskerry reputedly authorised the execution of three men and one woman at the siege of Kilfinny in County Limerick. In the final instance, Muskerry was accused as an accessory to the murder of Roger Skinner at Inniskerry, County Cork, in August 1642.

Of the three charges the first was the most serious. The initial prosecution evidence suggested that, despite the request by the English to go to Bandon, Muskerry refused, permitting them only to go to Cork instead, although it is later suggested that at least one of the colonists had family in Cork. On their way there, the colonists were murdered, although it is also apparent that the bodyguard company departed shortly after setting out. Muskerry in his defence stated that he had prosecuted those responsible for the murders during the war. The evidence of Mrs Hussey's daughter, Alice Stabber, was particularly damning, however, in that she claimed, despite her mother's request to stay at Macroom Castle, she had told her that MacSwiney, Muskerry's Steward, would have none of it, and Muskerry himself would not have 'any such wasps in his beehive'. The same witness would then implicate MacSwiney, albeit through hearsay, in the murders claiming that he had enquired as to whether the 'deed' had been carried out.

In Muskerry's defence, Edmund Stabber (Alice's husband) was called. He recalled that his brother had formed part of the bodyguard and they had indeed returned early (perhaps in fear of their own lives). He also added that soldiers from Blarney Castle had carried out the murders, and not any member of the bodyguard company. Muskerry, again defending himself with apparently trusted witnesses, put forward the evidence for his attempts to prosecute the murderers before leaving Ireland for a short time. Muskerry was subsequently found not guilty of the charge.

The second charge relating to the execution of the Irish at the siege of Kilfinny castle was denied by Muskerry, first in his claim that he had little responsibility at the siege, it being carried out by General Barry and secondly that in the six month siege, he had only been present for the last four or five days. There was little evidence, and Muskerry had in his time probably condemned many soldiers and civilians, most during the long war. For the articles and charges under consideration he was found not guilty, though was found guilty to the matter of fact. He was again cleared with regard to the third charge.

Sir Edmund Ludlow, who had been a commissioner at the trial, makes clear in his memoirs the importance of Muskerry being given the opportunity to prepare his own defence in the matter. Ludlow comments on the length of the trial;

> The trial of the Lord Muskerry was long, by reason of a clause which he urged in his defence from a printed copy of the articles made with him; which tho it had been unjust of me to grant in the terms there mentioned,

> yet would have cleared him, and thrown the guilt and blame upon me, for articles given ought to be made good. But this clause, upon search into the original, which I kept, appeared to have been inserted by themselves in the print which they produced for evidence, under pretence of having lost the original articles signed by me. Notwithstanding which, it appearing that tho divers of the English were murdered by the convoy appointed to conduct them safe to Cork; the Lord Muskerry had taken what care he could for their security, and had done what in him lay to bring the person who was guilty of that blood to justice, the court acquitted him and he was permitted, according to his articles to pass into Spain.

Ludlow casts a very different light on many areas surrounding the trial including the role of the bodyguards, Muskerry's role in the events and the entire question of his preparations and integrity. If there is foundation in Ludlow's comments, however, it should be remembered that Muskerry was fighting for his life.

He was discharged with a warning from the court as to his conduct in the rebellion, and to 'expiate' his conduct 'through repentance'. Muskerry's speech after his acquittal is interesting:

> I have not much to say, although I cannot say all I feel in the way of thanks to this Honourable Court, I must say that I have in these whole proceedings met with justice, without any leading to my prejudice, but that if any leaning hath been it hath been to my favour rather. It is one of the greatest providences that ever I met with this. I met with many crosses in Spain and Portugal. I could get no rest till I came hither, and the crosses I met here are much affliction to me, but when I consider that in this Court I come clear out of that blackness of blood by being so sifted, it is more to me than my estate. I can live without my estate, but not without my credit.

Muskerry was indeed free of that 'blackness by blood' that characterised the rebellion. By May of 1654, having being cleared of another charge, again of murder rather than simply complicity, he was free. In addition to Ludlow's comments there is a suggestion that Ormond had a hand in Muskerry's freedom. Lack of damning evidence had never been an obstacle to the Cromwellian courts to date, so the Ormond angle does have some credence given his relationship with his sister Eleanor, and his eagerness on other occasions to return her husband to her.[5]

Despite his newfound freedom, however, and, in common with many of the Irish who had fought in the rebellion, he had lost his estates in the upheaval of the Cromwellian invasion and its aftermath. What now for Muskerry? His family at least were safe in France, but his estates were gone and he had little hope of aid from the Cromwellians. His return to Spain would prove still fruitless as Ludlow continues:

> I have heard that upon his arrival in that kingdom a faction appeared against him upon account of his former opposition to the Pope's Nuncio in Ireland; so that he finding but cold entertainment there, entered into a treaty to put himself and his men into the service of the Venetians.[6]

Spanish memories of the Irish war and Rinuccini's treatment were still fresh and Muskerry had little option but to leave. Despite rumours of his murder in Dublin, the next few years would see Muskerry attempt a number of enterprising recruitment drives.[7]

In 1655 he attempted to procure a commission in France and in the same year obtained a licence from Cromwell to raise and ship 5,000 men to Poland for the service of the king. He also attempted to raise troops for Venice. All would come to naught, however, despite the apparent attempts of the Cromwellians to be rid of him from Ireland.[8] His patience and his past resistance to Cromwell's forces would be rewarded, at least in part. The monarchy in exile, now led by Charles II, made Lord Muskerry the Earl of Clancarty in 1658. Cromwell's death in the same year would signal the restoration of the English monarchy by 1660 when the exhausted English people turned in desperation back to their king.

Exiled with the monarchy in France were the rest of the MacCarthy family. Now secure in the knowledge that her husband had survived the Cromwellian examination, Lady Muskerry could perhaps be assured that there would be some future for her family. Her brother Ormond would not leave her isolated and would do all in his power to secure what estates were available to her husband, should the monarchy be returned to England.

Service in France

Loyalty to France and disenchantment with the apparently futile war against Cromwell and the English Parliament had driven many of the Irish to fight for the French during the 1650s. Charles II, with the monarchy in exile in France, also cultivated the creation of Irish regiments for the French. In this way many Irish could still fight for the English Crown against the Parliamentarians, albeit indirectly. By 1652 a regiment of horse and a regiment of foot fought under Turenne and the Duke of Lorraine. Many of these troops would later be placed under the command of Charles's brother James, the Duke of York, where they were incorporated into his own regiment. By 1653, with French armies fighting the Spanish, Irishman fought Irishman in a war where both sides employed the exiled mercenaries. The Duke of York's regiment fought bravely during the sieges that characterised this conflict. By 1656, however, the alliance between the English Commonwealth and France obliged Charles II to seek refuge with the Spanish court at Cologne while the Duke of York moved to Spanish Flanders. The Irish troops, now in the armies of Turenne and la Ferté, would have to choose between Charles, whom many still accepted as their sovereign, and the flag of France, the country for which they had fought so bravely. The Duke of York indicated initially that he would abide by the decision of the troops, though advised that the regiments should be kept together. It was of course in his best interests not to offend the sensibilities of the French. There were some interesting decisions made on the Spanish side. Richard Grace, who had fought in the Confederate War in Ireland before bringing 1,200 men into Spanish service, yet was apparently unhappy with the terms of his service, changed sides and the regiment joined the French army. On the French side, Sir John Darcy would not desert his French service despite protestations and commands from Charles.[9]

Cormac MacCarthy had carved a fine reputation in French service during the 1650s. We can be reasonably certain that Cormac led a battalion or regiment of Munstermen during the wars in Ireland in the 1640s and that he was the mysterious 'hostage' that Ludlow talks about prior to the siege of Ross Castle in 1652. It is also reasonable to assume that Cormac left with his regiment for the continent at the same time as his father left for Spain. In either event, he had become Colonel of his Irish regiment in French service. His men were mostly from Munster, a collection of loyal Muskerry fighters, tenants and dependants. Described as 'a very gallant officer, and most sensibly alive to the feelings of honour' and 'a young man of extraordinary courage and expectation … [with] the general estimation of an excellent officer', Cormac had an apparently bright future.

All this was to change, however, with Charles' treaty with the Spanish and the subsequent dilemma faced by the Irish regiments. Recent years of the Franco-Spanish conflict had been dominated by the question of what side Oliver Cromwell and the English Army would take. Siding with the French due to his hatred of Spanish Catholicism and in apparent pursuit of Spanish riches in the New World, Cromwell's treaty would be expanded into an offensive and defensive pact by 1657. The Spanish in turn had then courted the enemy of the English Republic, Charles II. Charles, disgusted by the apparent lack of complicity shown by his brother James in the Spanish affair, and his attempts to remain in French service, commanded that he attend him at Bruges. James was now in a very dangerous position and had little choice but to obey his brother despite his earlier promises to his Irish troops and to the detriment of his friendship with the French Marshal Turenne. Cormac had little time to contemplate his own decision at the time since he was under siege. In 1656, Condé, a small though well defended fortress on the Meuse River, lay besieged by the Spanish. The defenders were mainly Irish under Muskerry, and had held out against Don Juan of Austria, the Spanish commander, for many weeks. With the King of England now securely in the Spanish camp, Don Juan appealed to Charles with regard to ending the siege through his own intrigues. To this end Charles immediately despatched Cormac's uncle, the Duke of Ormond, to the town. We can never know the true nature of what occurred, suffice to say that many troops in the garrison surrendered, either due to their loyalty to Ormond or due to the dilemma caused by conflicting loyalties amongst the Irish in the presence of the nobles. Ormond also tried to convince Cormac to bring his regiment over to the Spanish side. The young MacCarthy replied that:

> It was not consistent with his honour that either he or his men should quit their colours, until, according to his articles, he should march into France; he would then leave his regiment in their quarters, demand his pass, which, by contract, he was entitled to whenever his own king should demand his services, and his regiment should be permitted to march with him.

Cormac saw his only choice in the delicate situation as that of showing loyalty to his king. He did not, however, know the decision of his comrade the Duke of York until later. Cormac returned to France. Cardinal Mazarin, the chief minister, who had in effect caused much of the fiasco through his agreement with the English Republic, pointed out that this entire scheme was but a pretext for engaging French troops in Spanish service. Mazarin, although pointing to the reality of the situation, could not dissuade the young colonel, despite promises regarding the benefits that would be made available for the regiment. Having obtained his 'pass', thereby ending his military contract with the French, Muskerry passed into Spanish service. He had made the decision alone and had only obtained permission for him to leave. His men and officers, however, showing a surprising degree of loyalty, deserted and joined him over the next few days, quitting their French quarters in small groups. A regiment of 800 men was available under MacCarthy for Spanish service by the end of the desertion. The effect of this event was compounded by events in other regiments, and the carefully crafted perceptions of honour and loyalty within the Irish regiments were thrown into complete disarray.

At St Gerlain the Irish garrison became Spanish troops overnight and turned the fortress over to their new allies. The hand of Ormond had again been involved as his secretary, Sir George Lane, had been present with the garrison. Despite arresting several Irish officers it was too late, and the governor, the Duke of Schomberg, was forced to surrender. In all, the Spanish had gained four Irish regiments who would fight in the sieges and battles of 1656 and 1657. They were however alarmed at the apparent ease with which the Irish troops had come over. Their apparent treachery at St Gerlain, and after the siege of Condé, drove them to insist that the Irish troops now swear an oath of fealty to the Spanish government. In their view, the Irish loss of honour in the affair could only be repaid through a religious oath, their Catholicism being a little more trustworthy. This stain on the Irish troops' reputation could not easily be glossed over, but the confused situation had meant that desperate decisions had been taken. Despite the changes 'French Irish' and 'Spanish Irish' would still face each other in the battles to follow.[10]

A curious episode also occurred upon Cormac's transfer to Spanish service. Despite his good relations with the Duke of York, the young Richard Talbot had also been a rising star in terms of the young James' favour. As already stated, most of Cormac's men were from Munster, his tenants and dependants. A vacancy for a lieutenant colonel had arisen in the regiment, and Cormac, quite understandably, had wished to appoint one of his own men for the position. Richard Talbot, a Leinsterman, and a man whose relationship with James would have a significant impact on the political future of Ireland, also applied for the position. When MacCarthy rejected Talbot, the two men chose a manner with which to settle their argument, which was all too common in the exiled court of Charles II. They fought a duel! Although the end result of the match is not clear, both survived. For Talbot though, the matter was clearly not closed, for he appealed directly to James, who in the end supported him. MacCarthy in turn appealed to his uncle, Ormond, in the hope of putting enough pressure on the Duke of York to make him see sense. A Leinster officer in a Munster regiment holding a position not approved by the regimental colonel would seem somewhat uncomfortable for all parties involved. Despite protestations to Charles himself, who would not interfere, the decision to promote Talbot was upheld. The enmity between Talbot and Ormond it seems was also fostered at this stage. There also may have been some antagonism generated towards the MacCarthys.[11]

Their reputation somewhat damaged, the Irish troops in 1657 and 1658 appeared to fare less courageously than had been previously suggested in earlier conflicts. The young Cormac MacCarthy was still heavily involved in the actions that did take place, however. At the siege of Ardres in August 1657 he led one of the Duke of York's Irish battalions in the assault. The Spanish army was forced to raise the siege by the appearance of Turenne and the French Army. Cormac directed his Irish troops in giving covering fire so that the Spanish engineers and miners could escape the French attacks.

By 1658, 6,000 English troops from Cromwell's New Model Army bolstered the French Army in Spanish Flanders. This year's campaign would concentrate on the channel towns of Dunkirk, Mardyk and Gravelines. Dunkirk and Mardyk would become English possessions if secured in return for Cromwell's assistance. Turenne laid siege to Dunkirk in May, triggering Don Juan's march to relieve it with around 14,000 men including his Irish regiments comprising 2,000 men. Critically, the Spanish commander would ignore General Condé's advice and leave his artillery behind. Condé, perhaps unimpressed, would change sides after the battle. Don Juan had arrived by June to face Turenne. In a final twist of irony, the French Army still had some Irish regiments (Dillon's for instance), who would now fight alongside Cromwell's New Model Army at the Battle of the Dunes.

Turenne, the meticulous planner, manoeuvred his army into position three miles to the east of the besieged town. Don Juan reacted slowly, despite James's warnings of imminent attack. A sand hill on the Spanish right was quickly reinforced with four Spanish regiments with James' troops to the left of this hill. The sand hill would undo the Spanish, however. In battle, a flank secured by a hill would be of major tactical importance. This flank, however, was on a beach, and the tide was going out. Turenne, though a master tactician, would not have taken long to realise that, given time, he could easily outflank the Spanish position. The English fleet was also within cannon-shot range of the hill from their anchored position offshore.

The English infantry assaulted the hill, pikemen attacking in force. The Spanish infantry broke despite a courageous cavalry charge led by James in an attempt to secure the flank. With the ebbing tide French cavalry surged along the strand, enveloping the flank and causing the Spanish line to slowly disintegrate. The French fought off Spanish attacks in the centre, and counter-attacked. The Irish troops, outflanked and with little support, could not sustain the position and broke. Cormac MacCarthy's regiment suffered heavy casualties, caught as it was, outflanked and assaulted from the right flank and front. Most of the Irish troops broke. Most of these were captured except Cormac, who escaped the French. Within four hours the battle was over.

The French had won a dramatic victory. Dunkirk fell, and the nineteen-year-old Louis XIV, who promptly handed the town to the English, watched as the Spanish garrison emerged. Other French objectives would quickly fall in the months to come. By 1659 Turenne's victories had convinced the Spanish to sue for peace. France would keep most of her conquered territory but, more importantly, she had now succeeded Spain as the dominant military power in Europe. Dramatic change was also afoot in England where the death of Cromwell would see the return of the monarchy and the coronation of Charles II.[12]

The Restoration & The Dutch Wars

The changes brought about by the death of Cromwell in 1658 were momentous to say the least. His heir, Richard, was unable to prevent radical military men and politicians from overthrowing him and reinstating the purged parliament, which would in turn re-emerge twice more before it would make the revolutionary decision to recall the exiled monarchy to a country exhausted by war and political upheaval. And so the decadent nature of Charles' reign began in 1660. We know little of the events surrounding the lives of the MacCarthy family during this early period of the restoration, although some points are clear. Donough had regained most of his estates through Charles' Act of Settlement. Ormond conveniently arranged most of this, however. Donough returned to Ireland and his estates with his wife. Cormac undoubtedly returned to England with the Duke of York's regiment while Callaghan remained in France to continue his studies. Of Justin there is no record at this time, but it is likely that he returned to Ireland with his mother and father. It is also quite likely that, in admiration of his brother, he was now keen to pursue a military career.

The first Dutch war had taken place in the early 1650s. In common with other conflicts of the time it had started as a quarrel and ended with a struggle over commercial interests. In October 1651 England passed the Navigation Act. This meant that goods and commodities imported into England could only be transported by English shipping or ships from the country of origin. It was a policy ultimately designed to confound Dutch trading interests. English harassment of Dutch shipping provoked a confrontation in 1652 which developed into naval warfare. The English ships were designed for war whilst the Dutch vessels were refitted merchant ships. By 1654 the war was over and little had been achieved; the Navigation Act was still in place. The quarrel between the Dutch and the English was far from over, however.

In 1665 the second Anglo-Dutch war broke out. The Dutch had not been idle in the interim and heavily armed warships had been constructed in an attempt to combat the English fleet. The restoration of Charles II had given hope to the Orange faction in the Dutch republic. Charles' sister Mary had hoped that her son, the young William III, would benefit from the king's support in his claim to be *stadtholder* amongst the Dutch. All was for naught when Mary died of smallpox in 1660 and Charles's hatred of republicanism instilled in him a deep concern for potentially damaging Dutch commercial influence. The Navigation Act of 1651 was reinforced in 1660 with a more rigid and, for the Dutch, a more damaging version. Mary had nominated Charles as her son's guardian, a relationship which would give the English significant influence in Dutch politics in the years to come. It was the republican element of Dutch politics rather than the Orangeism that concerned the English, however. The unrivalled commercial power of the Dutch also worried the English and perhaps made them a little jealous.

Unrest had been fomenting in English circles in the first four years of Charles' reign. Much of this enthusiasm surrounded James, the Duke of York. James was now Lord High Admiral of the English fleet and would thus command in any sea battle against the Dutch. His charisma and influence had meant that he was surrounded by a group of angry young Englishmen, eager for war and keen to show James their mettle. Cormac MacCarthy would also have moved in these circles. Incidents in West Africa and America between English and Dutch shipping exacerbated an already delicate situation. Both countries heavily miscalculated their respective eagerness for war however. On the Dutch side, de Witt, the Grand Pensionary of Holland, believed that Charles would never be voted the funds that he needed. Charles on the other hand believed that the Dutch would never fight another war, since it must have been obvious to them that they would lose significantly against his superior fleet. Both sides were to be proved wrong.

Pressure from the threat of trade in Africa and the Americas persuaded Parliament to vote Charles over two million pounds in order to provide a fleet to protect English trade. The English were spoiling for war. When news of Dutch reprisals along the Guinea coast reached England, ships were given a free rein to prey on Dutch interests in the channel and the North Sea. Attacks on Dutch convoys provoked reaction and the Dutch declared war in February 1665. Despite problems with manpower and provisioning, Charles had a powerful navy. He was also determined to use it. By April the English fleet had set sail for the Dutch coast to sit in such a position as to intercept Dutch convoys returning via the North Sea. By May the Dutch had managed to slip through the English net. The fleet returned home. Dutch preparations continued in earnest. They too now had a large fleet thanks to the lessons learned in the period between the wars. Their tactics differed too. They did not fight in line but in small groups, using their smaller size and weight to their advantage, and perhaps also due to differences between Dutch provincial groups. If an English ship became crippled, the groups could seize and board her though English 'line' tactics helped to prevent this to some degree. The Dutch also used 'chain-shot', where a short length of chain linked two iron balls. This was normally fired high and used to shred the rigging of the opposing ships, thus crippling them. As will become evident, such firing techniques could also be deadly for those standing on deck.

The Dutch fleet set sail in May under orders to seek out and destroy the English fleet, 'even to the mouth of the Thames'. In the event, this was a little ambitious. The two fleets, who had been hunting for each other, met about forty miles south-east of Lowestoft on the English east coast at first light on 3 June 1665. The English fleet was composed of three squadrons, each of twenty to thirty ships. The vanguard was led by James's cousin Prince Rupert, followed by James himself aboard the *Royal Charles*, with Lord Sandwich in the rear. The fleets passed each other, heading south-easterly, giving broadsides, but most shots fell short, the fleets still being too far apart to do much damage. By 6 a.m., the ships had re-organised, and the English, led by Sandwich, moved aggressively north-west. Again the fleets did not close until a third pass was made to the south-east. By now the two fleets were parallel and in range of each other. On the leeward side of the action, the Dutch were unable to use their fireships effectively or move *en masse* against the English flagships. Vicious broadsides erupted from both fleets, tearing gouges in timber and men. The thunder of the guns could be heard in London, where all listened intently but of course in vain, for some sign that would indicate victory. By midday, with hundreds already killed, and ships full of wounded and dead slowly sinking, the main action was still taking place at the rear of the English line. Here, Lord Sandwich in the *Prince* was supported by only one ship and fighting with the Dutch commander Obdam in the *Eendracht*, and several other ships. The Duke of York moved in to help aboard the *Royal Charles*. Sandwich pressed hard against the smaller Dutch vessels forcing open a gap in their line. Four Dutch ships became tangled together in the confusion and James unleashed a fireship to end the debacle. One of the Dutch ships exploded, when its powder store was hit, taking the mast of another with it. The vessels began to disperse, as the momentum of the Dutch defence was broken.

It was probably at this time as the Duke of York urged the *Royal Charles* to aid Lord Sandwich that the fire against the royal ship was at its most fierce. The Dutch would have thrown everything against the timely reinforcements. As the range lessened they would have aimed chain-shot against the rigging of the enemy vessels, or even at those English officers standing on deck urging the sailors on and eager for glory. Just at what stage of the battle the events occurred, we shall probably never know. As James stood on the deck of the *Royal Charles*, however, alongside his loyal aide Cormac MacCarthy and two English nobles, the Dutch fired. The chain-shot that flew towards the group killed all save James himself, 'Their blood and brains flying in the Duke's face – and the head of Mr Boyle striking down the Duke, as some say'.

It is not clear whether the shot had been a deliberate attempt by an enthusiastic Dutch gunner to kill the admiral on his flagship. What is clear is that had his aim been keener and the situation less desperate, he would have very significantly changed the history of the British Isles. Cormac was dead instead, a soldier who had fought through so much with the Duke of York, yet had not even been given a chance to fight back at the end. James retired to bed, quite possibly in a state of shock. Although chase was given to the remnants of the Dutch, the impetus of the attack had gone. It emerged later that this was partly due to the warning given to the duke's servants by his wife, Anne Hyde, that he should not get too close to the battle. James had obviously ignored this advice until too tired or too shocked by the death of his friends, to continue. Over 800 English sailors and noblemen had been killed or wounded, but the English had won a victory of sorts. The war would drag on until the signing of a peace treaty in 1667.[13]

After the battle, James's popularity in England would soar as he became a national hero. Cormac was buried in Westminster Abbey after a very public funeral. He was thirty-one years old. Having been a gentleman of the bedchamber to the Duke of York, he was buried with full military honours. Ormond wrote to his sister conveying his grief at the loss of her son, Lord Muskerry.[14]

> Dear Sister,
>
> It is not the length or words of a preamble that can abate the bitterness of the matter. I shall therefore without the affliction of circumstances, tell you it falls to my shame to inform you, that your son Muskery was killed in the late conflict betwixt the king's fleet and that of the Dutch. He was close by the duke his master's side; and with him were killed the Earl of Falmouth and Mr Richard Boyle, the earl of Cork's son. That your son is generally lamented and well spoken of, may aggravate your sense of such a loss; yet it must come to your knowledge, and I that partake in the loss, and am thought fittest to let you know it, cannot forbear to say it.
>
> It must be the work of some time, but principally of pious reflection upon the submission and resignation due from us to the good pleasure of God, to give consolation proportionable to such an affliction. That God, who gives and takes, and always for the best, (if it be not our own faults,) send you all the comfort you need, and make us all ready for that hour which we must all come to, and which your son has past with honour in this world, and (I doubt not) with happiness in the other.
>
> I am,
>
> My dearest sister, your most afflicted
> but most affectionate brother.
>
> Ormond

Donough, now the Earl of Clancarty, must have been devastated at the death of his first-born son in battle, especially as the family had come through so much in the preceding years. His grief would be short lived, however, for by August 1665, he also died. Cormac and Donough's tragic deaths left the family bereft of the titular heads of the family. Cormac's twelve-year-old son (also Cormac) would now lay claim to the Earldom of Clancarty. The child was a ward of Ormond, living in England. Tragically, however, in September 1666, a year after Donough's death, the boy also died.

Callaghan by 1666 was still in France studying for the priesthood. He would have been the next Earl of Clancarty but for his studies. Justin would then become the next Earl but for the unexpected chain of events that followed. In an unprecedented move, and in apparent anticipation of the wealth that the Muskerry estates would yield, Callaghan left the priesthood. It must have been a surprise at the French monastery too, as Callaghan had been on the verge of taking holy orders. There was more to come from the enterprising MacCarthy, however. Upon leaving the order and taking the title and estates of Clancarty, Callaghan changed his religion, becoming a Protestant. He then proceeded to marry Lady Elizabeth Fitzgerald, the daughter of the Earl of Kildare. Justin's world had been turned upside down in the space of two years. We can but imagine the effect that such events would have had on the young man. After a childhood where the family had lived in what was effectively an exile from their estates, waiting for a father who might never return, to the death of his revered eldest brother, father and nephew within a year; these events, capped by Callaghan's intrigues, a brother whom Justin must barely have known, can only have left him a little bitter with regard to the turn of events, to say the least. Such circumstances in rapid succession, even by ruthless seventeenth-century standards, cannot have been easy to deal with.

Any enmity between Justin and his brother was not immediately apparent, however, as he petitioned successfully on Callaghan's behalf for a reduction in quit rent due to the English Crown. Matters would take a turn for the worse as Callaghan displayed the kind of intrigue rich doubledealing that would set him and Justin at loggerheads. Donough had made provision for his youngest son in his will, charging his wife the duty of providing land for Justin to the value of £1,000 per year. Despite the Dowager Countess' attempts to further this request for Justin, Callaghan was unwilling to honour it. Ormond's intervention was required to settle the argument; however, he found in Callaghan's favour, insisting that the estate could not afford such an outlay. Land should instead be given to Justin for his own maintenance and that of his family, should he have one. Callaghan, however, displaying a degree of contempt for the entire affair, had to be persuaded to agree to any form of settlement.[15]

Justin seems to have been particularly close to his mother at this point, which is hardly surprising bearing in mind the recent turn of events. Callaghan's lack of 'brotherly love' and even respect for Justin is more difficult to understand. Future events would prove that the young man had become embittered by the entire affair. For now, it was clear that he would have to make a living for himself. Justin had looked on his oldest brother with admiration and had probably based his decision on Cormac's very successful military career. Any claim on his father's estate had disappeared and he would therefore shape his own future as a soldier.

Chapter II

French Service 1673–1678

Having spent time in France, and with little potential for advancement in the English army of the 1670s, French service seemed the logical starting point for Justin's military career. An Irish regiment still fought with the French army. Charles had improved his relations with the French after the restoration and an Irish regiment under George Hamilton had been recruited, with Charles's agreement, by Louis XIV. The English Parliament had readily accepted this, since it was clear that English officers would not accept Irish Catholics in the army establishment. Irish Catholic officers wishing to pursue a military career had little real choice then but to serve abroad; various oaths and acts precluded Catholics from public office of any kind in England after all. The Oath of Supremacy acknowledged the king as the head of the English Church while the Oath of Allegiance denied the Pope's right to depose kings. Catholics would sometimes have to take one form or another despite the protestations of Rome. All those who held government office were required to take the oaths, which for the most part excluded Catholics. Despite some leniency, and Charles's Declaration of Indulgence, matters had become more serious by 1673. With the French attack on the Dutch, the English Parliament, in argumentative mood, forced Charles to rigidly enforce the penal laws and withdraw the Declaration of Indulgence. Worse was to follow.

Parliament insisted that a Test Act be passed wherein office holders (and military officers) must declare their disbelief in transubstantiation, prove that they had taken Anglican Communion and take the oaths in court with witnesses present. When instituted in 1673 there were several resignations. Of these the most important was that of the Lord High Admiral, James the Duke of York, heir to the throne. The rumours that pervaded English society had proven true as James was revealed as a Catholic. That summer, two years after the death of his first wife Anne Hyde, he married Mary of Modena, a Catholic princess rumoured to be influenced by the French. The wheels of James's ultimate undoing had been set in motion.

Officers had little hope of pursuing their trade in Ireland either, even though the Test Act did not apply. The Irish army officer corps was still dominated by Cromwellians, and Catholic officers seeking experience had little option but to seek it abroad. Charles therefore was forced to offer his Irish troops to the French. The Irish, already in a form of exile, would fight for their king, albeit in the service of an officially foreign crown. It is striking when researching the early lives of these seventeenth century 'characters' how their lives and relationships are so closely linked. This is the inevitable result of what is essentially a relatively small family of Irish lords, the interwoven patterns and thus history of their endeavours telling a tale that leads the researcher to delve further, not only into their relationships, but to determine how they might have interacted with each other in the crises and political turmoil that beset Ireland during this period.

For Justin there was still considerable doubt over the future. It was clear that this lay with service to Charles, but not in the English army. Fate would play into his hands. George Hamilton was the eldest son of Sir George Hamilton of Nenagh in County Tipperary and Dunnalong in County Tyrone. His mother was another of Ormond's sisters, Lady Mary Butler, third daughter of Lord Thurles. This made George Hamilton Justin's cousin. The young George had married one Frances Jennings in 1665 (who would later become the wife of Richard Talbot, the Earl of Tyrconnel and whose sister Sarah would become the wife of the future Duke of Marlborough). It is also prudent to mention some of George's brothers at this point since they have a distinct bearing on the latter events of Justin's life. The family consisted of six sons and three daughters. Of the sons, James, in common with Cormac MacCarthy would die at sea fighting the Dutch in 1673. After George came Anthony and Richard, who would both achieve some notoriety in the Irish war to come. Of the daughters, Elizabeth, known as *la belle* Hamilton would marry Philibert, Count de Gramont, about whom Anthony would later have a great deal to say in terms of the intrigues of Charles II's court in his *Memoirs of Count Grammont*. Their father had been another Irish leader during the Confederate wars and in common with Muskerry, had served the interests of Charles I and later Charles II against the Cromwellians. By 1651 he was forced to give up his estates in Roscrea in County Tipperary and move his family to Paris.

It is likely that the Hamiltons and MacCarthys shared the years of exile together with the Duke of Ormond who seems to have had an understandably protective instinct with regard to the welfare of his sisters. The Hamilton boys were quite young during the years of exile (in 1651 George was seven, Anthony five and Richard three), and so they did not see the military service and experience that Cormac MacCarthy did during this period. It is also likely that the young Justin MacCarthy was well known to the Hamiltons and they spent their formative years in shared exile. By 1667 George had been commissioned in Charles's Horse Guards, but his military career was set for greater glory.

By the early 1670s Charles had a treaty with France by which Louis XIV could recruit English and Irish troops for French service in a similar manner to the regiments raised in the 1650s. The agreement was not entirely based on political goodwill, however, since English insistence on removal of 'Popery' from the army forced Charles to remove many of the Catholic officers from the English army and relocate them. The young George Hamilton was appointed captain lieutenant in November 1667 and later colonel. Subsequently, he moved his family to Paris where he was named a count. The Scottish troops that were recruited formed their own French regiment, the ancient *Companie de Gendarmes Ecossais* of the Royal Guard. The balance of troops formed the *Gendarmes Anglais*. In April 1671 Hamilton obtained permission to raise a company of Irish, *un Régiment d'Infanterie Irlandaise*, comprising fifteen companies of 100 men each, most of these recruited from exiles.

Additional Irish troops were recruited in 1673 when Charles ordered Essex, the then Lord Lieutenant of Ireland, to give Hamilton grace to recruit 600 men for the regiment. The extent of the treaty with France was to have been kept secret, the French ships being ordered to pick up the Irish troops in a remote corner of the Kerry coastline. Their appearance at Kinsale, however, gave the game away and plans were set back for a time. Eventually however, the troops were raised. Among them was the thirty-year-old Justin MacCarthy, a young officer forced to seek his fortune in the Irish military serving in France.[1]

He would get his first experience of war relatively quickly. The troops would serve under the French master strategist Turenne on the Rhine from 1673 to 1675. The campaign would show Justin the very worst aspects of seventeenth century warfare. The atrocities and strife associated with conflict in the 1600s had not disappeared with the Thirty Years' War, a fact that would become all too evident to the Irish officers. Louis XIV's Dutch War in 1673 was a complex and messy affair. Unlike his later wars, it was fought with the concept of *Gloire*, the French ideal of personal 'glory', forefront in Louis's mind. The wars in the 1660s and 70s formed the early part of his long reign; his youthful impetuosity, though no excuse for slaughter, tends to add credence to his insistent pursuance of his war aims. It was not only glory and greatness through military action that attracted Louis however. The Spanish Netherlands were also a prize worth having. In 1659 the long war with Spain had ended after the signing of the Treaty of the Pyrenees. The direct results of this treaty had given Louis a Spanish wife, the infanta Marie Thérèse, the daughter of the Spanish King Philip IV from his first marriage, and potentially heir to the riches of Spain.

The treaty had catered for this eventuality, however, removing Marie's claims to Spanish inheritance upon payment of half-a-million escudos to France. This enormous fee was never paid and hence Louis somewhat shrewdly insisted that from a legal point of view his wife still had her claim to Spanish inheritance. Of course such intrigues are typical of the language of the period's treaties and Louis would likely never have agreed to a covenant wherein the divine right of family inheritance was remotely questioned. In September of 1665, however, Philip IV died, to be replaced by the five-year-old Carlos II, his son from his second marriage.

Awaiting the inevitable perhaps, Louis signalled that he had no argument with the succession. He now, however, seized the opportunity that he had awaited. According to the law of the Spanish Netherlands, Marie, the daughter from a first marriage, had inheritance rights over Carlos in terms of Spanish property – in this case areas of the Spanish Netherlands. Marie's claims would later ignite the war of the Spanish Succession in the 1700s, but for now Louis would use his wife's claims on the Spanish Netherlands as a prelude to war. Louis began to build his army once more and by 1667 had 80,000 men under arms.

As Louis's plans took hold, he expected assistance from the Dutch in the Netherlands. He had after all supported them in the Spanish war, helped defend their borders and stood by them against the English. As far as Louis was concerned this part of the plan would not be a problem. The first moves took place in 1667 when Marshal Turenne once more led French forces against their old enemy, the Spanish. Louis watched events unfold from his carriage in the presence of his wife and mistresses, a young king basking in his conquering glory. The French war machine marched over the Spanish defences. There were a few skirmishes but the war was mainly concerned with sieges, though these were relatively short in nature and by the end of 1667 the result of the war was not in doubt. The Dutch, however, were not as close to Louis as he had believed. They slowly began to realise that a weak Spanish neighbour was a great deal more preferable to a strong and aggressive French one. Dictated by fears of Louis's ambition, they debated their reaction to the inevitable French victory. The Dutch had been fighting the English at sea, but French moves created the urgency for a treaty with England by July of 1667. By the start of 1668 the Dutch, English and Swedish had formed the Triple Alliance, threatening Louis with a war that would re-establish the borders set by the Treaty of the Pyrenees if he continued his aggression. Louis was incensed by what he felt was a Dutch betrayal, but there was little that he could do at the time. By May he concluded a treaty with Spain. He would not forget the Dutch, however.

Louis now fed his political ambition rather than conquer Spanish lands. By 1670 he had broken the Triple Alliance by paying off the Swedish and then Charles II with the subsequent Treaty of Dover. Charles's secret agreement allowed for payments to be made to his almost empty coffers on the basis that English aid would be forthcoming during the war with the Dutch. The secrecy of the treaty was all the more vital due to its second constituent, that of Charles's declaration of his likely conversion to the Catholic faith, assuming that the time was right in England. Whether Charles was serious about his conversion or not at this time – he could potentially call on a mighty French army to aid him if he converted – the consideration that he would not allow himself to suffer the fate of his father, must have been forefront in his mind. The Dutch, who had also been in talks with

Louis, were completely outwitted. Again, war was unavoidable. The preparations were complete by 1672 and a French army of over 100,000 men lay in wait. The war opened with an English naval attack in March and by May French troops were on the move.

Three massive armies headed for the United Dutch Provinces; Turenne led 50,000 men north along the left bank of the Meuse while the Great Condé led a force along the right bank and Lieutenant General Luxembourg led an army of French allies in Westphalia. Facing them was a small Dutch force of 40,000 men, mostly widely dispersed in garrisons. Commanding a force of 14,000, however, was the young William, Prince of Orange, who would by July be named *stadtholder* with executive authority, replacing the De Witts as bloody rioting shook the capital. It is unsurprising that civil unrest reached such heights as the French conquered more and more Dutch towns. Turenne had reached Nijmegen by July. The Dutch, however, had one card left to play as Amsterdam itself was threatened. They opened the sluices and dams that held back the floodwaters from the Dutch countryside. The resulting ingress bogged down the French assault and little progress was made as winter set in. The delay was timely as German states and troops from the forces of the Holy Roman Empire were able to come to William's aid. Charles II's treaty was also under threat as the English Parliament realised the full import of the alliance with France. Turenne's troops were moved to Germany in an attempt to hold back the Imperialist and Brandenburg troops who now threatened along the Rhine. The move confirmed that the Dutch invasion had lost its momentum. Turenne, however, was still able to forward French aims through entering the lands of the Elector of Brandenburg. The French troops' plunder of the countryside and towns would eventually force the Elector to sue for peace.

Irish and English troops under Hamilton had joined French forces in the United Provinces in 1672 and had been with Turenne during the Brandenburg operations. In 1673, however, they moved with Turenne to the Rhine. Louis divided the French army into three elements for the year's campaign. He led the first along the Meuse with 40,000 troops. Condé maintained pressure on the Dutch while Turenne's troops covered the Upper Rhine. The main success would be Louis's capture of Maastricht, but the Dutch objective was still inundated with floodwaters. Turenne's thankless task consisted of a massive delaying action in an attempt to prevent the Imperial army linking up with their Dutch allies, no easy feat since the renowned Raimondo Montecuccoli now led the 25,000 Imperial troops. Turenne's orders for his 20,000 men were simple in theory. He had to prevent the threatened link-up, whilst guarding the Alsace region, and stopping additional German forces from joining the enemy. Throughout the year, the two generals would attempt to outmanoeuvre one another and gain the upper hand. In the end the advantage fell to Montecuccoli who was better supplied. Madrid and Vienna signed alliances with the Dutch and Louis was forced to restrain his demands on them, but his enemies were now taking the upper hand. Towards the end of the year Brandenburg re-entered the war, and additional German states and Spain entered the fray. Louis now had most of Europe ranged against his ambition.

By 1674 the English Parliament had wholeheartedly rejected the French alliance, making peace with the Dutch through the Treaty of Westminster in February. The regiments that fought alongside the French troops surprisingly remained unaffected, however, and MacCarthy would gain the military experience that he so desperately sought. With the additional Irish recruits in 1674, Hamilton was reinforced. Justin MacCarthy completed his French service with many late seventeenth-century notables, amongst them the young John Churchill, later Duke of Marlborough. Hamilton had two battalions, one Irish, one English – around 2,000 men. Louis's strategy was now forced by the presence of the multinational Dutch alliance. He would attempt to withdraw from the Dutch provinces and try to seize his real objective, the Spanish Netherlands. Turenne, however, would repeatedly have to repel attacks against the Alsace region and along the Rhine in a defensive posture, something that the French had never accounted for at the start of the war. Turenne, now in his sixties, seemed at the height of his strategic genius, and barely impaired by his age. A veteran of the Thirty Years' War, he exhibited the best and worst aspects of that tragic conflict. Despite paying close attention to the welfare of his men, he gave scant consideration to the plight of the surrounding civilian population, a fact that would be clearly borne out in the 1674 campaign.

Turenne began the campaigning season on the offensive, crossing the Rhine in June and engaging Imperial troops at Sinzheim. This was the first engagement for the new Irish soldiers as part of a mostly cavalry raiding force of 2,000 infantry and 6,000 cavalry. The French force met the enemy force formed on a hill outside the town, in a strong position along the line of the advance. While the infantry took and held the town, the cavalry force attacked uphill, led by Turenne with sword in hand. Despite severe casualties, the Imperial troops were routed. Though the Irish infantry had not played a major role in the battle, Justin MacCarthy had seen his first real battle. After this victory French troops could convince Imperial troops to retreat simply by crossing the Rhine. Louis quickly reinforced Turenne due to his apparent success.

The army was quartered in the region of the elector Palatine, whose lands were defiled through the foraging, rapine and general plunder that accompanied seventeenth-century armies in the field. Turenne had wintered the army in the Palatinate and thus driven the elector into the arms of the Emperor. The army exploited the region on the far side of the Rhine throughout the summer. This early form of 'scorched earth' policy was symptomatic of the terrible reality of warfare in this area and exploitation of enemy resources was routinely carried out, most expertly by Turenne's troops. The Irishmen in this case appear to have been particularly adept at plunder and the ill-disciplined behaviour associated with it. The peasants, perhaps understandably, struck out in the form of bloody reprisals against the troops feeding off the populace. Small pockets of soldiers could be ambushed and killed by bands of peasants. When the Irish recognised some of their troops amongst the dead, they indulged in bloody reprisals of their own, burning towns and murdering the locals.

The elector, in desperation, wrote to Turenne in an attempt to stop the slaughter, even challenging the marshal to a duel. Turenne, despite stating that such acts were commonplace in war, and the natural consequence of his king's orders, had some of the Irish punished. Presumably some of the worst offenders were hanged, and this appears to have put an end to the worst of the excesses. It is not clear what part the officers played in this plunder, and how extensively they attempted to stop it. It is clear, however, that for the young MacCarthy, such sights were alien, and many of the officers would not easily forget the experience. That is not to say that looting and pillage were unique to the Irish troops. As late as September Louvois considered that villages and towns in the area who did not pay sufficient contributions were showing the French considerable disdain. Within a two-week period thirteen towns and villages were burned to the ground and the inhabitants killed or scattered. Unbelievably, despite the devastation, the acts would be repeated in the same area during the war in 1689.

Though Turenne may have had the upper hand, by late August 30,000 Imperial troops under Bournonville threatened the Alsace region. In a masterstroke Turenne blocked the Imperial advance, forcing them to subsist in the devastated Palatinate. The advance faltered and was abandoned by September. Bournonville had not finished, however, and moved his army south to seize Strasbourg which, despite previous neutrality, quickly fell and allowed Imperial troops to threaten Alsace once more. Turenne was now keenly aware that reinforcements were on their way to Bournonville and thus decided to attack. He moved to the north of Strasbourg, effectively splitting the Imperial forces. By October Turenne had arrived at Molsheim, threatening Imperial lines of communication and supply with Strasbourg and the main Imperial force at Ensheim. On the morning of 4 October he moved against the enemy. Bournonville's left flank was anchored by a wooded area and it was there that Turenne would concentrate his infantry assault. The battle in the woods began with French dragoons and skirmishers but, as Bournonville threw more and more German infantry into the fray the French, English and Irish troops were ordered to attack. Conditions were terrible as constant rain meant that matchlocks were useless and the battle for the woods must have quickly decayed into vicious hand-to-hand fighting. Turenne was forced to commit three more infantry battalions from his centre as well as supporting cavalry from his right flank. The French troops eventually carried the day and the Imperialists were forced back. Although the wood had been cleared, the French were hindered by Imperial fieldworks and could advance no further. Turenne's use of additional troops to secure the woods had weakened his centre, an advantage which Bournonville would not let slip. Imperial cavalry charged the French lines in the centre and the weakened left in an attempt to turn the flank and rout the army. French infantry battalions kept their composure, however, following their excellent training and drill and forming battalion-size squares, leaving no exploitable gap open to the Imperial cavalry. Despite some success against the French cavalry reserve, the Imperial charge was quickly spent and the mounted troops were forced back by successive French countercharges. Ostensibly the battle was over and the Imperials withdrew in the night, with the French too exhausted to pursue.

The Battle of Ensheim was over. George Hamilton had been severely wounded in the clash, most likely in the fight for the woods whilst leading his troops. The extent of his wounds is not known, though a French observer remarked that he 'had performed great acts of valour, having with a battalion of his regiment cut to pieces a hostile battalion and dispersed the dragoons who supported it'. In the rain with matchlocks, and dispersed in a wooded area, the fight would not have been decided by steady line and deadly volley, but with melee, and Justin MacCarthy must have had his first real taste of hand-to-hand fighting. Strategically, the fight had not been a great victory for either side. In Turenne's case he had not been able to split Bournonville from the Brandenburg reinforcements that could potentially change the course of the war. Turenne had little option but to fall back until reinforced with troops from Condé's army.

The French were not exhausted yet, however. As the Imperial troops went into winter quarters in the rich areas of the Alsace region, Turenne planned his next move. Winter offensives relied heavily on supply, since foraging was so limited and potentially disastrous for large field armies. Louvois, however, brought his logistical genius to the fore and Turenne prepared to attack Imperial troops in the region. By December the ablest and hardiest French troops, including the Irish, were on the move through the Vosges mountains. By the end of the month Turenne had emerged near Mulhausen, surprising and routing a large enemy cavalry force. He then marched north to Turkheim by 5 January 1675, where his 30,000 strong army faced a hastily arrayed Imperial force. The French, English and Irish troops had endured privations and forced marching across mountains, yet still they outflanked a similarly sized army and took Turkheim. George Hamilton and his regiment again distinguished themselves. The Irish clearly had something to prove and fought well for the French, despite the political turmoil in Europe and England. Turenne watched the Germans leave the Alsace region and put his troops in winter quarters, after perhaps his most notable success in the

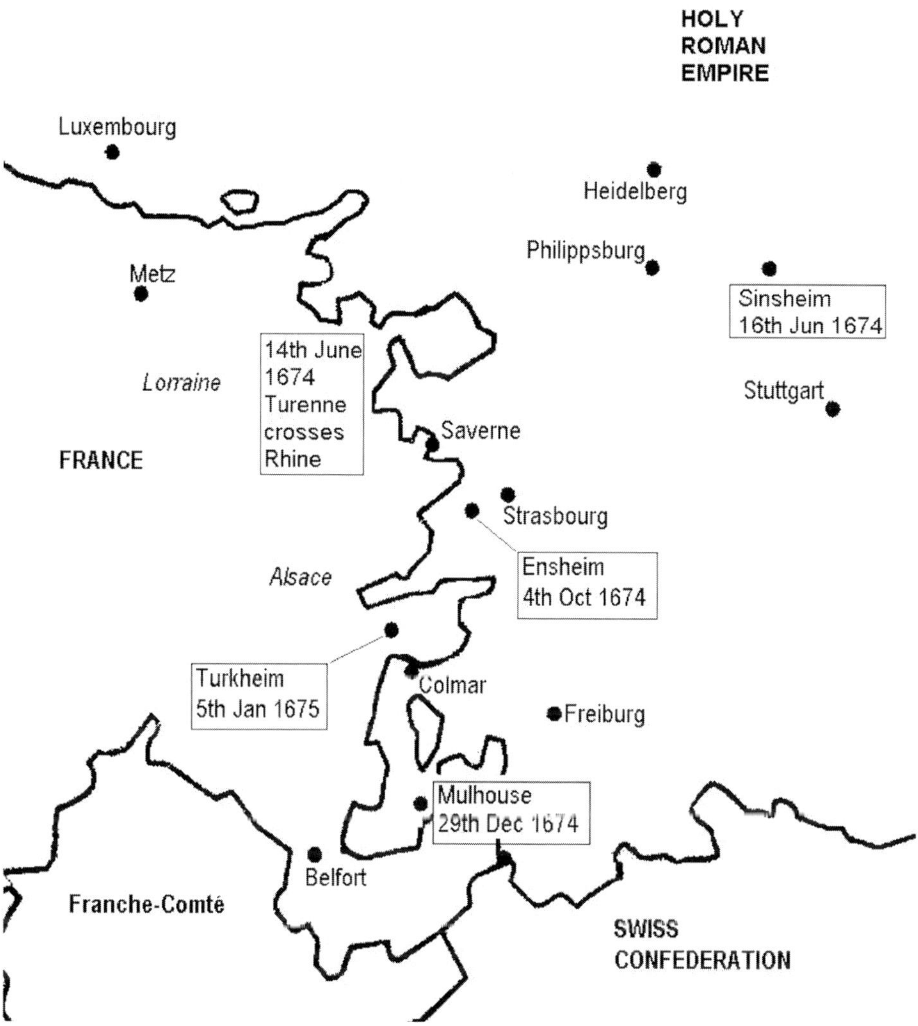

Turenne's campaign on the Rhine, 1674–75.

war. The Irish troops had in a few short months fought two major battles, marched across some of the worst terrain in Europe and been led by the greatest general of the age. For the officer cadre, including MacCarthy, the military experience would enable them to fight in any theatre in Europe. We can speculate that Justin was by this stage keen to advance in the military, having tasted victory, and not been frustrated as yet by the prospect of serious defeat. George Hamilton, who led by example, had by March been promoted to brigadier of infantry. It seemed that the Irish troops could reap real rewards and the advancement they so desired in the service of the French.

By 1675 the war was being fought in the Spanish Netherlands and the Rhineland, but Louis also had troops in Catalonia under Schomberg and an army in Sicily. In Germany, however, Turenne once more faced Montecuccoli. The Imperial troops had not forgotten his victory in Alsace in January and now sought to retake the lost territory. The old adversaries played a sophisticated game of cat and mouse as Montecuccoli attempted to cross the Rhine in force and Turenne countered his manoeuvre.

By late July Turenne had almost cornered the Imperial troops against the banks of the Rhine and wished to finish them before they could make any serious attempt to cross into the Alsace region. As Montecuccoli attempted to retreat east, Turenne intercepted and forced a confrontation at Salzbach on 27 July. Turenne rarely led from the rear. It was not in his nature. Such an attitude also applied to his scouting of the battlefield, and as the armies prepared for the battle, Turenne and St Hilaire, the French artillery commander, were observing an enemy artillery battery on the French right. Montecuccoli had moved 600 men with some cannon into a churchyard, covered in the front by a small stream. Turenne then needed to scout the lines and decide where to place his own cannon, since seventeenth-century field pieces, unlike their more manoeuvrable descendants, were rarely relocated once placed. Their tactical position was therefore of the utmost importance in this era. It is thought that George Hamilton warned Turenne of the danger of being so close to the enemy cannon, but to no avail. The enemy gunners would rarely miss such a chance and opened fire on the group of French officers. The cannonball tore off St Hilaire's arm and struck Turenne's body, killing him instantly. A French legend had been killed in the most unjust of circumstances. Hamilton immediately covered the body so that French troops would not feed off rumour and potentially rout but, despite this and additional French attempts to hide the truth until after the battle, word of the great general's death soon spread. Turenne's demise slowed the momentum of the French attack, and ultimately the campaign. By the end of July, and with the advantage of poor weather that hid their movement, the French troops were falling back, pursued with zest by Montecuccoli, who now pressed his advantage and chased the demoralised French army back through the Alsace region. A devastated Louis sent Condé to stem the flood and prevent a disaster.

Montecuccoli now sent his cavalry across the Rhine to Altenheim on a flanking manoeuvre in an attempt to cut off the French army. The French troops, though brave and determined for the most part to avenge Turenne's death, were poorly led, resulting in some disorder. They managed, however, to march as far as the town of Wilstet before pursuing Imperial troops caught up with them. A rearguard action was required and the rearguard of the near disorganised French army was made up from two regiments, the dragoons of the Chevalier de Bouflers and the English and Irish infantry of Count George Hamilton. Most of the French baggage and cavalry and the majority of the infantry had passed over the nearby river. Their safe passage and further retreat would require a hasty defence against the forward elements of the pursuing Imperial troops, in this case 4,000 infantry and 2,000 dragoons. Forming up in line of battle, Hamilton's troops repelled repeated charges from the Imperial mounted troops until it was judged safe to follow the main body. Montecuccoli would not be distracted and the pursuit would continue, in the hope that by the time the French had reached Altenheim, the Imperial commander's cavalry flanking force would be set to strike.

At the passage of the Schutter River another rearguard action was required. On this occasion, however, the Irish were not required to carry out the defence. Instead the Champagne regiment and a force of cavalry were engaged. In this instance the troops were surprised by Imperial infantry and cut to pieces. Most of the officers and the commander were killed. The situation was becoming desperate. Despite this success, Montecuccoli was cautious, to the benefit of the retreating French troops, giving them time to reform. Rather than take rapid advantage of the disastrous rearguard action, the Imperial commander pursued his cavalry action, pushing more troops along the mountainous route that would permit a surprise attack at Altenheim. The Imperial troops had taken too long to move, however, and the Irish and French infantry were waiting for them as they crossed the river. Volley after volley was poured upon the attackers, French training and discipline making the difference against numerical superiority. Late in the battle however, the Imperial cavalry appeared in the French rear. The Irish and French troops now fought surrounded by the enemy and Hamilton and his men must have thought that the battle was over. In characteristic style, the French cavalry from the main body returned to the fray and rescued their brave infantry. The battle raged throughout the day, but the desperate bravery of the French began to tell as the Imperial troops swayed then broke.

The French and allied troops remained victorious and retreated successfully across the Rhine. Hamilton had made a major difference to the rearguard actions and may very well have helped save the major part of the French army. Uncharacteristically, he was admired by the French for his valiant efforts and made a major general in February 1676. The French also spoke of him as having shown 'the greatest proofs of valour' and the Irish having performed marvellously throughout the campaign. The French celebrated *gloire* wherever they saw it and the Irish were rapidly gaining an excellent reputation. There can have been little better military experience for Justin MacCarthy. He had tasted both great victory and the demands of a demoralising retreat. The Irish troops, however, had remained loyal and stood against the enemy ranged against them. The Irish had bathed in *gloire* and found a taste for it on the bloody crucible of Louis's European battlefields.

The 1676 campaign would see a great many changes in the fortune of the Irish. Like so many of Louis's wars, although there had been great victories, there had been equally disappointing reverses. Although none of these were crushing – indeed the nature of the strategic seventeenth-century battlefield does not lend itself to crushing defeats – the to and fro nature of the war to date meant that it showed little real sign of progress. Louis was by now on the defensive. He had made some gains in the Spanish Netherlands but the Dutch provinces seemed part of a dream long forgotten. Luxembourg now replaced Condé in Alsace where the Irish troops still served. Charles of Lorraine once more commanded the Imperial troops. The campaign would see no major battles and would mainly be conducted through sieges, Philippsburg being the main objective of the Imperials. Some movement across the Rhine did take place, however. In October, again pursued by an Imperial force, the French forced battle at Kockersburg, between Strasbourg and Saverne. After a cavalry action and the withdrawal of some of the mounted troops, Hamilton was forced once more to check the advance of the Imperial attackers. At the last moment fresh cavalry came to the aid of the battered infantry and carried the day for the French. George Hamilton had been killed, however. His regiment had been involved in every major action in the Rhine campaign and had distinguished itself tremendously. For Justin, the death of his cousin and commander must not only have been upsetting but it must have seemed as if a chapter of his life had ended, his first taste of service in Louis's army.[2]

And thus, in a single stroke, the Irish troops were left without a regimental commander. It is at this time that the first real evidence of MacCarthy's growing reputation with the French becomes evident. By November of 1676 Justin's loyalty and apparent sound service in the regiment would pay dividends. The Duke of Monmouth was a lieutenant general in the French army and had led a regiment similar to Hamilton's. The illegitimate son of Charles II, he would become the puppet of the Whig conspiracy and the arch-rebel at Sedgemoor in 1685. For now, however, he was temporarily the colonel-proprietor of the regiment that had belonged to George Hamilton and had previously commanded the Irish regiment, within which Justin now served. Patrick Sarsfield, who would later gain fame in the Irish war, served under MacCarthy at this time as a lieutenant. Justin was a captain, in charge of a company of Irishmen.[3]

Monmouth had placed Lieutenant Colonel Scott in charge of the troops, though the continual ill health of this officer was a matter of concern. Charles II was also concerned. His troops in French service were apparently being ill-led to the extent that discipline and order were beginning to slip. With anti-French sentiment becoming an increasingly worrying trend to the English King, he sought a solution through Monmouth. Monmouth wrote to Louvois:

> The King, having reflected on Mr Scott's continual ill health, which is the cause that he cannot take the care necessary for governing the regiment well, the consequences whereof are many disorders and the relaxation of discipline, has decided to recall him to give him something else here, and has ordered me to appoint to his charge of colonel-lieutenant Mr Macartie, who will present you with this, and who is a person of quality and merit. He has already served in France, and his brother has commanded a regiment there, and I hope he will acquit himself so well as to deserve the King's good opinion of him. I beg you to give him a share of your favour and to obtain the King's approval of him. I refer myself to him to inform you as to the affairs of the regiment, begging you to listen to him favourably and to give him such orders as you may deem for his Majesty's service.[4]

Justin soon received his orders from the Duke of Monmouth. He was to go to Paris and meet with Louvois, with the Duke's letter of recommendation. Other orders related to the settling of accounts. Scott, it seems, had been somewhat lax with the paying out of French money to new recruits. In addition Monmouth ordered Justin to investigate further irregularities with Scott, with regard to the payment of 30,000 pounds to the regiment in 1675. There was perhaps more to Monmouth's remarks of Scott's 'ill health' than was immediately apparent. It seemed that the regiment had fallen into some disarray in the interim in terms of its readiness for duty, and Monmouth was taking immediate steps to rectify the situation. Stories of rebellious, ill-disciplined Irish regiments acting in the king's name in a foreign land, would provide too rich an opportunity for the anti-French lobby in England. Justin's last order from Monmouth seems to echo this sentiment:

> You are to take particular care that the discipline of the regiment be preserved, that both officers and soldiers behave as becomes them in their respective stations.

It is interesting to note that the young John Churchill was also considered for the post, though was turned down by Louvois, the future Duke of Marlborough being 'too addicted to pleasure'. It was clear that a no-nonsense professional soldier was required for the post and Monmouth was keen to see that the regiment did not disintegrate, urging Justin to push Louvois to permit one battalion to remain in garrison whilst two battalions would serve in the field. Louvois's meeting with Justin is not recorded, though it seems that his brother's reputation, as well as his own, spoke volumes. MacCarthy's military career and future seemed secure.[5]

The European war was not over, however. The majority of the two battalions fielded would be Irish troops but the nature of the war had changed. Though Louis's strategy had been essentially defensive, there had been some remarkable manoeuvres along the Rhine. Turenne, the master strategist, had gone, however, and the loss had affected Louis's strategic decision making. The war would now reach its conclusion, where significant gains would be minimised and each side would strive to finish the conflict in as powerful a position as possible. The scope of such a victory was significantly limited by this stage. The nature of the coalition and the odds now stacked against Louis meant not only that he would have to settle for a resolution, and soon, but that he would have to increase the size of his army to one-quarter-of-a-million men. Créqui would defend the Alsace region as Luxembourg had been moved to the north. MacCarthy, however, would lead his troops in the Spanish Netherlands for this campaign.

The ebb and flow of battle that had characterised the war of manoeuvre under Turenne was over and most of the engagements in the campaign were sieges, with only one major battle at Cassel. By 1678 peace negotiations were well underway, though the year would still see some of the most ferocious fighting to date, as each side competed to gain last minute territory. Louis took the Dutch city of Ghent by March in an attempt to secure peace before Charles II was forced to take the Dutch side in the war through the inevitable anti-French sentiment of his Parliament. Although the peace treaty was signed by 10 August, fighting did not cease until the 15th, by which time William had attacked French forces at St Denis, west of Mons. Fighting continued along the Rhine until October when the two shattered armies went into winter quarters. In Catalonia activity ceased by May.

Louis's taking of Ghent had the desired effect of increasing the pressure on all parties to sue for peace, though he would inevitably have to return it to its Spanish masters. The French too were under pressure to gain an agreement before English troops entered the war on the side of the allies. Despite the arrival of an English force in May, Louis reached agreement with Charles for English neutrality, though the bargain would not hold for long. The Treaty of Nijmegen signed with the Dutch was soon followed by agreement with the Spanish and Imperialists. Louis made a great many gains from the deal and obtained many valuable cities, only having to give up a number of seized fortresses, and dominion over Phillippsburg and Lorraine. The French retained Freiburg and a bridge over the Rhine. The Dutch regained all land captured by the French. The Spanish were the real losers, since the devastated Spanish Netherlands had been broken up amongst the main protagonists. Though Louis' initial aims had been somewhat downsized, he had made significant gains in the Netherlands and was still perceived as a significant threat throughout Europe.[6]

For Justin the campaign had seen him turned from a raw officer recruit into an experienced regimental commander. News from England regarding the turning tide of English support meant that the regiment that had fought and died for so long in French service would be quickly disbanded. Unsure of how matters would develop, but certain that disbandment of the French regiment could be problematic, Justin wrote from Paris to his uncle Ormond:

> I have once since my coming hither given your Grace the trouble of a letter, but I know not whether it came to your hands. And now, my Lord, I must importune you again, for I am so alarmed at the bill I hear that has passed the House of Commons for the recalling of us out of the French service that I know not what to do unless your Grace can by your interest get me particularly excepted, which is the only hope I have that can prevent my ruin, having been at vast expense to equip myself for the field, besides a certain disappointment of making my fortune, which I am in a good way of doing if I were permitted to continue here. I beseech your Grace, if nothing can be done in this business, at the least that I may have your advice how I shall carry myself, for without it I shall not stir.[7]

Monmouth had decreed that MacCarthy would deduct one *sol* per *livre* paid to his troops for himself. As long the troops remained in French service MacCarthy would be paid. Monmouth also commented on MacCarthy's 'good service' as colonel of the regiment.[8]

Justin's concerns did have some basis, however, not only with the ending of the Dutch war but with events in England. Despite the overtones of his preference to continue with his military career due to his investment and his potential within it, another point is clear: Justin by this stage much preferred the French service to that of his king. He had grown up in France, aware that Cromwell sought to remove his father's lands, and with the knowledge of his brother's service. These facts must have been forefront in his mind. He was also securing an excellent reputation with the French, something that he would have to earn from scratch, against stiffer odds and competition, if in English service. His feelings are perhaps understandable. The English had seen the Dutch as more powerful and benevolent allies than the French and the Dutch war heightened the desire to protect England against a dominant France and the fear of French *absolutism*. The political climate that would quickly develop would see a change in Justin's fortune once more, however.

Chapter III

A Return to England 1678–1685

1678 was a pivotal year in English politics with regard to the rest of Europe. Support for a Dutch alliance had increased significantly and Louis began to be seen as the enemy of England. Much of the change in attitude had started with the royal marriage in 1677 between William, *stadtholder* of the Dutch provinces and Mary, the eldest daughter of James, Duke of York. Not only did this ensure that the two countries would move closer together politically and militarily but it gave William a significant interest in English affairs, now that he was in effect part of the English succession and could potentially gain the crown. William, by virtue of the latest Dutch war, could not trust the French monarch and since it seemed that his lust for conquest could not easily be satisfied, the need for allies was crucial. That being said, William and Mary's marriage would not simply be a political charade like those of so many of their contemporaries.[1]

With the signing of the treaty, and the end of the Dutch war, the English and Irish troops of MacCarthy's regiment returned home to England. The regiments of *Gendarmes* had been disbanded. Justin's newfound career had been abruptly ended unless he could persuade the king to back an Irish regiment. Tragedy had once more struck the MacCarthy family in Ireland in 1677. Callaghan had died. His widow had written to Charles expressing her concerns regarding her son Donogh, then eight years old and the new Earl of Clancarty. The Countess expressed her wish to have the boy's Protestant religion guaranteed by Charles due to his lineage and she was concerned at bringing the boy up in an Ireland where the Catholic Church still held a significant degree of power. Charles wrote to Ormond, the Lord Lieutenant of Ireland:

> Having received a petition from Elizabeth, Countess of Clancarty, Dowager of Callaghan, Earl of Clancarty, lately deceased, setting forth that the guardianship of her only son Donnogh, now Earl of Clancarty, being about 8 years old is devolved on her as being his mother and a Protestant, and that she desires and designs to breed him up in the true Protestant religion, but has reason to fear her endeavours will meet with much opposition from the titular clergy and others of the Church of Rome, because his father and grandfather were both of that religion and praying our assistance and authority, we therefore require you at all times,

> as there shall be occasion, to use our power and authority to assist and countenance her in the education of her said son in the Protestant religion, and, if any persons whatever attempt to inveigle or take him away from her or to pervert him in the principles of the Protestant religion to cause such persons to be prosecuted with the utmost severity of the law.[2]

As events would show, the Countess need not have worried about the Catholic church, but instead those other forces that would determine the future of her son. The young earl would later write to Ormond requesting that he be his guardian.[3]

It is unclear whether Justin was aware of the turn of events or not, and it is by no means clear as to exactly what (or who) the Countess was concerned about. The events to follow would show just how perceptive she had been, however.

Having returned to England, there would be little hope for the Irish officers of using their military experience in English regiments. Their chosen religion meant that they would not be accepted for commissions in England. Charles, however, had no intention of wasting the experience that the men had gained in France. He would instead form a regiment of Irish troops, led by Sir Thomas Dongan. When relations with the French were restored, plans were put into effect to the extent that the regiment would once more be sent to serve under Louis. An Irish Catholic regiment had too much potential for trouble if serving in England as part of the army, no matter what the king's personal feelings on the matter might have been.

Paranoia in England, however, had been simmering during the war. Anti-Catholic hysteria had reached new heights, and matters were about to get significantly worse with the advent of the 'Popish Plot'. The plot would become one of the strangest yet markedly far-reaching events in British history. The minimal degree of tolerance that had been shown toward Catholics would be stretched to its limits as it took hold.

It is pertinent to outline at this point the particular form of paranoia that gripped the populace and led to the plot's credibility in the eyes of English society. Louis XIV dominated a large portion of a mostly Catholic Europe, a form of Christianity which Englishmen associated with absolute monarchy – an anathema to the ideals of the English Parliament. To many Protestants the aim of the Catholic Church was to impose such governing ideology on the world! After all, the Pope still retained his right (although not rigidly enforced) to depose monarchs and 'dangerous' ideas such as standing armies, which could back up arbitrary power stemmed from Catholic countries such as Spain and the new 'menace', France. With the civil war fresh in the minds of many, the parallel events that occurred in Ireland, a Catholic uprising in the British Isles, gave credence to the concerns of many Englishmen. Growing hysteria verging on general panic at the prospect of Catholic rebels usurping the throne and killing men, women and children was all too evident. When events conspired to light the touchpaper of anti-Catholic paranoia, such behaviour was accepted as the norm. The Catholic community in England had astonishingly managed to survive the onslaught of the preceding years although significantly reduced in size and influence due to the penal laws enforced throughout the sixteenth and seventeenth centuries. By 1673 the Test Act denying transubstantiation, the mainstay of Catholicism, would bar many devout Catholics from holding public and military office.

There were of course exceptions and some Catholics did take the oaths in contravention of Papal directives. Enforcement of the penal laws, however, had lapsed to a large degree in the 1660s and 70s. In fact, they had not been rigidly adhered to since the 1640s and, with Charles's accession to the throne, the laws had fallen out of favour somewhat. There had been scares and minor bouts of hysteria of course, Charles's marriage to the Catholic Catherine of Braganza, the second Anglo-Dutch war and the alliance with the French. Even the Great Fire of London had allegedly been an arsonist's plot propagated by dissenting Catholics or the French or any other convenient scapegoat. Many Catholics obviously wished for French support and Papal recognition of England. In reality, however, they were too few and lacked influence.

The public face of Charles's potential Catholic leanings after the 1670 Treaty of Dover would further fuel the anti-Catholic fires. In March 1672 he suspended the Penal laws to the horror of magistrates and high court judges alike. Louis's war on the continent had been a distant threat, yet now it seemed to many members of the English Parliament that he was at the back door. The Anglo-French naval attack on the Dutch drove Parliament to force Charles to remove his Declaration of Indulgence, and rigidly enforce the penal laws. The Test Act soon followed. By 1677 Parliament sought to ensure against future 'mishaps' through the introduction of a bill barring any member of the royal family marrying a Catholic bride without the consent of Parliament. Questions were raised over the English succession. William and Mary's marriage in November 1677 was shortly followed by the birth of a son to the Duke of York. Although the infant died within a few weeks, the perceived threat of a Catholic successor had become all too clear to Parliament, thereby threatening to displace Mary and Anne, James's Protestant daughters, from the English crown.

Such were the conditions within which the Popish Plot was born, an atmosphere of fear and doubt ripe for propaganda, anti-Catholic rabble-rousing and royal intrigue. Titus Oates had been an Anglican priest whose career had been beset with scandal and deception. He had been a brief convert to Catholicism, and together with his co-conspirator Israel Tongue, now claimed that there existed a Jesuit plan for the assassination of Charles II, which would leave the throne empty for James, a Catholic King. Oates was examined by the Privy Council in order to establish the truth of his claims. Although the account was fabricated, fate and coincidence would conspire to give credence to the whole affair.

Edward Coleman, secretary to the Duchess of York, was discovered to have written potentially 'treasonous' letters to Louis XIV's confessor, the French Jesuit François La Chaise. At worst, such communication implicated James in an apparently French design to impose Catholicism on England, while at the very least the affair played into the hands of the anti-Catholic movement. The events would bring James close to ruin. As if this was not enough to rouse suspicion, the unexplained murder of Sir Edmund Godfrey, a judge whom Tongue and Oates had first approached with the details of the plot, only made matters worse. Of course the murder was blamed on Catholic conspirators attempting to cover their tracks. Frenzied anti-Catholic hatred swept through the country, and treason trials led to the conviction and execution of twenty-four Catholics, while many died in prison.[4]

Although Justin had no direct part in the plot or the trials that followed its instigation, it would be almost impossible for a Catholic officer in England to remain untouched by the chaotic events. In October 1678, however, even in the midst of the plot, Justin was promoted once more. Colonel Thomas Dongan was commissioned as Lieutenant Governor of Tangier, leaving the command of the regiment open. Justin was subsequently commissioned as colonel of the troops, destined now to serve in Ireland.[5]

Charles's army was not trusted, however. Parliament therefore requested that portions of the local militia should be mobilised to keep order. Plans for shipping all Catholic officers who had returned from France to Dongan's (now MacCarthy's) regiment had been in place since February of 1678, since the king and Secretary of State Williamson had signed the commissions, but little action had been taken. Not all of the officers had left for Ireland, including the new commander. A proclamation was issued on 30 October reminding all 'popish recusants' that they should leave London forthwith. In November 1678, as the plot and hysteria had taken hold, Justin was walking outside the House of Commons. It seems unlikely that Justin did so with any intent, though in the light of the local fears of the time this seems a rash decision for any Catholic to take, even if he was a senior military officer.

Unsurprisingly, he was arrested and questioned, then subsequently told to leave the capital. In effect he could only be accused of ignoring the proclamation, in that he was a Catholic and had not left the city. In a bold move, however, he attempted to exempt himself from the terms of the declaration, being informed that he would have to do so at the Bar of the House of Commons. Within, Ormond was later told that MacCarthy had:

> Behaved himself so discreetly as to appease the House: yet for example's sake they ordered him to give obedience to the proclamation that night

> so that all the warriors despairing to come off so well are by his example withdrawn.[6]

Justin had the temerity to oppose the order but could do little against the forces ranged against him and his fellow Irish and Catholic officers. The force of public and Parliamentary opinion in light of the plot, however implausible, was too strong. The House also had the wisdom to appeal to MacCarthy's common sense. If he withdrew from London, many of his fellow officers would do the same, an elegant if somewhat unsatisfactory solution for all parties. Indeed, many of Justin's contemporaries saw the results of his appeal as a fair assessment of what they themselves might expect in similar circumstances.

Many of the officers took this as their signal to flee the country. Not all had been successful, however. Patrick Sarsfield, now one of MacCarthy's captains, was held under lock and key in Chester with several other Irishmen. Even Justin could not leave as easily as he had initially thought. As he made his way out of the capital and thence to Ireland, he was once more arrested at Barnet and imprisoned. He was eventually released via the Privy Council's decision and an immediate order from Whitehall, stating that Barnet was outside the ten-mile radius that had been outlawed for Catholics. Sarsfield was subsequently released also, and he too sailed for home.

Many Irish got away, but many did not. Some of those caught were subsequently executed at the end of the plot as news spread that Irishmen had apparently been involved in Godfrey's murder. Justin had escaped with little time to spare, as Parliament slowly became aware of the implications of the size and potential of the Irish officer cadre. The scandal had broken and it was made clear that the Catholic officers who had been detained had been excused both the Test Act and the Oaths of Allegiance. Despite Secretary of State Williamson's attempted implication of Monmouth in the affair, he was sent to the Tower.[7]

With increased tension in England, many Catholic officers, effectively out of a job since their return from French service, fled to Ireland. Justin's regiment was fast becoming a haven for disaffected Irish military men seeking some sort of protection from the still potent levels of persecution that were to be expected in an England still rocked by the plot. It is surprising that in the grip of such fears Dongan's men had remained intact as a regiment for as long as they did, given the feelings of the time. Charles undoubtedly had a hand in this, as he had made it clear that he did not intend to get rid of those officers who had so loyally served him on the continent.

In Ireland so many Irish officers now attempted to gather beneath MacCarthy's flag that several were detained. In reality they had little choice but to seek the apparent refuge of the regiment. Ormond, the Lord Lieutenant became further alarmed when informed that the number of officers claiming to belong to the regiment totalled more that those required to command it. Ormond had been given his own orders with regard to Catholics and the Oath of Supremacy now had to be rigidly enforced with the troops. Accused by his enemies of permitting Papist elements within his army, Ormond knew that he would be ruined should any of the soldiers take matters into their own hands or rebel. He wrote at the end of 1678:

> If any ill accident should happen either by the keeping on foot or disbanding MacCarty's regiment, the inconvenience and the blame too will fall on me; the inconvenience by the disorder that must follow the disbanding of so many men that know how to live upon their neighbours when they want bread, and the blame will be imputed to me; for people here are not so reasonable as to consider whether I have or have not orders; the smart will direct them to murmur at those nearest them, who they think might have prevented it.[8]

Much to his relief, plans were finally drawn up to disband the regiment in January 1679. Both Ormond and Monmouth sought to ensure that some form of compensation was given to the officers, though it is unclear how much of this was paid in the end. Although Charles had preferred to keep his Irish officers, in political terms they were now becoming a problem, if not an embarrassment. Charles's final note to Ormond in his letter of January 1679 closed the door on his Irish regiment:

> The arms being delivered up and all accounts adjusted, the Commissioners shall forthwith disband the respective companies and then the officers and soldiers are immediately to disperse to their own abodes and behave in all things as becomes dutiful subjects.[9]

The witch-hunt in England continued and the wave of anti-Catholic and anti-monarchist feeling enabled the pro-Parliamentarian 'Whigs' to gain significant ground in the Commons over the 'Tories' whose allegiance was to church and king. Ultimately the changes wrought by the plot would sow the seeds of the British party political system, replacing the older groups linked solely by family or background. Opposition to James would not simply end with the plot's intrigues, however. In 1679 the Earl of Shaftsbury, leader of the Whig opposition to Charles II, put forward the Exclusion Bill designed to keep James off the throne. His exploits came to naught as fears of a new civil war meant that opinion swayed towards the Royalists. Parliament was once more successfully dissolved in 1681. James would survive all of these attempts to circumvent his right to succession, though the frenzy stirred up by Oates's depositions would last for years. He would not be called to account and tried until 1685.

Nonetheless, Justin was once more effectively out of work and out of favour as a professional soldier. The Europe of the late seventeenth century, however, had more than its fair share of conflict and the market for mercenary officers across Europe was lucrative, and for many the only way of pursuing their chosen career. To this end Justin travelled to Denmark in 1679 to pursue service with the Danish Army. The Danes had been allied to the Dutch throughout the war, but also saw the opportunity to regain much of their territory lost during the earlier part of the century to their old rival Sweden. The Swedes had allied themselves with Louis throughout the Dutch conflict, and so the complex alliances in this case played into the hands of the Danes. There is little record of Justin's experiences during this part of the war though the clash between the Swedes and the Danes was dominated by Swedish success, at least on land.[10]

There is a three-year gap in the records regarding Justin's activities at this time. This may be due to his travelling in Europe or Scandinavia as a mercenary officer, in a similar manner to many of his contemporaries. He may even have resurfaced in France for a time, though this seems unlikely given the lack of records. It is interesting, however, to speculate as to the events of those intervening years because of what happened next. By 1682 Justin had returned to England. In May he returned to Ireland, having received word that his mother had died. There are few details with regard to the funeral bar that she was interred in Dublin. Her brother Ormond left for England shortly afterwards.[11]

In England Justin's name was connected with yet another plot, an apparently Irish one this time. His name appears in a reported conspiracy outlined in letters written by Viscount Preston to the Secretary of State. Preston outlined that a number of traitors in league with France would undertake the propagation of an English revolution of sorts with French arms and naval support and, most significantly, the heavy presence of Irish troops. Preston's mysterious informant related that the Irish would be led by *Colonel Maccarty* amongst others. The plans, reputedly laid down meticulously, and with French aid, would dictate the seizing of Cork, Limerick and Galway. Ireland, for so long feared as a stepping-stone for subsequent English invasion, would be used as a French base. Luckily, widespread news of the plot was kept secret, mainly because there was little evidence and, in terms of the logistics and preparation involved, the plan seems somewhat fantastic. Had word got out, similar scenes of panic to those that had accompanied the Popish Plot would have been repeated and the threat of another Irish revolution would have brought severe repercussions. By March 1683 Justin had returned to Ireland. Secretary Jenkins had little faith in the new scheme:

> his Majesty has every day more and more reasons to believe Tilly to be a cheat. I have no orders concerning Lord Clanricarde or Col Maccarty nor do I think, if they were here any trouble would be given them on an information as incoherent as Tilly's.[12]

Justin now had some difficult decisions to make. It was clear that the climate in England, and the damage that his reputation had taken, would have repercussions with regard to his future.

It is unsurprising then that he seriously considered giving up his military career. His future had shown much promise and his reputation amongst his peers had been second to none. His chances of successful establishment in the English or Irish military were, however, significantly reduced in the current climate. And so, at the end of 1682, Justin returned to what was left of his family. He approached Callaghan's widow, the Lady Clancarty, who had remarried in June 1682 to Sir William Davis, Chief Justice of the King's Bench. With little hope for the future, he asked if he could become the tenant of Blarney Castle and the surrounding area, having decided to return to Ireland. Justin was informed that the present tenant, an English clergyman, could not be 'put out'. Ormond was in London at the time.

The Earl of Arran, Ormond's son and Justin's cousin, acting as Lord Lieutenant in his absence, was apparently aggravated and disturbed by the entire affair. He wrote to his father that Justin had made it clear that he 'would deal with' the present tenant. Initially unsure of how to proceed with MacCarthy, his father having given him no warning of the events that would occur, he was determined not to see the Lady Clancarty 'exploited'.

> If M. will not be persuaded to desist, for I find my Lady Clancarty is unwilling to give him an absolute denial, I am resolved to interpose by telling him privately of the imprudence of the thing, and if I cannot prevail that way I will tell him plainly I will appear publicly against it.[13]

Whether Justin had attempted to bully Lady Clancarty or not, it was clear that the Ormonds were now set against him. Ormond wrote back to his son by January 1683 explaining that the greatest inconvenience of the whole affair would be Justin's religion, and he hoped that the whole thing would blow over. It was also clear that Lady Clancarty could ill afford to create friction since, if her only son Donagh should die, she would have to provide for her own future to a large extent. Ormond guessed that Justin had persuaded the young Donagh to write to him asking for guardianship, in the hope of gaining estates or, at the very least, responsibility for the boy. Despite Ormond's belief that Justin in all likelihood would improve the estate, his religion would preclude any further progress in the matter. Ormond's fears over the Irish regiment were still prevalent, especially over its erstwhile commander. Though he had some feelings for his nephew, Arran had little respect for Justin, considering him the 'improperest man in the world' to be employed in any fashion by his father.

In conference with Chief Justice Davis, matters were 'contrived' by Arran to the extent that the tenant in Blarney would not be removed. It is not clear exactly what transpired in this instance. What is clear is that Justin had lost all hope of gaining his father's estates, in any form. His religion and the scheming of the Ormonds had seemingly removed all hope of a future in Ireland and, by January 1683, Justin abandoned his attempts to retrieve the estates. His efforts at arranging the guardianship of the young Donagh, then being educated as a Protestant in Oxford, would also come to naught. We can never empathise fully with historical characters in these instances, since we have only second-hand knowledge of life in the seventeenth century. We can, however, understand that a degree of bitterness over the whole affair, so soon after the death of his mother, and with such clear prejudice and intolerance on behalf of the Ormonds, must have embittered Justin not only to them but to the religious and political systems that were in place in Ireland. Such feelings would inevitably lead to sympathies with the revolutionary change that was to follow.[14]

Lady Clancarty's fears over the young Donagh's upbringing in Ireland had meant that he now resided in Oxford, carefully tutored by the Bishop of Oxford, the dean of Christchurch. By 1684 Justin had returned to England which, though still markedly anti-Catholic, was not so consumed by the hatred that had prevailed during the Popish Plot. James had returned and was in the ascendancy, and many of his Irish friends had now also relocated to the court in London. Justin persuaded King Charles to write to Oxford asking if his nephew might visit so that they might see the sights of the capital. The Bishop agreed and the sixteen-year-old Donagh promptly travelled to London. The Secretary of State at the time was Lord Sunderland. It is not clear whether Justin's contact with him was by accident or design, though he would have a distinctive influence on Justin's prospects. Sunderland had served on various diplomatic missions for the king, and had been made Secretary of State in 1679. His support of the Exclusion Bill had resulted in his dismissal from the post, though he quickly regained it through the influence of the Duchess of Portsmouth, one of the king's mistresses.

He was now an important player in James's inner circle and in later years would declare himself a Catholic, and then subsequently renounce his beliefs as political expediency demanded. Donagh's arrival in London prompted the plan that Justin and Sunderland must by then have been discussing for some time. How much of the capital the young man saw is not clear, though he would not leave as he had arrived. In an apparent act of revenge, and in an attempt to further his own ends,

Justin saw the young man quickly married to Lord Sunderland's youngest daughter, herself merely fifteen years old.[15]

There is no clear evidence as to who conceived the scheme though it is easy to imagine that Sunderland would have designs on the Clancarty estates. It is also plausible that Justin saw both the Secretary of State's influence on his position and a chance for revenge against the Ormonds and Lady Clancarty. In any event the marriage and the scheme were to have far-reaching effects for MacCarthy. The entire affair seems out of character for an honourable military man. The same man, however, had become embittered towards many things in his life and in his dealings with the English and Irish noblemen. Donagh would return to Ireland, and later become a Catholic. Had Justin's aim been a subtle form of revenge, then it was complete. The next year would see significant changes in his prospects, and the birth of revolutionary change across the British Isles.

Chapter IV

Ireland and the King 1685–1688

It seemed that the ill luck that had bedevilled Justin had now been spent. He was married during this time in England to Arabella Wentworth, the second and youngest daughter of the Earl of Strafford (Thomas Wentworth, whose involvement in Ireland in 1633 as Lord Lieutenant had resulted in the loss of his head – see chapter 1). Arabella was an Englishwoman and details of the relationship and subsequent marriage, whether arranged or not, are sketchy.[1]

The couple would remain childless though Arabella, it appeared, would fully support her husband in the events that followed. By January 1685 the arrangement with Sunderland was paying real dividends for Justin. Two colonels were to receive commissions to command two new regiments in Ireland. Both were Catholics who had served on the continent. More seriously, both were employed in apparent disregard of the Test Act and the legislation that Parliament had so carefully put in place to prevent such experienced Catholic soldiers gaining command in the first place. Colonels Justin MacCarthy and Richard Talbot, however, in receipt of their new commissions, would not be disputing their new appointments, no matter what the reservations of Parliament.[2]

English Protestants viewed the actions at best as a clear flouting of legislation and at worst as the beginning of a pro-Catholic stance with regard to Ireland and the Irish army. Would the fact that a Catholic successor waited in the wings see a resurgence of anti-Catholic feeling in a similar vein to that which bedevilled England during the Popish Plot? Quite possibly, though Charles would hear little complaint with regard to the situation. The Earl of Halifax, the Lord Privy Seal, wrote to the king reminding him of the threat to the Protestant interest in Ireland if such appointments were the sign of things to come. Charles, however, would not be moved, insisting that MacCarthy had been removed from his previous post on his account and had similarly been removed from French service. He had now compensated the Irish officer for his loss. It is unclear what motivated Charles to pursue the appointments at this time. It is probable that the time that Justin had spent at court had not been wasted, however. The relationship with Sunderland proves this to a certain extent. This is further borne out by Charles's re-telling of the events with Halifax to Justin himself, promoting his subsequent angry confrontation with him.[3]

The implication of course is one of scheming and double-dealing within the king's court. Although popular history has highlighted this aspect of Charles's reign, political manoeuvring of this nature was the norm in courts across Europe. That Justin used it to further his own ends is no surprise. It seems that calculated political activity was fashionable, and used to great effect by Justin's fellow appointee to Irish command, Richard Talbot.

Talbot had used the system to further his own ends at every opportunity, but to a larger extent than MacCarthy could ever have dreamed of. The same man had fought a duel so many years before with Justin's brother Cormac over the command of a regiment in France, and by now had entered the inner circle of James, Duke of York. Kenyon outlines that, during the Popish Plot, James's close-knit circle of Irish comrades included a number of 'unscrupulous Catholic swordsmen and professional soldiers', among them Richard Talbot, Henry Jermyn and one Justin MacCarthy.[4]

James's liking for Irish adventurers had meant that Talbot (and Justin to some extent) had found noteworthy success and possessed some influence with the heir to the throne. Descended from an 'old English' family, Talbot had been brought up during the intrigue and faithless dealing that beset Ireland during the Confederate war. He had fought for Thomas Preston against O'Neill and the conflict had had a great influence on him, framing his political opinions and motivations. His old English loyalties meant that he possessed a degree of kinship to the church but was also keen to pursue the rights of Ireland. He was, however, looked upon with some suspicion by the native Irish. The twenty-six-year-old Talbot had met the then twenty-three-year-old Duke of York in 1656 in the same exiled court in which Cormac MacCarthy had served.

Talbot would form the principal influence on James's decision to become involved in Irish politics in later years, a decision that would ultimately seal his fate. Even in those early years James helped secure Talbot's military and, ultimately, political position. By the time of the Restoration and the monarchy's return to England, Talbot was a Gentleman of the Bedchamber. Such position and relative importance in the English court allowed him to focus on the Irish issues that were important to him. He had little real interest in the Catholic Church, his main focus being the Irish land question. He correctly assumed that the balance of power in Ireland would lie with those who owned and ultimately controlled the land. He had had his way to a large extent during the Restoration settlement, supported mainly by the 'old English' Royalists, many of whom regained their estates. Talbot had been heavily involved in the Acts of Settlement and Explanation, an affair which earned him as many enemies as friends.

The Irish had needed a powerful representative, a champion even, and Talbot had filled the role in a time when Charles II was keen to see at least some form of 'justice done' for his Irish subjects. Where Ireland was concerned, however, questions of justice and truth were transitory and ill defined. Talbot as Irish champion highlighted the cause of those Royalist Irish, and many would indeed benefit from Charles's reign. He disagreed with Ormond on many questions, but his unwavering loyalty to James and his relative importance in Irish eyes ensured that his position remained relatively strong. In 1680 Talbot married George Hamilton's widow, Frances Jennings, in Paris. His power and influence would reach its zenith during the mid-1680s and subsequent to the event which changed the lives of so many in the English court.[5]

On 6 February 1685 Charles II died from a stroke. Despite his faults and his apparent opposition to James's religion and his Catholic succession, he could not deny his brother his right. He had, however, been prudent enough to ensure that his nieces, James's daughters, had been brought up as Protestants. This ensured Mary's marriage to William and a Protestant succession if all else failed. James's second wife, the Italian Mary of Modena, had borne no male children after all, at least by 1685. He had also been farsighted enough to declare Monmouth, his illegitimate son and erstwhile commander of the Irish and English troops in France, officially a bastard, effectively denying his right to the throne. The subtle Charles had also remarked to William that he expected James to last no more than four years on the English throne. It may have been meant as an indication of things to come. William would certainly not forget his uncle's statement. During Charles's last week, as his stroke took hold, James took measures to ensure that, should his accession be threatened, the militia and the army would uphold order. Sunderland issued orders that those entering England via her ports were to be searched and at worst arrested. James need not have worried however.

Despite the opposition that had been manifest in the Popish Plot and the Exclusion Crisis, James II peacefully succeeded his brother in February 1685. He was not a subtle man and his determination to improve the lot of his Catholic subjects would heighten the ever-present fears amongst the Whigs that the new king's religion and 'Francophilia' would encourage absolute government. Although some degree of antipathy was predictable, England as a whole remained essentially Royalist, at least initially. Within months, however, James had a more pressing problem than the simmering fears of a Protestant Parliament, that of protecting his throne. Monmouth had been in Holland when Charles died and remained confident that the potential revulsion from the English population against a Catholic king would create support for his attempt to take the throne. His landing at Lyme Regis in June did not create the support that he had predicted, however, and despite his protests that Charles had been secretly married to his mother, that James had both started the Great Fire of London and poisoned Charles, his rebellion was limited to the West Country.

James's reaction was swift and by July, troops under Lord Feversham had routed the rebel force at Sedgemoor. Monmouth, the Protestant Pretender, was executed on 15 June. If he had been allowed to live, matters might have been very different, but James had gained confidence from the whole affair. His enlarged standing army had now grown to almost 16,000 men and had remained loyal, and convinced him that he could attempt to make the changes in English society that he had envisioned. Whigs saw the situation differently. A standing army could be used to enforce decisions, no matter how unpalatable. In reality, James lacked the finances for a very large standing army, certainly not on the scale of that of Louis XIV. Sedgemoor, however, had re-spawned some of the latent fears that had always remained hidden beneath the surface of English society. James did not immediately disband the troops after the threat to his throne was removed, leading to Parliamentary accusations that it would become a Catholic army. James protested that, with such threats to English security, he could hardly disband the force. He could have ridden the storm and bided his time. Instead, he played into Parliament's hands, in Ireland.

1685 would become a pivotal year for Ireland, and for those Catholic officers who had remained loyal to the crown. Richard Talbot would now take centre stage. In June James made him the new Earl of Tyrconnel and was perhaps fully aware that giving more influence at this time would cause suspicion. On the other hand, James did try to take the steps that would make the English army more accessible to Catholics. He dispensed the requirements of the Test Acts for many officers, creating his own troops of Life Guards – all Catholic. In reality the English Catholic officer population would remain at only ten to fifteen per cent of the army by 1688. In Ireland, however, the situation would change both rapidly and dramatically. The Irish army was almost exclusively Protestant at the start of 1685. Officers were composed of members of the Protestant aristocracy. This army was not a wholly professional organisation however. Despite numbering over 7,000 men, the quality of the troops was below average and even poor in comparison with their European and English cousins.

Most of the troops had had some training and were familiar with drill and at least a modicum of military discipline, but many common soldiers saw their military role as a 'part time' affair, and would pursue other trades or labour as the need dictated. Morale was also suspect and equipment in Ireland was in a very poor state. Matchlocks, pikes and swords were badly in need of repair. In essence then the essentially Protestant Irish army would have been useless at Sedgemoor, for instance, but had the potential at least to be turned into a reliable fighting force at home. James was determined however to 're-model' the Irish army. For such a task, however, the king, who had never been to Ireland, needed advice. He turned to his friend Richard Talbot, now Earl of Tyrconnel, an act which would have far-reaching consequences. It is understandable, though perhaps somewhat naïve on James's part, for him to believe that Ireland was the restless Catholic nation that he was destined to govern. He would never have this opportunity in Parliamentary England, that of righting past wrongs and supporting the Catholic population with the promise of their support in return.

Tyrconnel saw the situation quite differently. James's subsequent policy towards Ireland was a direct result of Tyrconnel's persuasion and he had quite different goals. His main aim was to overthrow the land settlement in Ireland, the cause for which this old-English Catholic had fought for so long. This clearly meant a replacement of the Protestant hegemony, a task which could only be accomplished through careful manipulation of the new king's wishes. The *interpretation* of James's wish to help the downtrodden Catholic population of Ireland was key to Tyrconnel's plan. Matters would hinge on disarming the militia and hamstringing the Irish Army. Ultimately, the military Protestant force would have to be replaced with a Catholic one, in terms of both officers and men. The unseen danger for James was Parliament's interpretation in turn, and their ultimate understanding of the events that were to unfold. If Protestant troops and officers were replaced with Catholics, was this a model for a re-structuring of the English army; would reform be carried out in Ireland to form a Catholic standing army, thus to enforce James's policies in England?

Tyrconnel's plans began in the summer of 1685. Having persuaded James to recall Ormond, that he needed to introduce some well chosen Catholics into the Irish Army, and that the existing officer corps could form the basis of Cromwellian derived resistance, if left in place Talbot was given what can only be described as a free rein over the reorganisation of the king's Irish forces. In July he instructed that officers in the militia were required to ensure that their troops' arms were kept in their own houses. This ensured that such weapons, belonging to the Protestant militia, could be easily collected at a later date. Within a few short weeks, Tyrconnel, with James's backing, assumed full control of the Irish military. What occurred next can be construed as a reform (although a drastic one) or more distinctly a purge. Tyrconnel's aim was to replace the Protestant officers with old English Catholics whilst sacking the rank and file Protestant troops and replacing them with native Irish. This endeavour was, however, at least initially, his own private interpretation of James's Irish and definitively pro-Catholic 'policy'. He did not have royal sanction for any reform or purge of the existing troops, although it is clear that James must have turned a blind eye to the proceedings. Tyrconnel of course had his own agenda, that of freeing Ireland from the 'Protestant yoke' and the divisive issues of the land question. He could not publicly reveal his intentions at this stage, though his standing with James and the king's pretence at ignorance of the affair allowed him to approach his goal. Despite protests from Clarendon, the new

Lord Lieutenant, public denial was the norm, although it was clear to many of the gentry what the ultimate aim was. New Catholic regiments were also created, most notably one of dragoons under Richard Hamilton, George Hamilton's younger brother, who had fought with Justin MacCarthy in France, and who would fight alongside his cousin once more in the conflict to come.

By the end of 1685, and with gathering impetus, the purge had reached new heights. Over 1,000 men had been replaced in the Irish army. 1686 would see more 're-modelling'. James had not been so naïve as to give Tyrconnel the lord lieutenancy of Ireland but pressure was mounting. He was well aware of the importance of the Protestant base in Ireland. It formed the basis of revenue, family connections and, more importantly, guaranteed the support of Parliament so long as it remained an English sovereign state. James, however, despite the fact that he had issued no clear instruction for Tyrconnel's activities, was slowly losing control of this most important of political aces. By 1686 the situation was wholly in the hands of Tyrconnel. Review and muster of existing troops became a byword for replacement and disbandment. In July over 300 men were removed from the Irish Guards in one day. By September over 5,000 men had been replaced. Excuses for replacement such as removal of old and unfit soldiers abounded, but there was by now little subtle masquerade left with regard to the purging.[6]

The Muster-Master-General wrote to Ormond in September 1686 regarding Lieutenant General Talbot:

> Concerning the Army. He sends an abstract of the Army as his Grace left it, and another as it now stands in his office, but the present rules and instructions for musters give the officers such a latitude that they make what alterations they please between musters, of which he is ignorant till the rolls of the next muster are returned to his office. The abstract of the Army as it now stands contains an estimate of Roman Catholics entertained to June muster, but since that there has been a general disbanding of the old Army, so that he is apt to believe that already two-thirds of the Army at least are Roman Catholics. He has marked the commissioned officers that are generally reputed to be Roman Catholics. The Lieutenant-General of the Army having power to make what changes he pleases in the Army under commissioned officers has lately appointed Romish chaplains to the regiment of guards, the Earl of Ardglass's regiment and Col Russell's regiment, and several others are expected. The writer may count some for Roman Catholics which are not such, yet on the other hand he is confident many more are omitted which might have been added. He should here put an end to his Grace's trouble, did not gratitude oblige and embolden him to lay hold of the opportunity

> of tendering his Grace his most humble thanks for all the favours his Grace has heaped on him, and particularly for the character his Grace was pleased to give of him to the Earl of Clarendon, who gave him to understand so much, and has confirmed it by real favours beyond what the writer could possibly diserve.[7]

Replacing two-thirds of the Protestant Irish Army with Catholics was by no means an easy task, even in the contemporary political climate. For Tyrconnel to have moved so far and so fast was indeed a major coup. The activity was so rapid in fact that some contemporaries, notably the Marshal of the Irish Army, Lord Granard, were convinced that he commanded royal authority in the entire affair.[8]

Tyrconnel's subterfuge was almost complete, however, and even if some guessed at his lack of royal prerogative they were relatively powerless in the situation that was developing. In September 1685 he dismissed all the officers of his own regiment who had received their commissions from Ormond. His pretence at surprise when asked about the affair was symptomatic of his ability to get away with it.[9] The purge would reach its height in the year to come.

Justin MacCarthy followed Tyrconnel's example with relish. He made radical changes within his own Irish regiment. He removed Captain Thomas Bingham, reportedly absent without leave, and replaced him with Thomas Nugent, who had been one of his officers in France. In addition, he forced the Protestant chaplain in the regiment to share his wage with that of a Catholic priest whom MacCarthy had appointed. The chaplain was given the choice of dismissal should he disagree.[10]

As with the balance of the Irish regiments, Justin's troops would not remain untouched by the purges across the country. Within a few short months at the end of 1685 Protestant officers and troops were replaced with old English officers and native Irish troops. Stationed in his native Munster, near Cork, Justin proved popular amongst his troops. This is not surprising since he was a well-qualified officer and experienced commander of men. His experience would have earned him significant respect, especially amongst those Catholics who were new to the military. In reality, however, the lack of experience amongst the rank and file would cause problems for the bulk of the army as matters progressed. The regiment was posted to Cork. There were, however, clear differences between Justin's reputation with regard to treatment of the populace and that of Tyrconnel, as evidenced by the Earl of Longford, a Protestant, who wrote to Ormond in September 1685:

> I was willing to take this opportunity of acquainting your Grace that from him your Grace may authentically have your account of my Lord Tyrconnel's proceedings with the Mayor and Corporation of Drogheda, and how insolently he treated Dean Pullein there on Sunday morning

> before he went to church. He will also tell your Grace what havoc he has made in Sir William's troop, and indeed in most of the troops of his regiment. His lordship was endeavouring to have several of his friends and relations made Sheriffs for the ensuing year, and proceeded so far as to give them promises of it; but I suppose the declaring of my Lord Clarendon Lord Lieutenant has stopped him in his career, and indeed it was but necessary and seasonable, his haughty carriage having so disanimated the Protestants and elated the Papists that the former, or many of them whose effects are only in money, were not only withdrawing from trade but also out of the kingdom, but since the confirmation of the Lord Lieutenant they seem now to assume more courage, and I hope will be so far satisfied as to fall to their trade again.
>
> Col McCarthy's carriage has been so differing from the others that he has by his great civility recommended himself highly to the affections of the people of Cork, though they are notoriously fanatic, and he is as well beloved by the officers of his regiment as it is possible for a man upon so short an acquaintance to be, for he is easy to every one of them and yet keeps them strictly to their duty.[11]

It seemed that, in some respects, MacCarthy's approach was quite different to that of Tyrconnel. Despite the common conclusion that 'might was right' in the delicate situation, Justin was well aware that the circumstances could get out of control at any moment and Parliamentary cries of 'rebellion' could quickly fall on Ireland, despite the relative power of the monarchy. His continental experience would stand him in good stead. He was relatively unique amongst the new Irish officer cadre, however, and this, in turn, created a new problem. The developing Irish army was untrained and unaccustomed to military drill, discipline and weaponry. The majority of the old English and Irish officers were inexperienced and unable to maintain discipline. The repercussions of the mistake would prove far-reaching. Despite Justin's relative popularity however, he still supported Tyrconnel's attempts to undermine the militia, requesting the removal and storage of weapons.

At the end of 1685, Justin was also involved in a discourse with a Tipperary magistrate. A group of Protestants had been charged with unlawful assembly at Borrisokane. Justin attempted to persuade Sir John Meade, the magistrate in question, to convict the Protestants in preference to allowing armed parties to meet with impunity. He failed in this attempt, though apparently wrote a letter to Tyrconnel regarding both the affair and the reliability of the magistrate. These events were related to Ormond by Sir Richard Ryves and, although they could be judged as hearsay, it would have been opportune for the Irish officers to extinguish the torch of resistance to the purges before it could become a serious threat to their collective aims. The situation was a delicate one indeed.

Clarendon

By the start of 1686 the next phase had begun. Lord Clarendon arrived in Dublin as the new Lord Lieutenant, yet his powers over the army were minimal. His position therefore would be difficult, if not untenable, in light of the military 'revolution' that was underway. If matters continued in this vein it would be difficult to see a stable future for the Protestant Clarendon. He was instructed by James to direct Tyrconnel, by now a lieutenant general, to increase the pace with regard to the restructuring of the Irish Army. Tyrconnel was instructed to review the army periodically and replace those 'unfit persons' with those more qualified for the post. Again, the interpretation of these ideas played directly into Tyrconnel's hands.[12]

Despite Clarendon's frequent protestations at the methods used, there was little that he could really do. Tyrconnel's browbeating personality seems to have dominated the softer Clarendon at every stage. Indeed, with James' policy at least appearing to back Tyrconnel, the Lord Lieutenant was relatively powerless.

Tyrconnel's methods are sufficiently summarised by his treatment of Blessington's troop in June 1686. Viscount Blessignton wrote to Ormond:

> I have the honour of commanding a troop in your Grace's regiment. I think it is my duty to give your grace an account of a proceeding, in my poor judgement, somewhat extraordinary. On Wednesday last, being at my quarters, I received orders from the Earl of Tyrconnel to have my troop by nine of the clock in the morning at the Naas on Friday, which was yesterday. In obedience to which I accordingly came thither at the hour appointed. Between two and three in the afternoon his lordship came and viewed us, who liked the horses so well that he was pleased to tell me he wondered where I could get horses of so large a size. After being viewed, and for some small time exercised, his lordship discharged us, and told me he liked the troop and that there needed not above two or three horses or men to be changed; but commanded me to send my quartermaster after him to the town of Naas by whom he would send me an account of what he thought fitting to be done. I paid obedience to his orders, but he was not gone half a mile before he sent for my lieutenant, Capt. Taaffe, who produced his commission but the day before at the head of the troop, and therefore must necessarily be a stranger to all the men, who brought me in the evening a letter from my lord, a copy of which I have

> here presumed to enclose to your Grace, with a list of about eleven men not thought fit to serve, by which letter your Grace will see I am not only commanded to turn them out, but also to take such men as my lieutenant shall provide. As to the men, excepting two, which I acquainted my lord I designed to discharge, I do aver to your Grace that there is not in the Army more soldierlike men, better equipped, or better disciplined, and I hope it will appear to your Grace very hard usage, that a lieutenant who came into the Army but the day before, should be consulted with about the men, and have power to provide others for their places, whilst the captain who has served with these men above eight year, and whose loyalty I hope was never questioned, should stand by as a cipher.

Taafe's reply to Blessington over the affair exhibits the power and authority that Tyrconnell had now developed;

> O my Lord, this order is not so strict but that my Lord Tyrconnel has left me a discretionary power to keep in whom I think fit ....[13]

Clarendon attempted to moderate the situation as best he could, but it was too late, and the army was not under his control. Despite his objections to Sunderland and James, he had, of necessity, to hold back from a clear attack on the policy since it was still unclear how much of the monarch's intent was actually being enforced. Throughout the summer of 1686 there was still an air of deception and subtlety, though this could not last for long.

Despite the obvious difficulties in the relationship between Clarendon and Tyrconnel, the Lord Lieutenant was on good terms with Justin MacCarthy, at least initially. Clarendon's letters of the time show many facets of the Lord Lieutenant's personality; a man whose relationship with Justin initially seemed close, yet whose weakness at being outmanoeuvred by Tyrconnel and James would undermine and ultimately destroy his authority. It would be unkind to criticise him for this since those prepared to 'take on' Tyrconnel with a view to amending policy, would of necessity have been rapidly dismissed by James. Clarendon's contact with Colonel MacCarthy related to his request to alleviate the problem of bandits or 'Tories' in the countryside around Cork. From this initial contact Justin appears to have attempted to befriend the Lord Lieutenant.

Whether the generation of such a relationship was in an attempt to gain favour or not, in the true seventeenth-century manner, it appears that Clarendon was impressed. In the early part of 1686 Justin spent some time at Dublin Castle. This was not wasted, as evidenced by Clarendon's communication to his brother, the Earl of Rochester, during February. Justin, in the knowledge that Clarendon had no regiment of his own, placed his Cork regiment at the Lord Lieutenant's disposal. Of course, this was no accident. Justin sought permission to go to England. He had been made acutely aware that change in the hierarchy of the Irish Army was imminent and it was time to seek further promotion, and Justin had 'powerful friends' in England, not least Lord Sunderland. The post of major general would be available and Clarendon recommended Justin over Sir Thomas Newcomen, Tyrconnel's brother-in-law, described by Clarendon as no soldier but 'wretchedly sordid and a brute'.

Clarendon described Justin as:

> a man of quality; for his being a soldier, according to his experience, I think, is not doubted; and he has behaved himself extremely well wherever he has been quartered, with great easiness and moderation, which every body has not done.

Justin's experience as a soldier and to some extent a clever politician had stood him in good stead. It is somewhat simplistic to ascribe Clarendon's remarks as a response to MacCarthy's flattery, although Clarendon's language can encourage the reader towards cynicism. There does seem to have been a friendship of sorts developing between the two; this would be tested, however.[14]

Justin also reported that muskets and pikes could be made much more cheaply in Ireland than in England, encouraging Clarendon to make this clear to the king in the hope that progress could be made. Again, it is not clear why MacCarthy wanted to force such a matter, though we can make an educated guess. Irish arms manufacture backed by English money could help secure the Irish Army. They would for the first time be able to fully arm themselves. Was this an attempt to strengthen the Irish position should James be deposed? There may have been more practical reasons for the request, however. The army's stock of arms was in a very poor state. With the purges very much in evidence, and the relative lack of experience in the army, MacCarthy may have been attempting to give the remodelled army a head start. It is not entirely clear, though it seemed that James was not interested in the request.[15]

Clarendon's recommendation of MacCarthy for major general was sent firstly to the king:

> This bearer, Colonel Macarty, is so well known to your Majesty, that there is no need of my saying any thing in his behalf, but what he will not give himself leave to say; which is, to give your Majesty an account how infinitely he is esteemed in all places where he has been in this kingdom, his obliging carriage having gained upon every body; which the bishop of the diocese, and several others have told me, and desired I would thank him for the favours they have received from him.

Relevant locations in seventeenth century Ireland.

And then to Sunderland:

> Colonel Macarty must not go hence without carrying my most humble service to your Lordship in a particular manner. I need not say any thing to your Lordship on his behalf: his own merit, as well as person, is sufficiently known to you; but yet I must not omit telling your Lordship (in justice to him) how extremely he has gained upon all people, among whom he has lived. The Bishop of Cork and several others have desired me to give him thanks for the civilities they have received from him. I am sure I need not move your Lordship to support his pretensions with the king; but I may assure you his Majesty can employ nobody, in his way, who will be more acceptable to people here.

With such recommendations, it would be unlikely that the position could go to anyone else. Although there is a degree of the extravagant character of the period in Clarendon's praise, it seems that Justin had made an impression. Clarendon's description also gives grace to the notion that MacCarthy was popular amongst the native Irish. He was not after all one of the old English and the combination of experience and leadership qualities appears to have increased his popularity amongst troops and the general populace. It seemed though, that Clarendon could not turn a blind eye to the purges, although he must have known that his complaint would not be heard:

> Colonel Macarty has spoken to me concerning the checks which are out upon officers and soldiers at their musters: that method has always been practised in the army here; but it is an imposition not laid upon the army in England. It does not become me to meddle with any thing I find, which is pretended to be for the King's service, without first representing it to his Majesty; but, I confess, I know no reason why it should be otherwise here than in England.[16]

Early in the year Justin complained at the distance that soldiers had to travel to receive their pay.[17] In fact he seems to have had a general problem with the entire structure and administration of army pay. Clarendon was very supportive of his new ally. If MacCarthy could find ways of improving the Irish Army, he would back him. He had, after all, little faith in or influence on Tyrconnel, and Justin must have seemed genuine in his loyalty to the Lord Lieutenant. By April the promotions so long discussed were made valid. Justin was promoted to major general of the Irish forces. Tyrconnel was promoted again, this time to lieutenant general, whilst Colonel Richard Hamilton (George and Anthony's brother) was made Brigadier of the Army.[18]

It seemed to all intents and purposes that, in Ireland at least, James was determined to have his way. Irish Catholics had been put in full control of the now Catholic force without the oath. James, perhaps unwittingly, was sowing the seeds of his own destruction.

Clarendon at least was happy with Justin's appointment as the Irish Major General.[19] Matters would be taken much further, however. James, determined to improve the lot and also the standing of his Roman Catholic subjects, now restructured the Privy Council in Ireland. The Irish Civil Administration was being restructured, again without the oath. Positions were allocated in May 1686 to Richard Hamilton, Tyrconnel and Justin MacCarthy, amongst others.[20]

James's reforms were far-reaching and significant, but was he proceeding too quickly for his own good? MacCarthy's good relationship with the Lord Lieutenant continued, however. Despite the purges and the slow erosion of discipline and experience in the army, Clarendon carried out a review of troops at Kilkenny in the presence of at least two of its most experienced officers. Previously, the Duke of Ormond's regiment, they were 'as adroit at their exercise as any men could be and that generally they were better mounted than the light horse in England'.

Clarendon's temerity, however, was such that he could not fail to comment on the grumblings within the army. Protestant officers and troops could do little as Tyrconnel continued to avail himself of the Lord Lieutenant's warrant:

> Lord Tyrconnel told me though the troops in the gross appeared well, yet he had marked several men, who upon account of their age, and for other reasons, were not fit for the King's service. I answered, that he well knew the King's pleasure therein, and that in obedience thereunto I had given him full power to put out and put in such common men, and non-commissioned officers, as he thought fit; and therefore I would not meddle in that matter: but I did desire, that whatever men he thought fit to put out, it might be done regularly, and due certificates made thereof to the Muster-master-general, whereby I might grant warrants for the pay of those men so put out; which had not been observed in several places in the countries, where the new officers had dismissed great numbers of men, some even whole companies, without giving them any certificates of what was due to them;

Clarendon still had little influence over the continued policy.[21]

MacCarthy's new-found popularity and authority now increased his ability to criticise and attempt to adjust policy in the king's name. Clarendon records his criticism of the Lord Chancellor, who was reticent to employ Catholics as justices of the peace. Invoking the king's instructions, and Clarendon's apparent confirmation of same, MacCarthy attempted to bully the Lord Chancellor into submission. His efforts were in vain, however, since many of the Catholics in line for the positions were seen as 'rogues'. He then referred to a bribe that had been rumoured that the chancellor had received from the Whigs, which was vociferously denied as a rumour put about by Tyrconnel.[22]

Justin, now fairly eminent and with the potential to gain great influence in the new Irish ascendancy, was playing a pro-Catholic and pro-Irish game. Indeed, this is unsurprising since both Tyrconnel and the king himself were doing the same thing, although to a greater and ultimately more influential end.

By August of 1686 Tyrconnel's main concern, the Irish land question, was being openly discussed. Among those present were the Lord Chancellor, Tyrconnel, MacCarthy and Richard Hamilton. Despite some debate, little was decided and Tyrconnel ended the matter promising that he would have discussions with the king and further investigate the Acts of Settlement and Explanation.[23]

During September 1686 Clarendon reviewed Justin's own regiment at Cork, after visiting Bandon and Kinsale. Of the regiment he remarked, 'I saw them exercise, which they performed as well as is possible for such new men' and 'as well as can be expected from men who have no longer been in service'. In conversation, Justin asked of Clarendon if he would take representations from the Bishop of Cork and from a number of Catholic merchants. His influence with the people of Cork must have seemed like a link with native Ireland to the Lord Lieutenant. Clarendon innocently hoped that all peoples would unite under the king, casting aside ancient fears and enmities. Instead he found that 'the natives will scarce hold any communication with the English, and will hardly treat them with common civility'.[24]

By October Clarendon was able to report on another meeting with regard to forfeited Irish estates. At this point the relationship between Justin and Clarendon starts to become strained. Justin left before the meeting ended prompting Clarendon to write, 'Major-general-Macarty, though he was there, went away at least half an hour before we broke up: how then could he sign a paper of what every body agreed to, when he was not there at the result, is worth considering.' As the purges in the army continued, Clarendon's comment on the lack of quality in the army is significant:

> This morning I saw the regiment of Guards drawn out and exercise; which they performed as well as could be expected from raw men, for much the greater part of them are raw.[25]

Clarendon's power and what little respect he had were rapidly being undermined by Tyrconnel, and the decline of his friendly relationship with MacCarthy is evidenced by his change in attitude towards his claim that Irish arms could be more cheaply made than their English counterparts. Earlier in the year he had considered the idea. By October he was prepared to 'forbid him going on in it' if necessary. Tyrconnel and Mr Justice Nugent now interfered with regard to the nomination of Irish sheriffs. Clarendon wrote to the king in protest that he should be assured of his Lord Lieutenant's obedience, but that such interference (obviously designed for Tyrconnel's own reforms) was not in keeping with the conventional way of doing things.[26]

These were unconventional times, however, and Clarendon's remaining Irish tenure would be shortlived. To the cynical it would appear that Justin no longer needed Clarendon, whether their friendship had been genuine or not. James was about to make him the Governor of Limerick and it seemed he could now freely complain to the Lord Lieutenant instead of displaying some glib form of reverence to the Protestant lord. In November he was concerned that he had not been informed with regard to murder charges levelled at one of his officers. Despite Clarendon's defence that matters were done this way on England, Justin's mocking reply was that 'it is not so in France'. Clarendon now wrote to his brother, obviously worried that he would be 'complained of upon that score'. The rot had set in, however, and later in November Clarendon once more wrote regarding Major General MacCarthy:

> And now, as to my stay here, for entertainment I will only tell you, that the reports the last letters of the 18th brought, are very various, even among the Irish themselves; some saying, I may stay as long as I please; others that Lord Tyrconnel is to succeed me, and will be here by Christmas: and I am assured, the Major-general offers to lay five hundred to one, that he will be here before March.

By December 1686 Clarendon was alone. That he and Justin had ever worked together with common purpose now must have seemed a distant memory. He now became embroiled in an argument over money. This began at a meeting with Sir Thomas Newcomen, at which Justin was present, over deductions that had been made from the regiment's companies. Clarendon's aim, as he remarked to Sunderland, was to ensure that the king should have 'as many men as he pays, and that those men should have as much of the money the king allows them as possible'. Clarendon delved swiftly into the matter, also investigating MacCarthy and his regiment. He was aware that his time would be cut short in his position, but he would make the most of exposing any 'slights' carried out by the new Irish ascendancy against the king. It does not appear that he had intent to ruin any of those involved, but it was clear that he would not go quietly. MacCarthy, however, had himself written to Colonel Hamilton, then in England, with regard to the small amount of subsistence money for clothing available to the Irish Army, implicating, though not blaming directly, the Lord Lieutenant. Clarendon then had to defend himself to Sunderland, insisting that MacCarthy had portrayed the situation inaccurately.[27]

Subtle accusation and counter-accusation followed, but Clarendon's time in Ireland was coming to an end. His poignant final communication on MacCarthy is telling, both to his friendship with Justin and his hopes for development of the army. It was all too late for that now, however:

> As to what you say of the Major-general, I do assure you he has not wanted courtship from me. I will venture to say, if he had been my most intimate acquaintance, and the man in the world upon whom I had most desired to build, I could not have applied more to him: which I did upon the principle of honest sincerity, in memory of his father, and his excellent brother; both of whom loved me very well, and of whose kindness and esteem I can give some instances. I thank God, I was never ungrateful: and I think it is known I love an old friend, and all that belonged to him. Upon this score I entered into this gentleman as if he had been a brother; which ought to

> have gained the friendship of a generous man. Whether ever I have had a reserve towards him; if I ever had a complaint of any of his officers, I presently referred it to himself and left it entirely to his own determination. In a word, if ever I have failed in any title of friendship, kindness, or civility towards him, I leave it to himself to give the instance. But I confess it has been apparent for some time, and observed by others, that he has withdrawn himself from me, for what reason I will not imagine at this time; of which I have never taken the least notice, but continued my frank open way to him. And even since our late ecclaircissement upon your letter of the 30th past, from the Treasury Chamber, being invited to a private entertainment, which does seldom happen, I spoke to him to be of the party; which he thought fit not to accept of, pretending to be ill, though every body knows he went abroad. But I do assure you I will never alter my way of living towards him, whilst he and I serve the King together. It may not be amiss to tell you upon this occasion, that I have never yet had any private meetings for select companies; but every body, Irish as well as English, have been equally invited and admitted: and there is scarce a day but both are at my table, whether a public or a private day. As to what you say of the heavings against you and me, God's will be done. Let them heave: we shall still be found honest men, and to have discharged our duties as such. God Almighty bless the King: he will quickly see who serves him best; and he is sure by experience what you and I shall always be.

The falling out of the two former friends was further exacerbated by the unwanted attention that MacCarthy was paying upon Clarendon's sister. It is possible that this may have been misinterpreted; MacCarthy may have been trying to talk to Clarendon through his sister or, indeed, the Lord Lieutenant may even have welcomed the display of such affection toward her at one time, but he would not condone it now:

> My sister told me, the Major-general had lately written to her: she gave me the letter. I directed her not to admit him to visit her; and if she met him anywhere, to tell him that she had no occasion to trouble him. I was very positive to her; telling her, if she would not be ruled by me, I would have nothing to do with her. She faithfully promised me to be guided by me.[28]

By February 1687 Tyrconnel had replaced Clarendon as Lord Lieutenant of Ireland. For the native Irish, it was a time for rejoicing. It would not be fair or accurate to say that Justin had 'duped' Clarendon. The friendship does, however, appear to have been a little onesided, implying a certain amount of deceit towards the end. In any event, Clarendon's inability to influence the continued purge of the army meant that little could now be done to stop it. By the summer of 1687 there was little need to further disguise or otherwise hide the reverses that were occurring. They were by now all too apparent.

Chester

James met with Tyrconnel over a two-day period in Chester in August. There is little accurate record of what was discussed though some educated guesses can be made. Despite the changes that had already taken place in the Irish military and society in general, James could not afford to give Tyrconnel free rein over the still very English dominion. Parliament would not stand for radical revolutionary change. He was eager to secure his throne, however. Speculation was rife that Tyrconnel had been summoned to England to be reprimanded over his policy in Ireland. This would not be the case, however, and, although there is no definite evidence as to what was discussed, French reports indicated that James not only backed Tyrconnel's actions but also agreed to his plan to put Ireland under French protection in the event of James's death. The Act of Settlement was also discussed, but James stopped short of repealing the act altogether.

Tyrconnel reviewed the army in the summer in order to establish how many Protestants were left rather than to remove any remaining unfit personnel. By the autumn of 1687 the purge of Protestant officers was all but complete – only two Protestant colonels remained. This, however, created problems of its own. When reviewing the army Tyrconnel paid little heed to the real problems that were being fostered. Rather than focusing on the decaying administration, reduction in financial support, and propagation of relatively poor Irish gentry who were unable to support their regiments, he focused on removing the last Protestants, effectively making his problems worse. His preference for old English Catholics over the Protestant gentry in the officer corps also had an influence on discipline and ultimately the level of training and thus readiness that had existed in the Irish army. This potentially devastating situation could only be exacerbated by the replacement of the rank and file. Ill-supported by untrained officers, lack of discipline and training would bedevil the fledgling Catholic Jacobite army and the cause of both Tyrconnel and James. Clarendon's reports related to MacCarthy and Hamilton's troops were not representative of the balance of the new army.

Results of the Purge

Throughout 1686 and 1687 civil disorder between displaced Protestants and Irish troops bedevilled Dublin. There was little alternative employment for the purged men and, despite Clarendon's requests for compensation, little had been done. Despite some deaths and the disorder many displaced troops travelled to England, the Anglo-Dutch Brigade and the Imperial army in Hungary. Some officers returned to their estates.

Many turned to brigandage, however, since in many cases the officers had put considerable amounts of their own funds into their regiments and were now destitute. Not all of the new Irish officers were inexperienced and Justin would have come into contact with many of the men with whom he had previously served in France, and who had served under him when he inherited Thomas Dongan's regiment. Around thirty-six officers from the French service would re-surface in the newly modelled Irish army, less than ten per cent of the officer corps. Matters were made worse by their wide dispersal across the different regiments, diluting their effectiveness. Had they been concentrated in two or three 'crack' units then matters might have been very different.

Ill-disciplined Catholic troops were now abroad throughout the country and in many cases they plundered both rich Protestants and trading ships. This was not simply retribution against the Protestant hierarchy which had for so long formed the ruling class, but an indictment against any serious use of the raw troops for protracted offensive or indeed defensive activities. Social distinctions that had previously existed in the Irish army, between officers and rank and file, were now not so distinct. Officers no longer inspired the fear and respect required to effectively run a seventeenth-century army, but in many cases encouraged and aided the unruly behaviour. It was clear that the purge had moved too far and too fast.

The Irish army in 1685 had lacked training but its officer corps was relatively experienced at least in running the organisation, a social elite of sorts in terms of administration and funding and part of the recognised establishment. Tyrconnel, with the intention of furthering his aims on the land question, overturned the establishment and in turn created an army that could do little to further his or James's aims. Experienced officers such as MacCarthy, Hamilton and Sarsfield were all too rare, and too thinly spread to make a real difference. Despite attempts at drill and exercise (most notably at the Curragh camp in the summer of 1686), their effects were diluted through the speed of the purge.[29]

Much of this must have been obvious to both Tyrconnell and James. To this end there can have been little intention to use the Irish army as any more than a vehicle to further the pursuits of Irish Catholics by 1686. It could not be used effectively in England, nor could it be used to exercise James's political will. To the English Whigs the events in Ireland were interpreted very differently. There had been rumours of James's intention to 're-model' the English army to favour Catholics; he had shown the Whigs that he could do this in Ireland. Added to this was the threat of a Catholic army across the Irish sea and the stories of displaced Protestant soldiers who had ended up in England, and the scene was set for yet another change in English politics. There was no evidence to suggest that James had any absolutist intent, but the Popish plot had shown that a Protestant Parliament did not need substantial evidence to foster anti-Catholic sentiment and, ultimately, a very English revolution.

The Path to the Glorious Revolution

The events of the 'Glorious Revolution' of 1688 had a measured effect on the events that followed in Ireland. There were many key issues in England with regard to James's future, but for William, there was only one key concern, that of the English succession. Until the autumn of 1687 Mary of Orange was viewed as the obvious successor. William's wife Mary, James's eldest daughter, was the natural successor, as James's young wife, Mary of Modena, had no surviving children. In 1687, however, she was pregnant again. A boy would secure a Catholic succession and mean that William's preference for an English alliance against the aggressive Louis would remain ill-founded.

The relationship between William and his uncle immediately became estranged; setting in motion a chain of events that would see Charles II's prediction of his brother's brief tenure on the English throne proven correct. At the beginning of 1688 James wrote to his son-in-law insisting that the English regiments then serving in Holland must be recalled, a plan apparently initiated by Tyrconnel. Suspicion of William's use of these troops was forefront in James' mind. William would not accept James's suggestion of an Irish Catholic commander for the troops, and the Dutch States General eventually agreed that the officers would return to England. Many of the rank and file were also allowed to leave later. Most of the Protestant officers and soldiers stayed, however. These and some of the disbanded Irish Protestant troops may have had some influence on William's decision to take action in England, though it seems less likely when taken in context with the other deciding factors. In any event, Tyrconnel warned James in August 1688 that a coup d'etat with designs on the English throne was being developed in Holland.

English opinion may have been swayed to a larger extent by the policies of the king. Late in 1688 James was urged by the French ambassador to bring Irish regiments to England to strengthen his position. The decision to use Catholic troops to protect the king in England with the commonly held view that the events in Ireland would be repeated there could only harm James's position. At the end of September 1688 Tyrconnel was ordered to despatch three infantry and one dragoon regiment to England. Amongst the infantry were the Guards regiment and Forbes's infantry regiment; Forbes's had been one of the few Irish units that had kept a large proportion of its Protestant troops, proving that

Tyrconnel was no fool. The Guards regiment also proved surprisingly popular in England, being well disciplined. Anthony Hamilton's dragoons also appear to have been well behaved, Hamilton having served with MacCarthy on the continent (under his older brother George) and being one of the few experienced Irish officers. Despite the fact that Tyrconnel appears to have despatched his most disciplined troops in the main, all of this goodwill was destroyed by the behaviour of MacElligott's regiment. These soldiers became known as the 'Terror of Portsmouth', drinking, robbing and assaulting the inhabitants of the town. An Irish soldier fired a shot into a Protestant church, playing into the hands of the Whigs. The Duke of Berwick, James's illegitimate son, later attempted to recruit some of MacElligott's troops into his own regiment while Governor of Portsmouth. Five Protestant captains were dismissed because of their refusal to accept the troops. Again, James would suffer as William used the incident to provide him with useful propaganda. Incidents such as this helped to alienate many of the Protestant officers against James's policy, and one cannot avoid the obvious comparison with earlier events in Ireland and the fear of 're-modelling' occurring in the English army.

A strong Tory Parliament had allowed James various freedoms and he was able to create a standing army which carried the day at Sedgemoor and defeated Monmouth, giving him the confidence to make changes in legislation that would improve, to a certain extent, the situation of the Catholic population who had been denied any ambition for pubic office via various acts of Parliament. James's 1687 Act of Indulgence repealed some laws against non-Anglican worship, though this combined with the king's interference in Parliamentary issues and the work of Tyrconnel in Ireland simply added truth to the supposed threats that the Whigs had been describing. Fears of a Popish King and a Catholic army allied with France did little to encourage belief in James's unbiased policy. Events would conspire to undermine his reign. William had been disturbed at James's conduct and the subsequent birth of a male heir in June 1688. Despite Whig attempts to discredit its authenticity there was enough evidence to convince William to listen to those who prompted him to take action. In addition, his potential loss of English support in the war against Louis would prove problematic, especially so if an Anglo-French alliance brought English troops into conflict against him. A combination of this threat and the fear that his wife Mary could be cut out of the succession, meant that William could not afford to remain idle.

William's fleet landed at Torbay on 5 November 1688, prepared to embark on a task fraught with risk. He could not admit openly to his European allies that he sought to depose James, nor could he be sure of English support, despite the propaganda and the best efforts of some Englishmen. He was sure, however, that England would be a vital ally in the War of the Grand Alliance. In return he would offer England a free Parliament and an end to Whig fears of absolutist monarchy. James resolved to fight but surprisingly lost his nerve, perhaps fearing widespread desertion in the wake of John Churchill and Sunderland's early defection to William's cause. In the main, however, military disloyalty at least would not have been as widespread as James feared. Most of James's soldiers remained loyal, despite the presence of Irish troops in England and the purges that had occurred in Ireland. Their allegiance never seemed seriously in doubt. Sufficient concern had been raised amongst a small officer corps, however, enough to encourage William and indirectly to defeat James. Whether there was a conspiracy in the army or not, the common soldier remained loyal to his king. The fact that a certain amount of conspiracy did exist, and that senior officers in the army had created it seems to have unnerved James at the critical moment and allowed the 'bloodless' revolution.

Churchill's defection had not been a spur of the moment decision. James had known that William had agents in his army but the scale of the problem and the conspiracies founded by secret quasi-military societies such as the Treason Club, the Tangerines (composed of ex-Tangiers officers) and the Anglo-Dutch Brigade seem to have been underestimated. Unlike their cousins of a later era, the officer in the seventeenth century was an opportunist, if not altogether a mercenary. As with the young MacCarthy, many officers served throughout Europe, making contacts at many levels. The fact that a military conspiracy could be hatched with influential English politicians then seems less surprising, especially since standing armies were such a new concept, and their loyalty was not always guaranteed. Misinformation characterised James's intelligence at the time of the invasion, though he had little choice in the disposition of his forces. Despite foul weather, William's landing was unopposed, and the advantages of James's striking early against an amphibious landing were lost. Despite further disagreement between Tory and Whig, there seemed little option but to crown William and Mary as king and queen of England. The country was now certain of one thing at least, it would join in the Grand Alliance's war against France, at the very least to ensure against James's return to the throne. By the end of December James succeeded in his second attempt to escape to France and join his family. William let his father-in-law go, mainly to ease the suffering of his wife, whose father's throne he had now taken. Despite fears over the number of Irish troops then in England, most of them got away and returned to Ireland.[30]

Chapter V

Munster

William's invasion had created a crisis. Tyrconnel's immediate fear was that Ireland would be William's next target. Irish Protestants immediately rallied both to the revolution and William as the events in England did, at least to some extent, provoke a reaction against Tyrconnel. Now that James was no longer king, Protestant rebellion against the changes that the Lord Lieutenant had wrought became a reality. Plans were made to seize Dublin Castle and kill Tyrconnel, but these came to naught. Ulster Protestants appealed directly to William. At Londonderry (or Derry, as it was known amongst the native populace – a distinction handed down the years, that famously sees favour on different sides at different times, dependent on the perceived political climate), the gates were famously shut against Lord Antrim's regiment. The promise of early action was quickly tempered, however, by rumours of pending massacres of Protestants to an extent not seen since the 1641 rebellion. Many people panicked and there was a rapid flight of families to England and Scotland. Tyrconnel issued a public statement with reference to such rumours in an attempt to isolate panic and to prevent the possible threat of Protestant action. By the same token, news of James's flight caused panic amongst the Catholic population, who became more fearful of a rapid Williamite invasion.

In the north many Protestants, who could form *en masse* in this region more so than any other, created armed associations for their defence. Events at Bandon in Cork would see the immediate involvement of Justin MacCarthy. In County Down in Ulster the objective was to preserve 'the public peace of the nation …. in these distracted times wherein no lawful government is established in the kingdom of Ireland'. In Sligo Protestants were determined to 'unite with England and hold to the lawful government thereof and a free parliament'. At Derry the gates had been closed, but Tyrconnel, ever the skilful diplomat and politician, reached agreement of sorts with the garrison, and discussion was re-vitalised by the admittance of the Protestant troops of Lord Mountjoy's regiment, the only other regiment aside from Forbes's troops remaining unaffected by the purges. Indeed, Mountjoy became a spokesman for the Protestant associations, bargaining with Tyrconnel over terms.[1]

Speculation was rife with regard to William and Tyrconnel, no longer with respect to invasion, but now in terms of negotiation over Ireland and its future.

Was Tyrconnel willing to submit? Many Protestants believed so, as did some Catholics in Dublin, at least initially, since the odds stacked against Ireland seemed too high. Through the Protestant Judge Keating and Sir John Temple, the Irish solicitor-general and brother to the ex-English ambassador to the Hague, word travelled to King William of Tyrconnel's intent to disband the troops that he had mustered and the levels of government that he had created. His wish was only that Catholics could return to the positions that they occupied at Charles II's death.[2]

Despite the apparent incredulity of the communication, it was taken seriously, to the extent that the previously captured Richard Hamilton was now sent to Ireland to negotiate. Many English politicians disagreed with the plan, believing that an invasion army or fleet would be more effective 'negotiating' tools. William disagreed, at least initially, and there seems to have been a real potential for ending the problem without a fight. This of course was in William's best interest. Ireland could be used as a staging post for James's attempted return to England, or worse, a French attack. Either way, a protracted fight in Ireland to avoid it becoming a thorn in William's side would use up military resources that could be more effectively used on the continent against Louis XIV. A diplomatic answer would have benefited William, possibly more than any other. Such solutions were not to be, however. Hamilton's arrival in Dublin was greeted with bonfires and celebration as he rejoined his brothers; the Irish belief was that he was worth 10,000 men.[3]

Whether Tyrconnel had been wholly serious or not, he had adapted to the circumstances of the political situation. The mainstay of the population seemed resolved to fight the matter out, and the French ambassador, d'Avaux, recounted that had Tyrconnel given in to William he would have been burnt out of his home. Irish public opinion seemed a great leveller in terms of diplomatic solutions. William's hesitancy over military action in Ireland then had been based on his faith in just such a diplomatic solution. Had he realised that this would never have worked, he would most certainly have tried to take action quickly, decisively, and before the arrival of James in Ireland, despite the problems with the English army, funding and Parliament's political wrangling. The Irish Jacobite view was very clear with hindsight. If William had acted quickly he would have 'easily effected what afterwards cost him so much blood and treasure'.[4]

Ireland was now in the position where Tyrconnel and his most competent generals, including Justin MacCarthy and Richard Hamilton, had the opportunity to prepare the army and the country for the war which must now come. French aid was essential, and James's imminent arrival could also be effectively utilised to both preserve Louis's support and give the army a figurehead. If all went well Ireland could sue for terms through its propagation as the 'thorn' in William's side. Tyrconnel acted swiftly, at least initially. Through his own scheming he disposed of Mountjoy, the potential Protestant leader, by sending him to James in France on

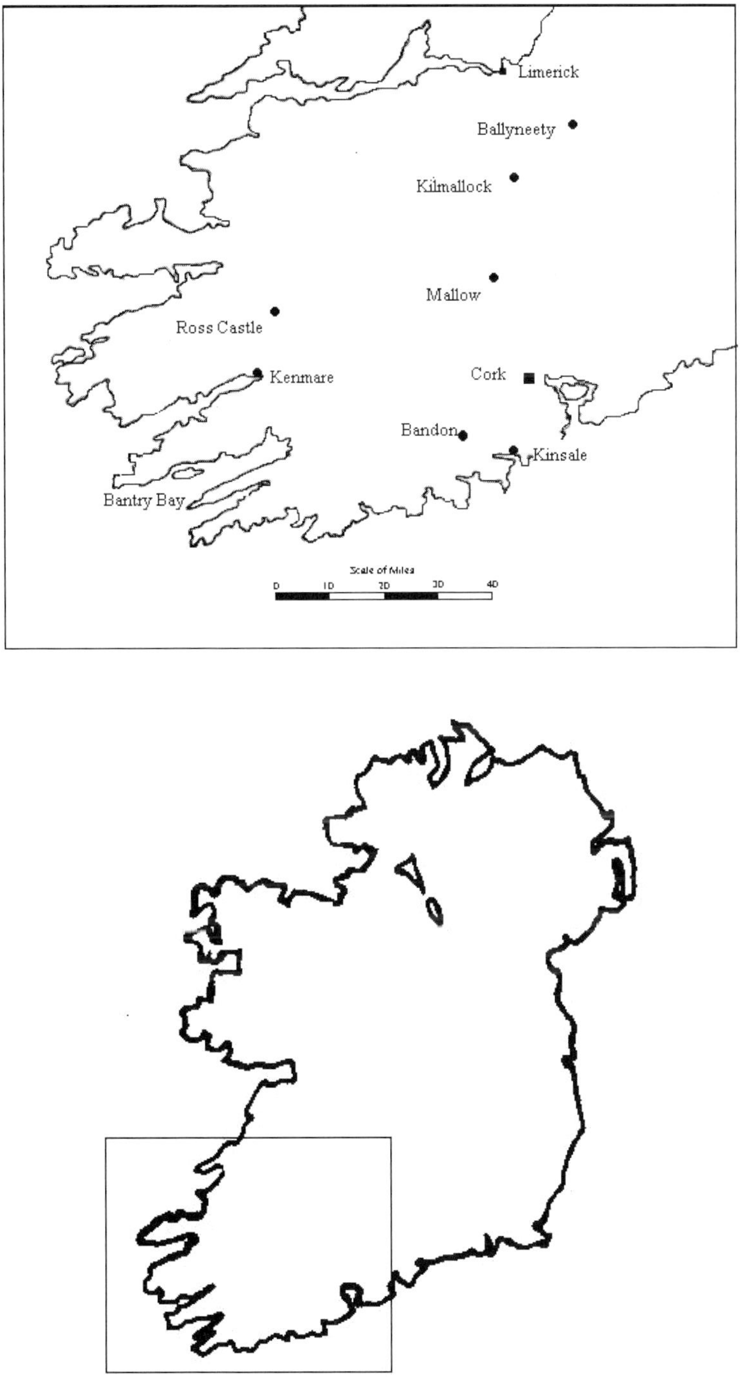

Munster, showing Cork, Bandon, Kinsale and the surrounding area.

a fool's errand. He was quickly imprisoned in the Bastille. Promises of French aid encouraged him and, by the end of January, he wrote to James to relate that he had given commissions for almost forty regiments of foot, with four of dragoons and two cavalry, a total of almost 40,000 men.[5]

This was the Catholic army that James could now lead. The French, however, noted that men were of poor quality and that most were very poorly armed, though their enthusiasm was obvious.[6] Enthusiasm alone did not win wars. Tyrconnel agreed that, rather than French arms, French money was the priority. He asked James to pass on the plight of the troops to Louis, promising Irish land as security. It seemed that the situation was becoming desperate. The men were not paid and despite Tyrconnel's best efforts, ill-disciplined Irish troops began to fend for themselves, making the Protestant associations for defence appear all the more necessary in the wake of the sense that it was time for many old scores to be repaid. Justin would now find himself at the centre of just such a clash.

Bandon

Justin MacCarthy, who had worked so hard in terms of his own career, future and his standing within what he had considered a new Irish ascendancy, now found himself once more cast adrift through the dangerous repercussions of Irish politics, with only the French as a potential ally. The war to come would settle little, but would open the old sore of the Irish question – for both its land and its people. Ormond records that in October 1688 a vision was reported in the Dublin skyline. Two armies appeared in the clouds, firing at each other. The sound of cannon-fire was reputedly heard by sailors at sea. All of this conjecture seems almost laughable, were it not for the fact that Ormond reports that MacCarthy also saw the vision, reporting it to the Lord Deputy.[7] If detractors had required proof of the validity of such omens, the ferocity of the Irish war to follow would surely shake the convictions of even the most sceptical.

Although the mainstay of Protestant association and resistance was in Ulster in the northern part of the country, the province of Munster had its own share of armed Protestants, centred on the small town of Bandon. The town lies around fifteen miles southwest of Cork on the southern tip of Ireland. It had also been known as Bandon Bridge as it spanned a river. It was a walled town, tracing its ancestry back through the 1641 rebellion. The charter that had been granted to the town by King James I had now been superseded by his grandson James II. Many of Cromwell's soldiers had settled in Bandon and the surrounding area, and many had regarded the local Irish population with some hostility. James's accession had meant that many of the Irish now felt that it was time to return the favour, and accusations of treason against the Protestants increased significantly.

Tyrconnel's new Catholic authority, now immersed in making the changes in government that would ensure a very Irish future, had created new charters for towns such as Bandon. Indeed, events there were to exhibit in microcosm much of the activity that exemplified the clash then occurring between the two religions and cultures, a clash that would ultimately lead to war.

Few towns in Ireland had remained so devoted to the English crown as Bandon. A mainstay of Protestant power in Munster, the town had a reputation as both loyal and English. Richard Boyle, the first Earl of Cork, had left his mark there, founding a deep-seated religious and political heritage. Clarendon had visited the town in 1686, remarking 'it is a very pretty town, and well seated upon a fine river; it is an English plantation, made and settled by the old earl of Cork.'[8]

The changes in Ireland as a whole would see a complete reversal of the basis of authority in the town, however. By the new charter that had been conferred upon Bandon, Teige MacCarthy from Aglish in Muskerry would become the new provost in 1688 and twenty-four local burgesses would sit with him, appointments which would fire up confrontational Protestant feelings in the town. Catholic authorities were now permitted to function under Daniel MacCarthy Reagh, while Captain Daniel O'Neill would command Jacobite troops. News of MacCarthy Reagh's imminent arrival, carrying the new charter for Bandon, had reached the ears of those Protestants who could be easily stirred into action.

Rumours that he also intended raising money from the townspeople and enlisting soldiers to serve in the Irish army provided additional encouragement for the Bandonians. If any further persuasion were required, it was also made clear that a Catholic priest would be travelling with MacCarthy Reagh. The Bandonian 'adventurous spirits', supported by locals from Kilpatrick, awaited the approach of the party near the Brinny river, pretending to fish whilst planning an ambush, intending to burn the charter and make the men prisoners. MacCarthy Reagh, however, either through local knowledge or a warning, was made aware of the planned ambush, and thus avoided it, taking a different route to the town. Although in many cases Tyrconnel's selection of those who now took their place in civic office was questionable, in terms of their means and reputation, in the case of Bandon this was not the case. Those appointed held both social position and had a degree of experience. The provost was a member of one of the oldest and most respected noble houses in Ireland. Colonel Charles MacCarthy, one of the burgesses, was one of the few officers with experience and would later sit in the Irish parliament. Tyrconnel's methods and his delegation of Catholic authority, however, was still brusque. MacCarthy removed the Protestant provost, Mr John Nash on 20 March 1688. New constables were appointed to preserve the peace.

The next step for the new provost was to establish James as the accepted monarch of the kingdom, no mean feat given what had already occurred. On 23 March the populace was offered the freedom of the town if they would recognise James as their king. Only forty-two people signed the agreement, taking the oath of allegiance to James. The authorities took the further step of publishing a proclamation in June 1688:

> Whereas several summonses have of late been given to the inhabitants of this corporation to appear, and take the oath accustomed for freemen, and for as much as they refuse and condemn the said summonses, now we, the said provost and majority of the burgesses, having taken into consideration the wrong and injury that happen unto the corporation thereby, do and, by our mutual assents and consents, have ordered, that every person of what trade soever shall pay six shillings and eightpence sterling per diem for using every such trade or occupation, either private or public, after the fifteenth day of June next, after the date hereof; and the same to be levied on their goods and chattels, and to be disposed of according to law, or their bodies to be imprisoned, through the choice lying in the provost.

James's reforms had been quickly implemented. The new authorities in Bandon were determined to stamp out the potential for resistance one way or another. Six names only were added when the new proclamation was issued. It appeared that the Protestants would remain defiant. By 1689, and with events in England having been made clear to the populace, their underlying feeling to resist was strengthened, their feeling that William's next martial step would be to Ireland, helping reinforce their convictions.[9]

By early March the rebellion of sorts in the northern part of the country was echoed on a smaller scale in other parts of Ireland, most especially in MacCarthy's home county of Cork. In Bandon matters were slowly getting out of hand. In Munster as a whole, unlike their counterparts in Ulster, the Protestants were in a distinct minority. Despite rumours of elaborate plans and conspiracy, intent upon the seizure of Cork, all schemes were betrayed and thus fell short of any form of open rebellion. At Bandon, however, continued harassment from the ill-disciplined Jacobites together with a number of robberies committed against the townspeople did little to promote good relations.

Matters at Bandon had been in development for some time. The Jacobite garrison under Captain Daniel O'Neill had little reason to feel altogether safe. The town's corporation had been reformed and Protestant remonstration against the fact that members had not taken the oath were of course not taken seriously. O'Neill asked that all arms be given up, a request which was for the most part ignored. It is not clear whether O'Neill then called for aid, or if he was forced to accept reinforcements. His garrison after all consisted only of two companies of foot and a single troop of horse.[10]

In the event, however, the news of what lay in store for the residents travelled quickly. A few days after O'Neill's statement news reached Bandon that Jacobite reinforcements threatened the population with force if O'Neill's request was not obeyed. At first glance the news appeared serious, though hardly enough to instil open rebellion. The factor that tipped the balance was the commander of the reinforcements, Lord Clancarty.

Donagh MacCarthy, the young Clancarty, had been married to Sunderland's daughter, Lady Elizabeth Spencer in 1684, through the machinations of his uncle Justin MacCarthy. He had become a devout Catholic when James ascended the throne. Since then, and in light of the revolutionary events, the young earl had obtained a somewhat violent reputation in Munster. Stories abounded of his and his horse troopers' brutality. He had attempted to take the horses of a butcher in Mallow. When the man refused, the horses were seized, only to be returned when the butcher complained to the authorities. The troopers later returned, however, tossing the butcher inside a blanket where they 'suffered him to fall upon the pavement, till he was so bruised, that he was left quite dead on the spot'. Clancarty himself had also had a Clonmel man strung up by his hair for offending him. Whether such stories were true or not, when it is considered that a substantive amount of rumour and supposition must also have been added to these stories, the Bandonians' reaction to the young Clancarty's approach is perhaps predictable. At the end of February 1689 Clancarty marched with his cavalry troopers and six companies of foot toward Bandon.[11]

The remaining Protestants in the town wasted no time, fearing the approach of the earl. Buoyed up by the proclamation that William had now ascended the English throne, the Bandonians resolved not only to prevent the arrival of Clancarty's reinforcements but on removing those Jacobite troops already in the town. Further impetus seems to have been given to the Protestant scheme with O'Neill's announcement that the Sunday after Clancarty's arrival would witness the celebration of mass in Bandon's Kilbrogan church. An assembly was held in the home of Katty Holt, a Protestant widow who lived near the church, and reputedly the local gossip. Hardinge, a Presbyterian minister, was elected chairman and the disarming of the garrison was unanimously agreed to. On the following Monday morning at dawn it was agreed that the church bell at Kilbrogan would ring, signalling the insurrection. The leaders left the meeting and within a few hours most of the male inhabitants had been enrolled in the scheme.

The following morning, however, despite the rising of the sun, the bell did not ring. A local story records that Jack Sullivan, the local sexton, had apparently lost his nerve. His wife Nancy, however, had not and, after some degree of arguing, she rang the bell herself. The 'Black Monday Insurrection', as it came to be known locally, could hardly be called bloodless, but it was effective, for the most part because the garrison was completely surprised. The job was made all the easier since the Jacobite troops were not quartered in barracks. Instead they lived amongst the local populace, in ones and twos, making the seizing of arms, ammunition and soldiers all the easier.

By night O'Neill's garrison was overpowered, and their arms and horses taken. Matters did not go smoothly, however, and there is some disagreement in the sources as to how many Jacobite troops were killed in the incident. One source indicates a sergeant and two troopers lost their lives. Another suggests that eight troops were killed. Of these, one Sergeant John Barry and two horse troopers were actually Protestants who still remained in the army – perhaps in Bandon in an attempt to keep the peace. In any event, the fact that soldiers had been killed changed the level of the insurrection from rioting to rebellion, making the action treasonous. O'Neill and his troops were forcibly ejected from Bandon and the gates of the walled town were shut. The Protestants quickly manned the walls, looking to their own defence against Clancarty. They had little with which to defend a town against any military force. Apart from matchlocks, they had six rusty cannon. The Earl of Cork had supplied these pieces fifty years previously, but they were in such disrepair that they were likely to do more harm to those who fired them than to any attacker.

Bandon was not alone, however. Captain Henry Boyle, father of the Earl of Shannon, began to set up defences around his house at Castle-Martyr (also in County Cork) with 140 men. William O'Brien, the second Earl of Inchiquin, was also inspired to take action, rounding up a number of Protestants and arming them. O'Brien had been brought up as a Protestant in England. He was an experienced soldier and had lost an eye in a sea fight, had fought in Spain and once headed the Tangier Regiment of Foot, where he had also been Governor. He was not simply a disgruntled colonist, and could be a real threat in Munster. Another rising began at Kenmare where the population near the local ironworks felt that a repetition of the 1641 rebellion was inevitable. Bandon then was not alone and, if Protestants were also to rise in Cork, Justin MacCarthy would have a real problem in Munster. A large party of Irish horse and foot entered Cork at midnight in early March and disarmed all Protestants in the town. There is no evidence that Justin gave orders for such actions, but it is likely that he instigated the move. So much could be altered by an armed insurrection now. In the event the ill-disciplined troops broke into the houses of prominent Protestants and pillaged the nearby villages, taking money and goods. Despite the fact that these events could not have endeared the Protestant population to MacCarthy's and thus James's cause, the action had prevented a co-ordinated rising, at least initially. There was still work to do, however.

MacCarthy, using much of the horse that had been taken in Cork, created a fast moving mounted force which could quickly move around Munster preventing the spread of the uprising. With two cannon (actually small field-pieces, but they would prove highly effective without firing a shot), MacCarthy moved towards Castle-Martyr and Henry Boyle. The events that followed could have proven decisive for matters in Ireland. As it was, no serious event had occurred which would further harm James's cause or otherwise to his enemies. Had Castle-Martyr and later Bandon seen massacres of Protestants, the echoes of murder combined with the use of international seventeenth-century propaganda would have doomed the Jacobite cause forever. Justin MacCarthy was a good deal subtler than this. Rather than further propagate a Protestant revolution in Ireland, he convinced the defenders of Castle-Martyr that neither 'their persons or estates should be molested' if they submitted. In the face of MacCarthy's cannon, Boyle surrendered. Boyle and his followers were transported temporarily to Cork, though his house was plundered. It seemed that MacCarthy could not keep all of his promises, but matters could have been much worse.

He then moved quickly toward Bandon with his artillery pieces in tow. With the capitulation of Henry Boyle, however, and the fact that MacCarthy's reaction had been so rapid and co-ordinated, Inchiquin could now see little option but to give up the action, effectively before it had started in earnest. He advised the residents of Bandon to seek terms with MacCarthy upon his arrival. This was not an easy prospect since MacCarthy's somewhat delicate handling at Castle-Martyr was not to be repeated so quickly. The cannon again decided the issue and the Bandonians sought terms.

Justin, however, was no longer in such a congenial mood. He demanded that the leaders should be given up to him. They had after all killed soldiers in the Irish army. The besieged, however, although having no objection in the face of MacCarthy's force in terms of discussing the delivery of the town with honourable terms, would not give up their leaders. MacCarthy took the town easily. As there is no record of further loss of life, it can be assumed that this was done without a fight. He was in no mood to debate the issue. Although he would not provoke a massacre, restitution for the matter had to be sought. He immediately informed the populace that ten of the town's principal men would be hanged, after which Bandon would be burnt to the ground. This situation would surely have instigated further violence were it not for the intervention of Dr Nicholas Brady, a local minister. Brady was reputedly a follower of James's policies. Whether this was instrumental in his persuasion of Justin or not is not clear. Upon discussion of the matter with Brady, however, MacCarthy backed down, to an extent.

Having perhaps appealed to his merciful side, Justin's initial anger and frustration at his potential loss of control in Munster had now abated and he agreed to an indemnity of 1,500 pounds paid by the residents of Bandon. Such terms may have been dictated by Brady himself as they hardly seem to have been derived from the seventeenth-century military mind, which was more consistent with direct action (or execution). In addition, the town's walls would have to be destroyed at some stage, lest further insurrection should be planned and all arms and equipment removed from Jacobite troops would be compensated for or returned. Most of the Bandonians involved borrowed money from Protestant friends in Cork, including William Chartres, an alderman of the city. Many other residents of Cork became personally liable for the debt. Articles of peace were signed on 2 March between the inhabitants and Justin MacCarthy on behalf of 'His Most Gracious Majesty King James'. The matter, however, was far from over, so far as Tyrconnel at least was concerned. James too would become involved upon landing in Ireland

At Kenmare, the remaining outlet for Protestant frustration, Irish Tories (bandits known locally as *rapparees*) had been attacking and robbing mercilessly. Despite appeals to MacCarthy prior to the rising, little was done, although Justin did have Sir Valentine Brown, Governor of Kerry, issue warrants to the townspeople so that they could pursue the robbers themselves, a rash action in hindsight. Since there were forty miles of rough hills between them and Bandon, the townspeople similarly prepared to defend themselves. Led by Richard Orpen, some of the miscreants were captured and goods returned, but the matter was not over yet. On hearing that the Cork Protestants were disarmed, Castle-Martyr had fallen and Bandon would also fall, and that no word of help from England had yet come, Orpen had little option. He agreed to terms, stating that his garrison would not be 'plundered or molested' and to 'leave the country or stay in it, as they thought fit'. In the event, the town was plundered and the residents had little choice but to leave the country. No mean feat, in that they were given two small boats with which to accomplish the task. Orpen was also ordered to pay a bond of £5,000, but sailed without paying, his thought being that he would be back in Ireland with William's army. Indeed, many of the escaped Protestants who fled back to England enlisted with William's forces, resentment creating the need for revenge.[12]

Justin's rapid intervention had saved the Jacobite cause in Munster and Cork. His muster of a rapid moving mounted force complete with cannon had prevented the insurrection becoming co-ordinated and effective. The matter became more critical when word of the imminent arrival of King James from France reached Munster. Tyrconnel, however, was not at all happy with Justin's handling of the situation. He wrote on 10 March, concerned

> that a treaty was entered into with the people of Bandon, until the authors of the disturbance were brought to justice, to which end the army we shall new model when the King arrives, and till that be done it is impossible to make them useful.[13]

The Bandon incident was to represent a clear turning point in the relationship between MacCarthy and Tyrconnel. James would later insist that the Bandon insurrectionists be tried for treason. To his credit, Justin successfully resisted both James and Tyrconnel's insistence on this matter. He had after all given his word to the Bandonians and this could not honourably be reversed. It is a testament to his own honour that he successfully argued their case. The matter, however, did little to endear him to Tyrconnel and it may have been the point at which relations with James would also start to become strained.

James's Arrival in Ireland

The situation by March of 1689, in Tyrconnel's terms at least, was not perfect. He still faced difficulties in Ulster. Despite his skilful manipulation there were many questions still to be addressed. MacCarthy had successfully stopped the Munster rebellion before it started. Tyrconnel had successfully disarmed the Protestants in Dublin. The massive army of 40,000-50,000 men, however, would remain on paper only. Those who were assembled were unruly, poorly trained and causing more harm than good.

The Munster situation was indicative of what could happen should the Protestant 'associations' gain an opportunity to band together or resist. Such activity could quickly get out of control, especially where Protestant numbers were high. In Ulster, this is exactly what was occurring. Derry and Enniskillen had become centres of Protestant resistance. The sporadic breakdown of law and order and the perceived need for the Protestants to protect themselves against rogue Jacobites made the situation worse for Tyrconnel's administration. Despite this, he was particularly concerned to show that he was striving to be impartial and objective to both sides.[14]

Ormond's diary entries for 27 February and 8 March 1689 (O.S.) are particularly enlightening however:

> This morning some sugar plums were given after the portion, for the letters of the packets were given out, though searched and opened before, but no Gazettes delivered, and the Lord Deputy had, as it was reported, three letters from the King to be kind to his Protestant subjects that were loyal. This evening the sham of the King's landing and the French was laughed at, it being a mere device to amuse the Protestants while they were disarmed; but the thing being done, out comes a declaration, a mere ridiculous thing, and a detachment was sent to Ballinderry in the county of Wicklow, in which many Protestants were got, but it was given up and many of them made prisoners, John Price, etc., and this evening bonfires

> were made for joy of an express to the Deputy that the King would be here on Saturday or Sunday, but this was quashed, the business being over, and the soldiers punished that began the thing, but the party was found still for the King's coming, the Lord Mayor ordering all the streets of the city to be mended and gravelled, which made Protestants to believe that there was some farther design on foot, so that had there been shipping and free passage many thousands would have left the kingdom, their discontents being heightened by some reports of raising a contribution for the army and plundering the city. This great work of disarming the Protestants gave thousands of arms to the Papists, and made them not fear doing what they pleased, for now they quartered upon private houses and prepared for an expedition into the North.
>
> The forces began to march to the North, and next day the train of artillery, consisting of seven brass pieces [and] two iron ones with empty carriage. More of the forces went daily. An express brought a declaration from King William and Queen Mary, commanding all to lay down arms, and come under their standards, else to be prosecuted as robbers and traitors; on the 7th out comes a proclamation against several Lords and gentlemen of Sligo and Ulster, as Lords Massareene, Mount-Alexander, Kingston, etc.[15]

Bandon and the potential for rebellion that had developed in Munster was but a pale imitation of the protracted fight that would develop in the north. Isolated pockets had sought to converge on Bandon at the start. MacCarthy's quick thinking had stopped this. In Ulster Protestants from outlying regions flocked to Londonderry and Enniskillen. In the east of Ulster, the centre of resistance lay at Hillsborough in County Down. A 'supreme council' led by the Earl of Mountalexander was ineffective and schemes to disarm Catholics at Belfast and Carrickfergus came to naught. By 14 March, however, Richard Hamilton had routed Mountalexander's troops at 'the Break of Dromore'. The mismanaged affair broke all resistance in eastern Ulster and the earl escaped to the Isle of Man. In the far north Coleraine held the Jacobite advance in check for a while, but ultimately the defenders fell back on Londonderry. By the end of March Tyrconnel controlled the country, except for the continuing resistance in the two towns. Again, it was not a perfect situation, but good enough to herald the landing of King James.

For James, the 'Glorious Revolution' in England had confounded his resolve and all but crushed his will to resist. The courageous commander who had fought at the Battle of the Dunes and at sea near Lowestoft seemed incapable of reacting fast enough. Ireland was his last chance. William's insistence that he not be used as a hostage to secure Tyrconnel's cooperation had been to prevent further strain on his wife Mary, James's daughter. Both Tyrconnell and Louis XIV of France wanted James to go to Ireland. Tyrconnel knew that he would rally the Irish cause and help to channel the vital French aid. Louis may have had some feeling toward a deposed Catholic monarch but William's seizure of the English throne was a more important matter, and a severe blow to his war effort in Europe. If James could be restored to power, he could be a staunch ally. The effort required for such a task, however, would be enormous for the French. The threat of James in Ireland, a pawn in Louis's grand European strategy, would be enough to slow William down.

Louis's ministers were divided over French attempts to help James and the Irish cause. Louvois, for instance, looked gravely upon any attempt at aid, preferring to concentrate on the continental aspects of the war. Seignelay, the Minister of Marine, in contrast maintained that French naval power could make a real difference in Ireland. Louvois, however, had been held responsible for many of the reverses and defeats in the European war and was out of favour. William's lack of action against Ireland also prompted a decision in favour of an expeditionary force. Seignelay sent the Marquis de Pointis, a naval gunnery officer, to report. Pointis brought word to Tyrconnel from James in January. James hoped that Tyrconnel could defend Ireland until the summer, but there was little hope at that time that James himself would come. Playing to the erstwhile monarch's pride, Tyrconnel's attempts at persuasion are worth repeating:

> if, sir, your majesty will in person come hither and bring with you those succours necessary to support the country.... I will be responsible to you that you shall be entirely the master of the kingdom and of everything in it; and, sir, I beg of you to consider whether you can with honour continue where you are when you may possess a kingdom of your own.
>
> if your majesty would take a step here to arrange our affairs, you could again return afterwards if you found it necessary.

Pointis's report indicated that Ireland would not hold out for long against William unless French military aid was forthcoming. Later reports focused on the importance of James's presence in Ireland. Not only would it act as a catalyst for Irish resistance against William, but the Catholic king would be an important figurehead. English Jacobites would also support James in Ireland, where they would never condone French intervention in isolation. The additional value to France was the prospect of dividing King William's military resources, with the resultant delaying effects on the important European war. After some discussion, French plans were drawn up for Ireland and for James. Louvois eventually proposed that a small expeditionary force be sent under Major General Maumont, with arms and money, together with those Irish and British troops who had rallied under

James in France. The expedition would return immediately should there be any hope of a 'deal' between Tyrconnel and William, though there was little real hope of this now. Otherwise, the expedition was to determine the nature of Irish defensive policy, if any. Preferring rapid defensive preparations, the French wanted to urge Tyrconnel to pay for the army and administration through the seizure of Protestant property. For the French, such decisions were easily made, as Louis's persecution of French Hugenots had shown.

Matters in Ireland were somewhat different. Promises of French reinforcements were made. If the Irish could resist until the end of the year, French troops, the seasoned professionals that Tyrconnell needed, would come and ultimately help James invade Scotland and then England, an ambitious plan indeed. The immediate requirement, however, called for the preservation of Ireland to William's detriment and additional arms and money would be sent by the summer.[16]

James had also resolved to go, perhaps having regained his nerve in the face of Irish and French persuasion. Vauban wrote poignantly to Louvois:

> I have an idea that when a man plays his last stake he ought to play it himself or to be on the spot. The king of England seems to be in this condition. His last stake is Ireland; it appears to me that he ought to go there, where with the help that the king can give him he can get on his legs again and be supported by those of his subjects who remain loyal to him.[17]

In the end, Maumont would not lead the expedition. Rosen, of German heritage and born in Livonia (modern Latvia), would command. He had joined the French army as a mercenary in 1646, and was brusque and direct, lacking the subtlety and refinement that such a mission demanded. Accompanying him would be le Comte d'Avaux, as French ambassador, whose letters would give such an insight into the early part of the Irish affair. D'Avaux had a difficult, if not impossible, task allocated to him by Louis. He was to help arbitrate between James's supporters, Irish, English and French, all of whom had different aims and ambitions. In addition he was ordered to make attempts to resolve differences between Irish Protestants and Catholics while simultaneously highlighting James's impartiality to both populations. Also, he was to make contacts where possible amongst potential English and Scottish allies. D'Avaux was under no illusion that the mission would be a difficult one! He also controlled the French purse strings, looking after around 60,000 pounds of French money.[18]

James left St Germain on 15 February 1689 in preparation for his journey to Brest and thence to Ireland. Despite poor weather conditions, which held up progress, James and his attendants arrived at Kinsale on 12 March, the first English king, albeit without a kingdom, to set foot in Ireland in almost 300 years.

His entourage, together with vital French supplies, sailed with him in a fleet of twenty-two ships. The small fleet had remained unmolested throughout its journey, an indication of how little the opposing fleets were able to interfere with each other's strategic movements at the time, largely due to mass desertions of Royal Naval crews and friction between Louvois and Seignelay. There were few sea battles and many potentially exploitable situations were missed. The once Lord High Admiral, a Catholic king without a throne, had landed at Kinsale in Munster. Travelling from France with him were a multitude of around 200, including relatives, loyal retainers and Jacobite supporters; amongst them, his two illegitimate sons, the eldest James Fitzjames, Duke of Berwick, and Henry Fitzjames, the Grand Prior. Also present was John Drummond, the Earl of Melfort, a Scot who would be appointed Secretary of State for Ireland, and who would prove most unpopular with French, Irish and English. Amongst the Irish officers who accompanied James, both Patrick Sarsfield, now a colonel, and Roger MacElligot were present.

The French military were also represented. Lieutenant Generals de Rosen and Maumont together with three other experienced officers, Lieutenant General Pusignan, Captain Boisseleau and de Léry. Pointis also joined the expedition to further the interests of Seignelay. Despite the number of adherents, James had brought urgently required arms, ammunition and military stores from France. A clear demonstration of the rivalry between Louis's ministers is evidenced by the fact that the stores delivered were split between those supplied by Louvois and those supplied by Seignelay. The goods were secured in a fort at Kinsale where James ensured that a full record was given to de Pointis. He could not afford to make enemies of the French at this stage, although d'Avaux's report of the situation would not be favourable.[19]

Upon landing, James was received by the young Donagh MacCarthy, Earl of Clancarty, and his uncle, now Lieutenant General Justin MacCarthy. James enquired after the state of the country and was informed by Justin that Ireland was secure, albeit for the two centres of resistance at Derry and Enniskillen in the north. James was entertained by the Earl of Clancarty who was rewarded for his loyalty by being made Lord of the Bedchamber and by his appointment as Clerk of the Crown and Peace for Munster. His infantry regiment was also made a Royal Regiment of Guards. It appeared that the young man had made an impression on the deposed king of England. Justin was ordered to establish a regular army as soon as was practicable. James also gave orders for him to arm the local levies and new arrivals in the area with some of the newly disembarked French equipment. The balance of the stores and equipment would be sent to Dublin. Apparently concerned about his delicate position upon landing, James also gave orders that Kinsale should be secured against sudden enemy attack (however unlikely).[20] Appointed to command under Justin was the gallant French Guard Captain Boisseleau, who would so successfully defend Limerick later in the war.

James called a council at Kinsale with d'Avaux, Melfort, Lord Chief Justice Sir Thomas Nugent and Lieutenant General Justin MacCarthy. Tyrconnel had given orders and commissions to raise men 'all whom either the love of their religion, their king, or their country, incited to accept thereof'. Of these raw levies, James gave orders that seven regiments of foot should be raised and that James Cotter's dragoons should be armed. He resolved to travel to Cork, twelve miles from Kinsale. English officers who had landed with James gathered up the best horses in the surrounding area and left for Dublin before the crowds that would inevitably inundate the king and his retinue made travelling difficult. French officers remained at Kinsale with the arms, ammunition and stores.[21]

D'Avaux's comments on the Kinsale landing indicate how fully aware he was of the potential problems with the fledgling Franco-Jacobite alliance. His initial report to King Louis XIV centred on the key aspects of the Irish issues of the time. He reported of the assurances made by Justin MacCarthy and others with regard to the 'sound disposition' of Irish affairs. Despite such assurances, d'Avaux was still concerned not only with the fact that resistance existed in the north, but of how such resistance might develop. From his point of view, however, external issues with Protestant rebels were only part of the problem. He cited James's frequent indecision and his particular concentration of the minutiae of Irish affairs whilst ignoring the more pressing and critical issues. The king's eagerness to set off for Cork before, in d'Avaux's view, arms and ammunition had been fully unloaded, or matters with local troops taken care of, boded ill for the future.

Although James may have been more interested with quickly rallying his Irish support, he had made a bad start with the influential d'Avaux. The French ambassador was also concerned with the growing rift that had developed between Tyrconnel and Justin MacCarthy, and the resultant effect that such a split could have on James's authority and the overall effectiveness of the French expedition. D'Avaux, as per his orders, would strive to keep matters in check. The split had not been severe enough to prevent MacCarthy and Tyrconnel's agreement on the matter of two senior Protestants intent on leaving Ireland for England. Inchiquin, the experienced military commander who had helped provoke matters during the Bandon crisis, was one and he had been allowed to leave. D'Avaux again disagreed with such actions, believing that such men would only return as part of William's invasion force.[22] For MacCarthy's part, it was probably better to reduce any further chance of rebellion in the south and he was quite happy to be rid of such an influential Protestant.

James proceeded to Cork where the Irish greeted him with great celebration. He finally met with his old colleague the Earl of Tyrconnel, the two conferring once more on matters and conditions in Ireland. He was rewarded for his continued service with a dukedom. James would stay in Cork for six days, lodging with the Dominicans, while the Franciscans escorted him to their new chapel, where he would hear Mass. The events at Bandon, possibly the root cause of the rift between MacCarthy and Tyrconnel, would once more come to the fore. Chief Justice Nugent, having been made aware of the articles of surrender at Bandon, promptly cancelled them. When James was made fully aware of the details he too was dismayed. Dr Brady, who had convinced Justin to be lenient at Bandon, now asked the king if the walls, previously condemned to destruction, could now be spared. Despite d'Avaux's protests the request was granted.

The leaders of the insurrection also pleaded for the king's mercy, in the main receiving a pardon for their actions during the rebellion, since the intrigue of Nugent had seen them once more indicted for treason. James was by now conscious of the importance of appealing to Protestant sensibilities. As much a political move as an act of reconciliation, he would later say 'let the people of England judge us by our conduct in Ireland what they may expect from us'. The Protestants of Munster would receive much harsher treatment from their new French governor, Boisselau, who would later be accused of sending 30,000 pounds worth of Protestant goods to France from Cork. Despite a later order to destroy the walls once more, it was only partially obeyed and they remained for the most part untouched.

The pardon, however, had not been universally granted and some of the Bandonians were to be indicted for high treason, a crime that could be punished by hanging, drawing and quartering. James left word that those unpardoned be severely dealt with. Nugent would later attempt to ensure that the Bandon men would be arraigned and face a jury, which would show little mercy. Brady, however, with characteristic aplomb, once more approached MacCarthy, reminding him that his act as a general had been done in the king's name. Justin at once felt bound by his agreement. If he let the matter pass, his honour, a concept still held in high regard by many, especially those in the military, would be ruined.

Whether he would lose face amongst the Irish or the French for aiding those accused, he acted, perhaps feeling that he would be an accessory if he let matters pass. To this end he urged Nugent to abide by the articles of surrender that had been agreed to in Bandon and signed by himself on behalf of the king. Nugent refused. MacCarthy, taking matters into his own hands, marched into one of Nugent's court sittings and demanded that he back down. Such bonds could not be broken. There is no record of what was said but MacCarthy's tactics worked. Nugent gave way and the twelve remaining Bandonians were released. MacCarthy's honour had been maintained and he had won a victory of sorts, but at a cost to his relationship with his fellow Jacobites. He was no stranger to bullying the bench of course, having at one stage threatened Sir John Meade in 1685. The Bandon incident was different, however. The issue was not with bringing about the verdict that he desired; MacCarthy would not stand to have his honour questioned, no matter what the repercussions to his relationship with the other leading Jacobites.[23]

While at Cork James had the garrison strengthened, distributed some of the ever diminishing stores and paid some of the monies owed to the local troops. He heard a petition requesting permission to trade wool with England. This was denied, but liberty was given to transport the goods to France. It was clear that such decisions could take second place when a bloody Irish war was now inevitable, but for James the role of the King of England in waiting was to make such decisions in his loyal Irish dominion, the views of the French ambassador notwithstanding. Tyrconnel reported to James once more, bringing news of victory in the north, that of Richard Hamilton at Dromore. Despite the continued preparations for resistance at Derry and Enniskillen, the news may have given a lift to spirits, but there was much work still to do.

James left Cork on 20 March en route to Dublin, which he reached by the 24th. The entire journey was accompanied by cheering crowds and the king got his first glimpse of the Irish army. The condition and quality of his these troops was exemplified by their appearance, many seeming like bandits, and armed only with the ubiquitous Irish *skeine*, a half-pike.[24] This would be of little use on the contemporary battlefield facing the well-drilled formations and numerous muskets of the Williamite forces. Justin MacCarthy had meanwhile been tasked with the transport of all remaining French arms and military supplies to Dublin. The king had awarded honours to the earls of Clancarty and Tyrconnel, but so far little notice it seemed had been taken of the lieutenant general. In terms of the prospective military future of the numerous Irish nobles, however, the French had only one man in mind.

Even before James had departed for Ireland the ever-enterprising Louvois had contemplated the Irish plan. If French troops would ultimately follow the expedition to Ireland, then Irish troops would replace them on the continent. Louvois had written to Justin in February making him fully aware that French aid would require an exchange of troops and would not simply be a one-sided affair. He had the end of 1689 in mind for such an exchange, depending of course on how matters proceeded in Ireland. Justin was also invited to command the Irish troops that would go to France. Louvois had played his card despite the earlier disagreements with Seignelay. There were few experienced officers amongst the Irish but, knowing his military machine, Louvois was fully aware that an Anglo-Irish soldier would not be accepted in the French establishment. A Franco-Irish officer, who had come of age in France, fought in and for France, and yearned to return to France, would be required. MacCarthy's reply gives an indication of lack of action regarding the early decisions made at James's arrival. He had always wished to return to France and French service and would endeavour to pick the best officers and men from the Irish troops.[25] That the Irish army could not afford to lose such men seems to have been the last thing on his mind.

It is clear that even at this stage, he was aware that neither the scheming Tyrconnel, despite his overtly French leanings, nor King James, who was more concerned with regaining his lost kingdoms, was the solution for Ireland. His country could only be saved from William's invasion in one way. That path lay in cooperation with the French and if that meant that he must fight William's armies on French soil, in the hope that professional French troops could win the day in Ireland, then so be it. Justin had also written to Louvois regarding the state of Ireland, implying that it was quite secure and that William would not dare to come. This, however, depended heavily on James putting the Irish army in order, a matter which could only be brought about through French arms and supplies.[26]

Again, MacCarthy and Louvois were fully aware of James's preferred intent to regain his kingdoms of Scotland then England via the loyal Irish army. If this was the case then Ireland's security could only be ensured through close co-operation with France. Who better to champion such a cause than MacCarthy? Louvois did not share Justin's optimism on the Irish situation and the potential of an invasion of England or Scotland, however. He wrote to Melfort of his concern that James's attempt to retrieve another kingdom would result in the loss of all three.[27]

Indeed, neither James nor the Irish army was ready for such an undertaking, as events would show. For Louvois this was of little importance. The exchange of French troops would make little difference, though the French would have their preferred commander no matter what the result of the Irish distraction.

James arrived in Dublin on horseback amidst great celebration and ceremony. A flag flew over Dublin Castle inscribed with the legend 'Now or Never, Now and Forever'. Ormond would record in his diary:

> March 24 – The King came to town with far less splendour than the Lord Deputy used to do. He rode on horseback, and Tyrconnel carried the sword, his two base sons riding on each hand of him. He was very courteous to all as he passed by. It is said that he wept as he rode into the Castle.[28]

Such spectacle and hope for the future of Ireland were far from d'Avaux's thoughts. He had to stay alongside the sovereign and persuade Irish Protestants that there was nothing to fear. James's neglect of important issues had done little so far to impress the French diplomat. There was clearly much work still to be done, with bands of irregular troops and bandits roaming the countryside apparently out of control. Newly-raised, though as yet unpaid, troops only made the situation worse.

Troops near Dublin had still not been armed or even divided up to form regiments. Despite the number of untrained levies however, d'Avaux, in concert with his master, Louvois, had noted enough potential amongst the Irish to contribute significant numbers of men for French service abroad. He also wrote to Louis XIV in relation to the difficulty of his task. Distinguishing between loyal and non-loyal Protestants was proving a difficult business, especially so when the Irish maintained that none were loyal and there was some disagreement over what should become of Protestant estates.[29]

James formed an inner council comprising Tyrconnel, d'Avaux and Melfort. Tyrconnel and d'Avaux both thought little of Melfort, both his influence over James and his preference for a rapid yet dangerous move against the mainland contrasting sharply with their more individual and cautious aims. Melfort's partiality of course played to James's own leanings with regard to his lost kingdoms. James then preferred to listen to such reckless advice whilst to all intents and purposes ignoring the more sober counsel of d'Avaux and the now more taciturn Tyrconnel. Indeed, d'Avaux thought Tyrconnel now 'well intentioned, though lazy', perhaps developed through Tyrconnel's own realisation that his influence and position in James's favour had been somewhat usurped by Melfort. His resentment caused him to take a back seat in decision-making and council. Many Irish Catholics felt similarly and d'Avaux noted that should James go to Scotland many of the Irish would not now follow.[30]

James's subjects who had remained loyal, many of whom did not sail with him to Kinsale, waited for the return of his ships to Brest, then sailed by the end of April. Additional money, ammunition and arms would also come. On this occasion, however, the Royal Navy was sighted and the French vessels headed for Bantry, forty miles to the west. The French managed to land their precious cargo prior to engaging the English men-o-war. Around 2,000 men including French officers and engineers had been landed. The subsequent sea battle, involving over forty ships, was relatively inconclusive, though the successful French landing of men and stores makes it a victory of sorts. James would have preferred the successful French fleet to proceed north in order to prevent aid from reaching Derry, or to transport vital siege guns or troops, or even to guard the Irish sea against English invasion and reinforcements. He was not, however, the admiral of the French fleet, and the ships withdrew. This would not be a naval war.

There were still considerable problems with the Irish army. The rapid and unco-ordinated raising of troops had left many regiments oversized, understaffed with officers, and poorly trained. D'Avaux recorded that some regiments had as many as forty companies, each of fifty to sixty men, rather than the more conventional thirteen. Inexperienced men commanded for the most part. D'Avaux noted, however, that the rumour of a 50,000 or even 100,000 strong army in Ireland had deterred a rapid invasion from England and given vital time to the Jacobite cause. Had William known the true nature of some of the troops then he might have reacted sooner. The army clearly needed reorganisation and the time that had been given could not be squandered. The military would be reduced to a 35,000 strong force by May, including thirty-five regiments of foot, seven of horse and seven of dragoons.[31]

Tyrconnel was ironically given the task of reorganisation and disbandment, the second occasion on which he had carried out such efforts. The first time he had attempted to ensure loyalty but now, with a Williamite army gathering in England, his task became one of determining quality. Many of those troops disbanded, however, would be required again within a few short months as the Jacobite army was significantly depleted at the siege of Londonderry and in the north. The appointment of provosts accomplished little, as disbanded troops held sway on the countryside. In the main the army did improve. The quality required to face William's seasoned professionals, however, would not emerge for another two years, by which time the war was almost decided. French weapons that had been supplied were in the main poor. Local supply was controlled by Protestant armourers who, despite the earlier claims of Justin that arms could be more cheaply manufactured in Ireland, could not now be trusted.[32]

When Justin's potential departure was discussed with James he immediately opposed the idea. He could not after all afford to lose an experienced general, either from the defence of Ireland or, more seriously for James, from the Irish army that he still hoped would help him in Britain. The wily d'Avaux, in keeping with the spirit of his orders from Louis, persuaded James that disciplined French infantry battalions and officers given in the exchange were just what the Irish army needed. In a further letter to Louvois he reaffirmed his intention to choose the best of the Irish to send to France. It was initially envisaged that this would not occur until December when French troops would have finished the campaigning season and be in winter quarters. Louvois once more insisted that only the best officers should be included. Louis would only want men of noble birth while James wanted to send Irish officers of poor quality and experience. This would obviously be in his best interest. D'Avaux then continued to play a delicate political game with the benefits of the Irish diversion in mind and with one eye on events occurring in the Irish army.

In the midst of such turmoil and an approaching war, the calling of an Irish Parliament may seem with hindsight a ridiculously extravagant notion. On the other hand there were many matters to discuss, although hurried legislation to counter the years of English dominance in Ireland would do little to breach the walls at Derry. James had issued a declaration on the day after his arrival that an Irish parliament would be summoned on 7 May. The Irish envisaged what they had waited so long for, a repeal of the land settlement and the return of their estates. Such measures and the removal of the anti-Catholic laws that had become an intrinsic part of English dominion had been what men like Tyrconnel and MacCarthy had been working towards for so long. Such decisions, however, which would champion the Irish cause, would destroy any remaining support that James had in England. He was fully aware of this, as was d'Avaux, whose interest stemmed from the potential for French dominance as propagation of the European war. It is unsurprising then that the parliament would find itself involved in factional and divisive infighting and many of James's objections, rooted in his English heritage, would upset Irish plans. Such discussion should, however, be taken in context with events in the north at Londonderry and Enniskillen. Jacobite attempts to overcome the defences at Derry and stop the raiding from Enniskillen were failing. While in some quarters the parliament was felt necessary, John Stevens, an English Jacobite who had sailed from Brest, and O'Kelly would both observe that the summer months were wasted in unproductive discussion when, if more time had been devoted to the siege and resistance in the north, matters might have been very different.

> To satisfy the humours of the people a parliament was called, which having sat many days granted the king a subsidy that never turned to any account, but the chief thing they did was repeal the Act of Settlement. Nothing could be more pernicious, or a greater obstruction to the king's service than was this parliament.[33]

Indeed, the actions of the parliament would create many more problems than they would solve. The factions were determined, however, and on 7 May the event that would see the zenith of the Catholic resurgence in Ireland took place. English opinion would frown upon James's tampering with the erstwhile English colony, but he had little choice. He needed Irish backing, both militarily and financially.[34]

The Irish Parliament

Were it not for the differences between factions, the Irish parliament could have been more effective, since Tyrconnel had restructured most of the local authorities. Representation from Fermanagh and Londonderry was notably absent, however. James opened the parliament in a former convent in Dublin wearing official robes and a crown that had been made locally. He gave a speech in which he thanked the Irish for their continued loyalty. Declaring 'liberty of conscience' a right that he would see enforced by law, he affirmed that there should be 'no other test or distinction but that of loyalty', perhaps a reference to that which he had lacked in

England. He would relieve the suffering of those affected by the Act of Settlement 'as far forth as may be consistent with reason, justice, and the public good of my people'. To James, his people of course included English, Scottish and Irish, and he must have seen the difficulties inherent in making any far-reaching decisions in an Irish Parliament. There would be little room for compromise, however, since if he did not fight for the Irish they would not fight for him.[35]

Around 250 members sat in parliament. Of these, six were Protestant. More surprising, however, was the breakdown between old English and Gaelic Irish. Two thirds of those sitting could be considered old English, including Tyrconnel and Patrick Sarsfield. The young Clancarty would sit in the Irish House of Lords. Though underage, he was given royal dispensation to do so. Justin MacCarthy would represent County Cork at the proceedings and would bring the bill from the Commons to the Lords for the repeal of the Act of Settlement. On the second day of proceedings, a new peer was introduced to the parliament: Justin was elevated to the Irish Peerage and made Lord Viscount Mountcashel and Baron of Castleinch. He would represent County Cork at the proceedings.[36]

Justin, however, would spend little time in discussion. After James's landing in Kinsale, he had been responsible for the transporting the stores to Dublin. With Count Renaud's successful landing at Bantry, he was called upon once more to supervise the transport of French stores and arms to Dublin. By 20 May he would be recognised for his efforts and his interest in this field and promoted to Master General of Artillery in Ireland.[37]

Meanwhile, the Irish Parliament had continued. Richard Nagle was chosen as Speaker and James acknowledged the aid that he had received from Louis XIV. What the Irish really wanted to hear, however, was James's solution to the land question; a concept that James's loyal English supporters felt was unassailable since its basis underpinned English control in Ireland. Initial attempts at compromise were rejected. When an attempt was made to introduce a bill providing for half the land in question, it was quickly defeated. Further complications were introduced by the presence of a number of judges who had bought land since the 1641 rebellion and would thus lose it through a bill that promoted Irish repossession. James's siding with the landowners prompted several members to remove their backing for the war. After further discussion, the act was passed and the Acts of Settlement and Explanation were effectively repealed.

Those who had possessed land prior to 1641 would be permitted to take steps to recover it. In addition, all transgressions that had been carried out during the rebellion were declared void. The act also included for lands that had been forfeited by Protestant landowners, who had fled to England, Derry or Enniskillen. Even those who had communicated with rebels could lose their land. The act would neither pull punches nor take chances and the Irish felt that centuries of persecution had to be answered for, but only to an extent, since the Gaelic Irish who had lost land prior to 1641 would receive nothing. In fact, the old English majority in the house were the main beneficiaries of the act. Lands taken by Cromwell had now been restored. The permanence of the entire episode, however, would depend on the outcome of the war, since William had already stated that such repossession would be reversed in favour of those who supported him if he gained success in Ireland. Stevens once more sums up the main point of the debate:

> First it [the Parliament] drew to and kept in Dublin all that time the nobility and principil gentry who before were dispersed at their posts, raising or encouraging and exercising their men or upon actual service. Secondly, the Act of Repeal being passed, private interest outweighing the public good, every one quitted his command to enter upon his estate, to settle his house, and improve his fortune. And the estated men not content to forsake the service themselves kept with them for their own use all the better sort of country people, so that none but the most rude and useless sort of mountaineers took to the army. Thirdly, the Protestants, who before might have perhaps stood neuter or hoped for some reconciliation, their estates being taken away, were in a manner necessitated to espouse the rebellion, which alone could restore them to their, although unjustly yet long enjoyed, fortunes.
>
> Thus it appears by the sitting of this parliament, the army was much damaged and weakened, the king lost the assistance of many of his friends and gained a vast number of irreconcilable enemies.[38]

Worse was to follow for those Protestants who had refused to acknowledge James. The Act of Attainder listed over 2,000 names of those who had taken part in rebellion against him, armed or otherwise. Ormond headed the list, the meaning of which was to imply that those concerned were traitors. They had to surrender to a judge by 10 August where, after due trial, they would probably be acquitted. Again, it seemed that James was being led by the Irish, whose memory of Cromwell's 'Adventurer's Act' was all too recent. The English Parliament would later influence William in a similar manner, and with dire consequences.

Matters did not all go the Irish way, however. Williamites had criticised the Irish parliament since it sat outside the requirements of Poynings' Law, wherein all legislation had to be certified in England. James opposed the bill introduced to repeal the law on 15 May. He still attached importance to English opinion, while the Irish saw the law as another example of English dominion. James would only go as far as declaring that the English Parliament had no right to pass Irish laws. French interest was mostly economic and they sought to achieve the position over

Ireland that had been the monopoly of England, though James of course fought against French commercial bids, if the result would be the removal of English interest. Similarly, he resisted French suggestions to naturalise all Louis's subjects in Ireland. In terms of religious freedom, James removed the requirement for the 'oaths' but would not go so far as to remove Elizabeth's Catholic penal laws, and restore the authority of the Pope. He was still at heart a very English king.

The entire affair had done much to dampen the enthusiasm of the Irish. It was clear that James had little real concern for Ireland other than as a stepping-stone to his former glory. If Poynings' Law remained intact, then England could still exert control over the parliament. Though the land question had been settled to a large extent, self-government remained questionable. One reason for assembling the parliament in the first place had been to get money for the war and 20,000 pounds per month was agreed. This proved not only inadequate but also difficult to gather. The event had done more harm than good, and not simply due to the Irish realisation of James's real interests. The Irish had hoped to regain their land and hold out against William with French aid. Even the French were concerned only with their king. Had James, the French and the Irish been more focused on a single goal, they might have succeeded, at least temporarily. Even then, the English colony would have been ultimately reduced and destroyed. Protestants and Williamites who had felt that the Irish parliament had shown little mercy, despite James's initial clams, would show even less when they ultimately gained the upper hand. The Irish parliament was prorogued on 18 July. It would never meet again. Twelve days afterwards, Londonderry was relieved. Two weeks after that, and Schomberg had landed. The dream in the north had ended.[39]

The Irish Military

Although James's time in Ireland was far from over, many of the decisions that would affect his all too brief tenure had been made. The factions that would decide the Irish question had for the most part been disappointed by the events in the Irish parliament. What effect this would have on the defence of the country and the subsequent attempt to reclaim the throne remained to be seen. Even with the imminent arrival of Williamite forces, strategies for defence were ineptly handled and poorly directed, a fact that would inevitably be made clear to Justin, the new Lord Mountcashel. The French had many strong views with regard to Ireland and its untested army. In contrast, the French army at the end of the seventeenth century was a living example of how effective a well-disciplined and efficiently drilled military machine could be. It was justifiably feared and respected throughout Europe, its threat in conjunction with Louis's ambition helping to create the Grand Alliance of European allies required to curb French imperialism. The rank and file that composed the Irish force then did little to impress the pompous and proud French officer cadre. De Rosen was especially contemptuous.

> Nearly all are without arms and quite naked: the greater part of the officers are miserable fellows without courage or honour, a single cannon shot passing at the elevation of a clock tower throws a whole battalion to the ground and the only way to get them to their feet is to send horses over their bellies.[40]

D'Avaux, however, with a keen eye for exploiting the situation to the benefit of the French, saw things quite differently. In contrast to de Rosen, he saw the great potential of some of the military 'raw material' within the rough regiments of the re-modelled army. Although his choice to command such troops had been made, his reasoning requires some explanation. D'Avaux and many of the French dignitaries knew that the secret to foreign troops' success was their commander, whose role was as much that of a diplomat and ambassador as that of a general and leader. Where a French-trained general who remained popular yet firm with his troops was available, Louis's emissaries would strive to obtain him. D'Avaux would later comment:

> I can assure you that he [Mountcashel] will be very useful in getting rid of a great many bad officers and in recruiting others to keep the Irish troops dutiful and disciplined.[41]
>
> Sir, If I had not believed that it was important to have a man so liked in his Majesty's service, so loved and influential in Ireland that he could keep dutiful the Irish troops in France. He could draw recruits in this country and even raise as many new troops as we would wish. If the King of England would give permission to all those who wanted to follow him, you would have the best officers in the army ...[42]

Even the implacable de Rosen had to admit that Mountcashel was 'a very good man and the only one that we can rely on, but he is unluckily in the same position as myself, of being looked upon as stating his mind and outlining the disorderly state of things'. If Justin was unpopular amongst Tyrconnel, James and their followers, it was not only due to his representation of the native Irish faction, but the fact that he told the truth of the situation that he perceived – that James would leave Ireland and the old English would return to their lands if they could. In essence, not only would little be ultimately settled, but the very real threat of William's invasion was not being effectively dealt with. In Mountcashel the French recognised the qualities they themselves considered sacred. Outspoken he may have been, but he was loyal and a patriot and displayed the courage of his convictions, truly noble virtues which would have impressed those pompous French who felt that many of the Irish were little better than savages.

For his own part Mountcashel's concerns were made quite obvious to his Gallic colleagues. In June he wrote to Louvois that 'my simple belief is that without French help then all is lost', pointing out also the dearth of both good officers and money. In fact, Justin saw only one solution: 'The only way to finish the affair is to send a good body of regular troops led by a good general ….' who should be:

> a man of character with a patient and diplomatic temperament, for rudeness with an ignorant people who do not have the required skills, repels instead of giving instruction, and to teach them obedience they should admire as well as fear you.[43]

Mountcashel was under no illusion as to the Irish army's requirements, and was ostensibly in agreement with those more positive elements of the French cadre. He would also highlight the importance of d'Avaux in the country, perhaps by now his closest ally.

Mountcashel wrote to Louvois again in July. He complained of idleness and the indecision that now existed in Jacobite Ireland. James's schemes, supported by Melfort, were hampering the preparations. Factional infighting was preventing not only coordination of the disparate Irish elements but diluting leadership.

> If we are not restored by the King of France or Divine Providence, there is a significant risk, since it is a terrible thing to see the efforts with which we seek our own ruin![44]

Again, different parties had different aims, James even considering the native Irish, including Mountcashel, somewhat inferior. There also appears to have been some distrust of the Irish general, his motives and loyalty perhaps regarded as 'questionable' due to his close dealings with the French. D'Avaux was quick to point out the apparent gulf that was slowly developing between the English and Irish, describing them as 'irreconcilable enemies'.[45]

Mountcashel had for instance offered his services to James to undertake a mission to France where further requests for arms, money and reinforcements would be made. The weak Lord Dover was sent instead when a man of Mountcashel's French experience and reputation might have made a difference. Despite James's insistence that William's imminent invasion meant that he could not release the general, Mountcashel remained unmoved.[46]

Many of the Irish military were by now more deeply concerned with the prospects for resistance than continued loyalty to the deposed king. Many, including Mountcashel, felt the greater potential that could emerge with French alliance and protection rather than with that of the English Jacobites, a force that was all but spent. For Lord Mountcashel, however, who, with Sarsfield and Berwick, was one of the ablest commanders in the field, and despite the concerns and attention of the French, the Irish war would begin in earnest. Many other matters had been discussed at the parliament, including plans for Derry and Enniskillen. Despite the lack of focus, the disagreement and the time wasted in pertinent though poorly timed debate, the Jacobites resolved to take action. Mountcashel would take the lead and meet the Enniskillen militia head on in a battle that would see a turning point in the war.

Chapter VI

Enniskillen

As the Enniskillen militia play such an important part in the military events of 1689, it is important to look at those actions which led them to battle. The clear similarity with events at Bandon can be easily recognised in the early days of the stiffening of resistance at Enniskillen. The result of the continued growth of such efforts, unchecked, gives an insight into Justin's reasoning behind moving quickly in Munster earlier in the year. Events would show how important it was to take rapid and decisive action in such instances. It would also be ultimately highlighted to the Jacobite forces how disparate and confused strategies could bring little reward.

By April 1689 the province of Ulster would become the focus of the war as it reached its height. Both Londonderry and Enniskillen would become centres of fierce resistance to the Jacobite aims. In Enniskillen the population had been making preparations since January while, at Londonderry, what had in early days been a relatively low-key affair became a protracted siege by April. Both towns had resisted the imposition of Jacobite garrisons in the previous December 1688, in the hope of receiving help from William, soon to be crowned king in London after wresting the throne from his father–in-law. At Londonderry Lieutenant Colonel Robert Lundy, an army officer, became the town's governor. William in turn supplied limited arms and money for the defence. Although there were plenty of eager defenders, military experience was lacking. Lundy, having some experience (being a veteran of the siege of Tangiers), and perhaps more aware of the savage manner in which a siege would develop, sought to open negotiations with the Jacobites and their commander Richard Hamilton.

English reinforcements arrived too late to help Lundy, and the pessimistic governor attempted to negotiate the town's freedom. Both James and Tyrconnel were fully aware that a siege, although perhaps necessary, would certainly be difficult, tying up manpower in an army that lacked both experience and the equipment for such activity. Lundy's plans were to come to naught, however. While negotiating with the town's authority, and despite assurances that Jacobites would not advance during the meetings, James himself with an escort of dragoons appeared on Windmill Hill (in apparent ignorance of any agreement – it having been previously negotiated with Hamilton – and in the belief that he could appeal to the town in person). This well-intentioned though ultimately disastrous mishap created upheaval within the walls. 'Treachery' was the word on the lips of the besieged Protestants. This event is symptomatic both of the ill fortune and lack of communication that was to hamper the Jacobite cause in Ireland. By 18 April, and James's arrival, the siege had begun in earnest.[1]

At Enniskillen events were to unfold somewhat differently. There would be no protracted siege. The population were also to see more active forays against the Jacobite forces when compared with the besieged defenders farther north. The Jacobites' failure to act would prove decisive, and a cohesive plan to deal with the Enniskillen troops (the 'Inniskillingers' as they would become known in regimental lore) and their cavalry raids would not be formulated for some months. The Inniskillingers would become bolder, strengthening the town's and the surrounding area's defences, equipping themselves and raiding Jacobite positions. Londonderry was strategically important since it was a major port, and James's goal of returning to the English throne via seaborne invasion of Scotland was still very much in his thoughts, despite the odds against its success. The concentration on Londonderry, however, was to result in a tying-up of necessary resources which would find the Jacobite forces wanting, and unable to respond cohesively to the threat from Enniskillen where early action may have thwarted all opposition and changed the course of the war. Lord Mountcashel, whose fate was entwined with the activities of the Inniskillingers, was by now an essential part of the new Irish ascendancy, both in military and political terms. Impending events would see the first real battle of the war and stunning examples of how the Jacobite strategy could be un-coordinated and ineffective despite the presence of good, and even exceptional, commanders such as Mountcashel.

Resistance in Enniskillen

The events that lead to the clash between MacCarthy and the Enniskillen forces can be traced back to the spark that ignited Enniskillen resistance at the end of 1688. In December a letter from Tyrconnel had been intercepted by the Provost of Enniskillen, detailing the requirement for quarters for two companies of foot, loyal to James, within the town. Such actions were common during the early stages of the war and similar events occurred all over Ireland. At the same time, rumours of an impending massacre of Protestants had spread. This is a common theme throughout the Enniskillen sources of the time and there appears to have been a general fear of a recurrence of the events of the 1641 rebellion. Given James's later behaviour with regard to his Protestant subjects, and his attempts to dilute the volatile religious situation, it is unlikely that an organised massacre was ever planned, at least not to the extent feared.

Of course, with armed bands of Jacobites being raised across the country, led by soldiers loyal to Tyrconnel, a certain amount of concern is not surprising.

A contemporary map of Ulster, showing inset of Enniskillen Castle. (*British Library*)

The slow erosion of Protestant authority in the army and public office must also be considered. The effect of the order therefore was to reinforce resistance within Enniskillen and the surrounding area. (MacCarmick, however, records a different chain of events. He suggests that the reaction of the Enniskillen townsmen in taking up arms nightly to protect the town actually instigated the despatch of the Jacobites in the first place and it was believed that Anthony Murray, Guardian of the Friary, was a Jacobite spy.)

Not all of the Protestants were motivated to resist, however, and Captain Corry, a 'leading gentleman of the country', would not take sides. Indeed, it seems that a small nucleus of the population, at least initially, formed the movement to resist. These attempted to rally support in the surrounding countryside and took it upon themselves to finish the town's drawbridge and to prevent the winter ice forming a natural bridge to the island town. By 13 December Captain Corry had made his decision and attempted to persuade the populace to accept the Jacobite garrison. MacCarmick admits to the presence of a 'divided multitude' and a consensus was not yet apparent. In preparation for the worst, however, the minority Catholic population were turned out of the town and Murray (now believed in most quarters to be a spy) was seized. Now, with two Jacobite companies of foot less than twenty miles from the town, and the enforced absence of the detractors, the decision was taken and the town would resist. There is some dispute as to what occurred next, whether there was a show of cavalry force or the displaced Catholic population contacted the Jacobites. What is certain is that the approaching companies of foot withdrew.[2]

By the end of 1688 news had reached Enniskillen of James's flight to France and William's arrival in England. The Inniskillingers began to prepare in earnest for the siege that they believed would come, encouraged perhaps that with the impending coronation of William of Orange, the Protestant cause in Ireland would be rigourously supported. This of course helped William's European objectives, through securing the English throne and thus providing English troops for the continent. The town began to prepare for war. Unlike Londonderry, Enniskillen's only fortification was its castle, built by the Maguires in the sixteenth century, and the town had no walls to speak of. The resulting actions of the Inniskillingers were therefore forced upon them to a large extent. Cavalry raiding and support of outlying towns in the region would be required to prevent the Jacobites forming organised forces that could take Enniskillen. The holding and fortification of Ballyshannon, for instance, held open a supply route on the Donegal coast. By the start of 1689 victory was by no means assured, though the Jacobite forces in the area were poorly led and lacked cohesion.

Led by Gustavus Hamilton, who was part Swede and the new Governor of Enniskillen, and Thomas Lloyd, the town began preparing for war. Lloyd would become an excellent leader in the months to come and carve his reputation as a cavalry raider. Both Hamilton and Lloyd had ironically been sacked from the Irish army during the purges. Both were experienced and able to train and lead the Enniskillen populace. They were also perhaps eager for revenge, though thoughts of immediate defence must have been paramount in their minds at this time.

There were few firearms to speak of but increased efforts were made to fortify the town against attack and siege. By the start of 1689 Enniskillen was also becoming the focus for assembling Protestants in the surrounding area and word was sent to England requesting arms, ammunition and money. Fortification continued into February 1689 (while Mountcashel was engaged with subduing resistance in Munster in the southern part of the country). Jacobite attempts to reduce Enniskillen and the towns of Fermanagh continued. Lieutenant Colonel Lundy was placed in charge of newly-formed Protestant regiments by virtue of the general council held at Hillsborough. His first act was to request the Enniskillen garrison to join him at Derry, a request which Gustavus Hamilton politely refused. March saw an influx of frightened Protestants into the town as Lundy ordered the evacuation of Cavan due to the presence of Lord Galmoy and a large part of the Irish Army.

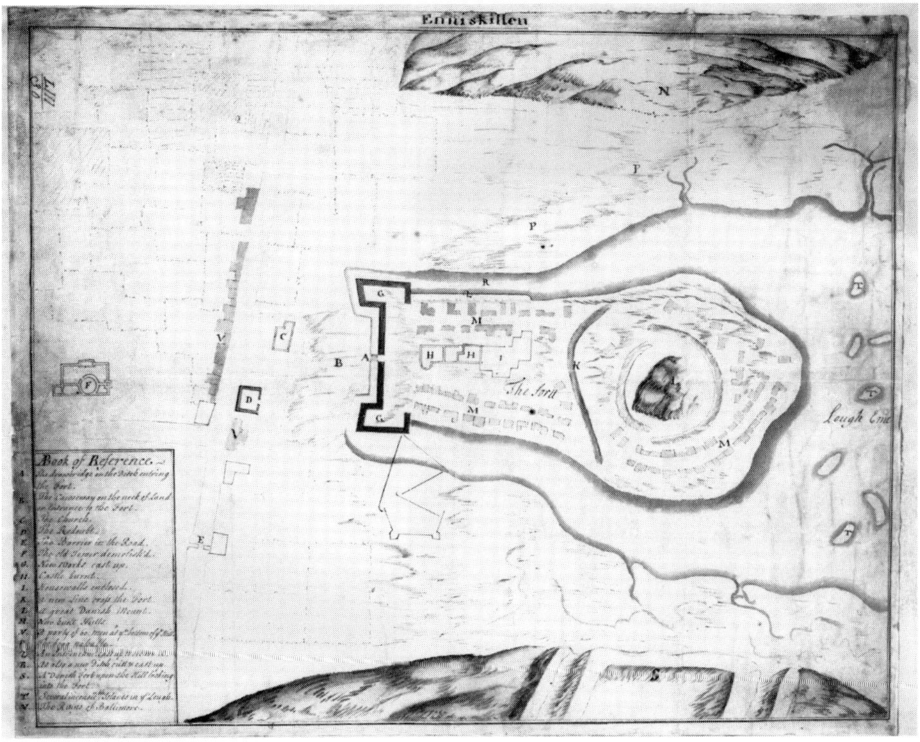

A period outline of Enniskillen, the island town, and MacCarthy's ultimate objective in Ulster. (*British Library*)

Piers Butler, Lord Galmoy of Kilkenny, unlike Mountcashel, was to lend credence to those Inniskillingers who feared a recurrence of the 1641 atrocities. Despite news from Cavan that he had burnt towns and threatened the local populace, Galmoy did not have enough troops to seriously threaten Enniskillen, (MacCarmick describes him as having a regiment of horse, some dragoons and some local 'rabble') and suffered from the fact that most able Jacobites were heading north to Londonderry.

Galmoy now advanced to Belturbet, twenty miles from Enniskillen. As Cavan men and women found refuge with Hamilton, Galmoy was planning the first siege of Crom Castle. Crom commanded Lough Erne and strategically was an important base of operations for actions against Enniskillen, only sixteen miles away. Colonel Abraham Creighton garrisoned the castle with two companies of foot. It was not, however, designed for a protracted siege, having no outward fortifications and it was in range of musket shot from high ground nearby. The area around the castle was boggy and impractical for transporting siege guns, and Galmoy must have realised that his threat would need to carry greater weight for the siege to work

By 22 March Galmoy, still besieging Crom, issued a letter to Gustavus Hamilton asking him to surrender Enniskillen and advising that James had arrived in Ireland. Better conditions (and thus quarter) would be available now rather than later, should Enniskillen have to be taken by force. Hamilton rejected Galmoy's offer and began to make preparations for both defending Enniskillen and relieving Crom. He formed his troops on a large hill outside the town in order to fight rather than be surrounded and cut off. Galmoy seemed unprepared for battle, however. Advancing to Lisnaskea, only ten miles away, and finding through his scouts that the Inniskillingers had come out to meet him, he retreated to Crom (burning the village before leaving). Undeterred, Hamilton sent 200 men towards Crom. These arrived both in boats and by land during daylight. Despite Jacobite fire they were able to enter the castle and thus reinforce the garrison. The Inniskillingers subsequently attacked the besiegers, driving them off.

Galmoy retreated to Belturbet, then asked for a prisoner exchange. Captain Brian MacConogher MacGuire had been held in Crom and Galmoy wished to exchange him for Captain Woolston Dixie, a captured Enniskillen man. Creighton agreed and released MacGuire, little realising that Dixie would be put on trial with another officer – Edward Carleton, for levying men in William's name. They refused to side for James, and were hanged and decapitated despite the released MacGuire's protest. This event of course hardened the resolve in Enniskillen.

By the 23rd the County Cavan men had left the town to journey to Londonderry as ordered. A chance for re-supply proved ill founded on the 25th when intelligence suggested that Captain James Hamilton had delivered arms to Londonderry. Lundy, however, took almost everything and the Inniskillingers were left with broken firearms and five barrels of powder. They would not be properly re-supplied until July. By now Tyrconnel controlled all of Ireland except the north. In other parts Protestants had been disarmed and a Catholic army and administration was in control. James had landed and made his entry into Dublin and Richard Hamilton had routed the north-eastern Protestants at the 'Break of Dromore', causing Lord Mountalexander to flee to England. Enniskillen's allies were becoming fewer and fewer.[3]

By April Londonderry was besieged and, despite rumours of the town having been taken, Enniskillen raiding parties set out. Thomas Lloyd's first foray was to Omagh and Augher where the Jacobite garrison was dispersed and the local Jacobite supply of cows and sheep was raided before the men returned to Enniskillen. Lord Kingston, previously of Sligo, and now at Ballyshannon, sent additional foot companies to Enniskillen to help reinforce the town. Ballyshannon was strategically an important stronghold since it held open the waterway that was to become Enniskillen's lifeline with English re-supply and reinforcements.

Around the same time Jacobite forces were garrisoning Trillick, nine miles away. Lloyd again set out with a raiding party reinforced with Kingston's men. Arriving early in the morning, he discovered an enemy group approaching him. The small Jacobite force retreated, leaving their baggage train which was subsequently relieved of all arms and provision in true cavalry raiding style. Lloyd gave chase in vain and the troops dispersed. He set out again at the end of the month upon hearing that a Jacobite garrison had entered Augher Castle. Again he pursued the small garrison of Jacobite troops through Monaghan and Cavan, cattle raiding as he went, returning to Enniskillen by the end of the month. Such raiding and attacks on Jacobite strongholds were now typical of the kind of war being waged.[4]

By May the Inniskillingers were preoccupied with events outside the town when Jacobite dragoons killed a number of farmers. The effect again appears to have underlined the feeling amongst the garrison that articles of surrender would not be kept and hardened the resolve of the population. There was no reduction in the number of Jacobite probes. At the start of May, Captain Folliot, Governor of Ballyshannon, warned Enniskillen that a large party of Jacobites under the renowned Patrick Sarsfield, Mountcashel's old friend from his days in Dongan's Regiment, had come from Connaught to besiege the town.

Lloyd set out with twelve companies of foot and some troops of horse towards Ballyshannon. Sarsfield had to take chances and move quickly. He knew that Folliot had refused to surrender because he could expect help from the larger force at Enniskillen. Castle Caldwell held 400 Inniskillingers and was only nine miles away. Between the two lay Belleek, and Sarsfield was obliged to split his force, drawing the largest part of it to Belleek. There, almost completely surrounded by bogland and water, they held a well defended rampart, leaving only a narrow causeway through the bog for means of access. Lloyd was preparing to undertake the dangerous task of attack over the swampy ground when a local man informed his scouts of a safe route through the bog. Lloyd wasted no time and immediately sent his men across the safe passage, out of musket range, and much to the dismay of Sarsfield's men. An orderly retreat back to Ballyshannon turned into a rout as the Jacobites fled. Sarsfield withdrew to Sligo, having lost almost 200 killed and wounded with sixty men taken prisoner.

Later in the month, amid reports that the Irish had garrisoned Redhill and Ballynacarrig in County Cavan, Lloyd set out with 1,500 men and news of his approach, together with exaggerated rumours of his number, convinced both small garrisons to flee or surrender. The Inniskillingers released their prisoners after disarming them. Rumours of the size of Lloyd's force put their number at 15,000 and capable of threatening James at Dublin. In reality, Lloyd's force was a raiding party and he returned to Enniskillen with firearms, and herds of cows and sheep. The privations at Londonderry would not be repeated in Enniskillen. Sarsfield, who was by now camped at Manorhamilton (sixteen miles from Enniskillen) with 7,000 men, sent an express to the town requesting a prisoner exchange. The earlier events with Galmoy obviously made Gustavus Hamilton cautious and he requested a list of names of Sarsfield's prisoners. In an uncharacteristic move Sarsfield rounded up the Connaught Protestants and jailed them in Sligo, sending their wives to Hamilton to plead for mercy. Hamilton relented but the episode did nothing to endear the Jacobite cause to the Inniskillingers and was another example of 'faithless dealing' in their eyes. The situation was improving, however, and the holding action that the Inniskillingers had been fighting would reap benefits. Major General Percy Kirke, formerly of the Tangiers garrison, and a veteran soldier, had reinforcements and supplies for Londonderry and Enniskillen – though had taken refuge in Lough Swilly. The situation was therefore far from safe and waterways had to be kept open to permit such valuable resources to reach the garrison.

By June, further raiding opportunities were available. The Inniskillingers received information that the Irish army at Londonderry grazed their horses near Omagh, only eighteen miles away. Yet again raiding troops were used to steal horses (and yet more cattle), effectively disabling three troops of enemy cavalry. By this time several messages had been received from Londonderry to ask for relief. Hamilton felt his force in no condition to attempt such an undertaking, with 2,000 men, few arms and very little gunpowder. Understanding the importance of the continued siege, however (since without it, all eyes would be turned to Enniskillen), Hamilton felt compelled to do something. He hoped to supply the town with much of the sheep and cattle that had been taken and avoid further starvation. By 10 June Hamilton marched the bulk of his men to Trillick and then to Omagh. The scouting party was ambushed, however, and one man taken prisoner and subsequently killed. Enniskillen was left defended by Lloyd in tandem with the system of fortifications and earthworks in place at the fords and bridges. By 12 June the Jacobites had fled Omagh town and Hamilton began to lay siege to the nearby fort.

By now, however, news had come of Jacobite movements close to Enniskillen. Scouts reported that Sarsfield with 5,000 men was besieging the strategically vital Ballyshannon. In addition, Sutherland had arrived at Belturbet, twenty miles to the south of Enniskillen. Hamilton was left with little choice but to return, arriving by 13 June. By the 15th reports from Belturbet indicated that the size of the force there was increasing. For the second time the Inniskillingers decided against isolation within the town but would fight outside it, although their chances of defeating the ever increasing numbers were becoming more remote. Hamilton ordered Lloyd to march against Sutherland at Belturbet with as many troops as he could spare. By the 17th Lloyd had reached MacGuiresbridge, halfway between

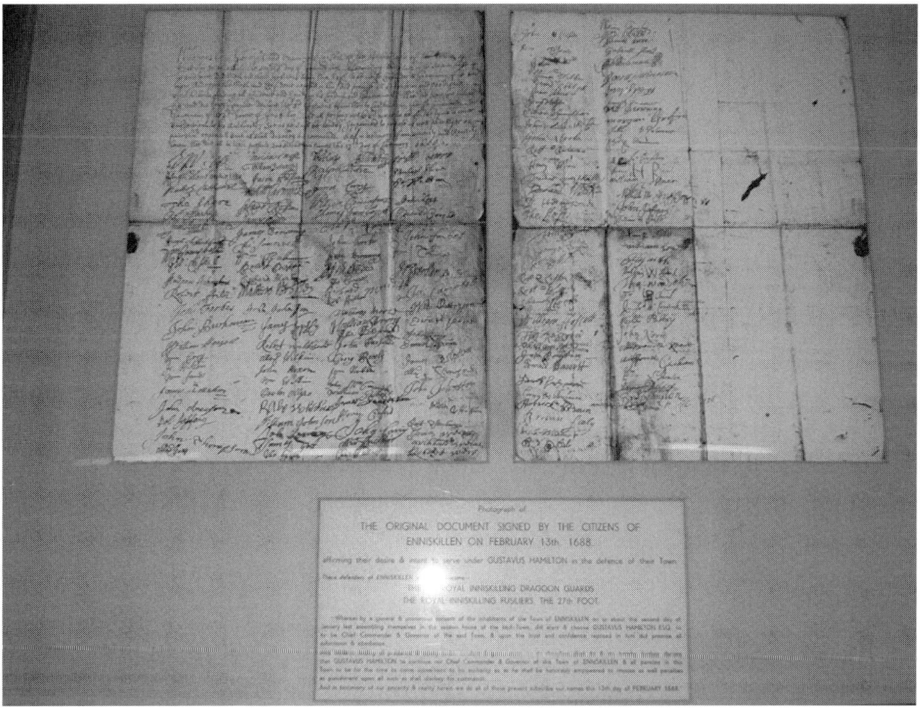

A copy of the document signed by the people of Enniskillen in February 1688, related to their unity in terms of defying the Jacobite moves toward them. (*Enniskillen Castle Museum*)

Enniskillen and Belturbet. Irish picquets, seeing the advancing troops, advised Sutherland, whose force consisted of two regiments of foot, a regiment of dragoons and some troops of horse.

He also carried some cannon, additional arms and powder with which to equip new levies, and provisions. Again the Inniskillingers benefited from false rumours of their number, and without any suitable fortifications at Belturbet and seeking to protect his cannon, most of Sutherland's men pulled back (leaving 200 foot and eighty dragoons at Belturbet church). On the 18th rain prevented any further advance and gave Sutherland time to retreat. The next day Lloyd sent two troops of dragoons forward. They were ambushed by Jacobite dragoons within two miles of Belturbet. These later retreated back to the church. Inniskillingers reached surrounding houses, however, and, firing from the upper floors, overwhelmed the defenders within two hours. The surrendering Jacobite officers were taken prisoner while the troops were disarmed and released, the Enniskillen men taking their red coats, a few hundred muskets, powder, horses and provisions.

By July Enniskillen was in its strongest position since the start of the war and was about to be re-supplied. News reached the town of the ship sent in May, now at Ballyshannon, its aim to determine Enniskillen's condition and to re-supply if necessary. Lack of powder was the biggest problem and so a party of horse and foot, led by Lloyd, was sent to meet Captain Hobson aboard the *Bonadventure*. On 5 July the Enniskillen representatives boarded the ship, acquainting the English captain with Enniskillen's condition. The party received thirty barrels of powder and some muskets. Two men would be sent on to Kirke for commissions, supplies and, more importantly for the battle to come, experienced officers. John Rider and Andrew Hamilton departed with the *Bonadventure* on 8 July arriving with Kirke at Inch Island by the 12th. By now Enniskillen had seventeen troops of horse, thirty companies of foot and a few companies of dragoons. Kirke provided a further 1,600 firearms and additional powder, eight light cannon and ammunition. This was the first real supply that the Inniskillingers had received. Before this their raiding was forced upon them to a certain extent, since their lack of equipment precluded their fighting a pitched battle. Kirke could not supply men but, more importantly perhaps, he supplied experienced officers. Colonel William Wolseley was made commander in chief and colonel of horse, while Captain William Berry was made lieutenant colonel of horse. Additional officers included Major Zachariah Tiffin to lead a foot battalion, Charles Stone as major of horse, and James Wynne as colonel of dragoons. These were very capable English soldiers. Berry and Tiffin had served with Kirke in the Tangiers garrison and both were experienced leaders. Commissions were also made for existing Enniskillen officers.[5]

New English Officers

The fifth son of Sir Robert Wolseley, William Wolseley was born around 1640. Little is known about his early years but his first commission is recorded in 1667 when he was appointed captain-lieutenant in the Marquis of Worcester's Regiment of Foot, although the regiment was disbanded as a result of the signing of the treaty of Breda. William had the same rank in 1673 in Lord Worcester's Regiment during the Dutch war, although the regiment was again disbanded in the following year. It is not until 1679 that William's military career flourished again, when he was made a lieutenant of an independent company of foot in Chepstow Castle, under the command of the Marquis of Worcester. Promoted to captain in June 1685 in the Duke of Beaufort's Regiment, he was later to become the colonel. 1688 and the Glorious Revolution was to see a change in Wolseley's fortune. In August, while quartered in Scarborough, he was instrumental in the public humiliation of the mayor as revenge for similar indignities carried out against a Protestant clergyman. The mayor complained to James himself and Wolseley was summoned to London, his requests for pardon being dismissed. William's fortunes were soon to change again, however. At the end of 1688 the headquarters of the regiment (now

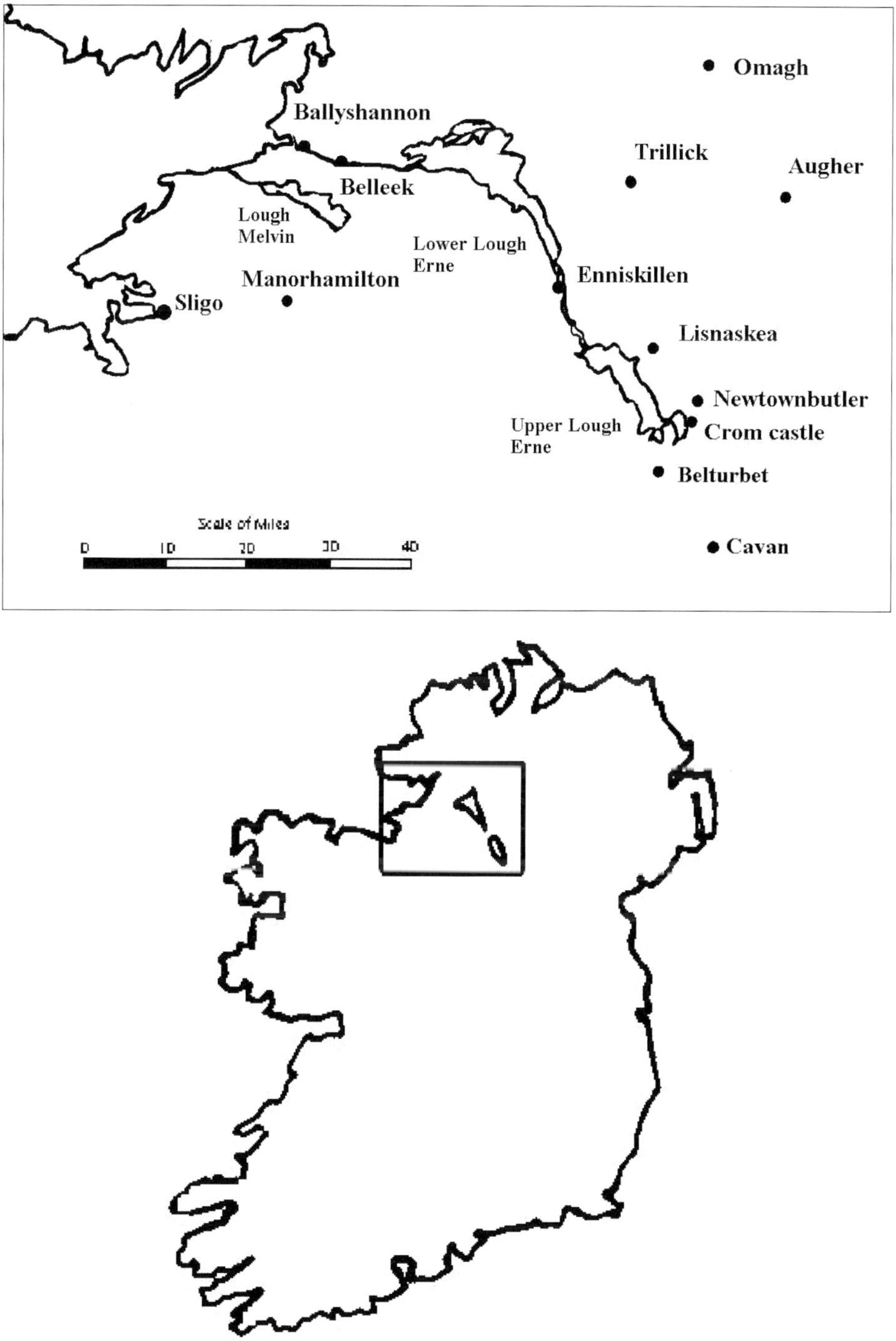

Enniskillen and the surrounding area, the focus of Mountcashel's Enniskillen campaign in 1689.

Montgomery's) were in Hull. On 3 December Colonel Montgomery and Lord Langdale, both Catholics, were arrested and detained by the Protestant officers. Wolseley was then desperate to join with William's forces in England, but this was delayed by rumours of atrocities and confusion throughout the country. By early 1689, however, he had secured the rank of lieutenant colonel in his old regiment (now Sir John Hanmer's). In May they accompanied General Kirke's expedition to Ireland. It is clear that his experience and the supply of arms and equipment to the Enniskillen garrison would allow them to fight the pitched battle that was by now inevitable and in which Mountcashel would play such a vital part.

Captain William Berry was another of Kirke's 'Lambs' who had accompanied the regiment on its Irish expedition. Another experienced officer, he had served with Kirke's Regiment in Tangier and was a lieutenant by February 1681. By December of the same year he had been promoted to captain-lieutenant. He also served as lieutenant of a troop of independent horse in 1685. He was an experienced cavalry officer and would have an important role in the battle to follow.[6]

The Skirmish at Cornegrade

Had the Jacobites formulated a strategy around the Enniskillen problem? Jacobite forces were converging on the town for the first time. While the Enniskillen party was at Ballyshannon, their home garrison was warned by scouts of the approach of Berwick's forces. Hamilton immediately ordered two companies of foot and two troops of horse under MacCarmick to defend the straight pass at Enniskillen Mill, through which Berwick's force would have to approach. He also prepared the remaining garrison for the coming battle. According to one source, MacCarmick's scouting party did not stop at the easily defended pass, however, and advanced a mile further on to a hollow between two hills (near Cornegrade Castle), where they were ambushed by Jacobite horse and dragoons. The two foot companies were routed and the Enniskillen horse, seeing their fleeing companions, 'wheeled about without coming to their relief'. Around twenty-five Inniskillingers were killed and the same number captured, a significant defeat for the town's garrison. Gustavus Hamilton later reached the area at which point Berwick's forces withdrew to Trillick with their prisoners. It had been a significant blow, albeit in a small skirmish, for the Inniskillingers. Hamilton, looking to the welfare of the captured troops, sent messages to Berwick indicating that if his men were not treated as prisoners of war the Irish prisoners held in Enniskillen would suffer. Within a few weeks another prisoner exchange had been agreed. (MacCarmick, captured at this battle, tells a different version of these events. Rather than being surprised, two companies of Enniskillen foot were deserted by their horse during the skirmish, and the prisoners secured their own wellbeing.)

At Londonderry events were moving quickly. Kirke's arrival had encouraged the demoralised Protestants somewhat, though his lack of movement, and thus intervention, was frustrating. Rosen, the French commander-in chief, now feared a pincer movement between Kirke and the Enniskillen troops in the south. Sarsfield moved his force closer to Ballyshannon again, with over 3,000 men. Despite further Enniskillen probes, he remained strong and the Inniskillingers would not risk facing him, while leaving their town unprotected. Berwick's victory at Cornagrade had shown that well-led Jacobites could face the Enniskillen troops and win. The situation was becoming critical now. By 28 July, however, the new officers had arrived at Enniskillen. The arms and ammunition were to follow soon afterwards.

Mountcashel had also arrived at Belturbet, as part of the Jacobite forces gathering in the south. It was his turn to make the Jacobite strategy work, and move against Enniskillen. On the night of the 28th Enniskillen received an urgent message from Crom Castle. For the second time in the year it was under siege. Mountcashel had arrived from Belturbet. Enniskillen faced enemies on two sides. The battle to follow would determine the fate of the town.[7]

A Dutch print of the Battle of Newtonbutler, the town in the background being slightly misrepresented; it is thought that this may be a depiction of Enniskillen.

Chapter VII

Newtownbutler 1689

The Jacobite Strategy

A reading of the events from the Enniskillen side promotes the view that Jacobite probes and attacks were ill conceived and carried out in an ad-hoc manner, and there is some evidence to support this view. To blame the Jacobite activities (or lack thereof) on poor planning, however, is to suggest that there was no strategy at all. This was not the case and it was to Mountcashel's credit that he strove to carry out the plan as far as was practical and meet the Enniskillen garrison in open battle.

The siege of Derry was immensely important to the Jacobite cause, not simply because of its strategic importance as a port. After the events of April it was important for James to leave no active centres of Protestant resistance in the country, especially in Ulster where the Jacobites could not afford to lose ground. In England William was preparing an invasion force. The initial blockade and siege of Derry meant that Enniskillen and the nearby towns of Ballyshannon and Belleek near the inlet to Lough Erne became strategically important. It was clear that the Jacobites realised this and Sarsfield's attacks in the area were indicative of, at the very least, a concern with the potential for supply and reinforcement from Britain. The will was present, though the quantity and quality of troops was lacking, and the Inniskillingers appear to have had such a demoralising effect on the Jacobites in the early stages of the war that their forces were hamstrung for the most part. In the event, Enniskillen would prove to be a greater thorn in James II's side than Londonderry. This was not to become apparent to James until June, however, by which time it was too late to divert sufficient resources to the capture of the town. In retrospect, it may have been more prudent to take the poorly-fortified Enniskillen early in the campaign, a town which lacked a defensive wall, and whose troops lacked even powder for their matchlocks prior to July.

Though considered a secondary problem, plans were discussed in May and June in the hope of sending around 8,000 men to take the town. As with many Jacobite strategies, however, the protracted siege of Derry and logistical problems would prove decisive. By mid July, the Dublin parliament gave serious consideration to a concerted attack. Plans were formed for a three pronged assault, Berwick from the north, Sarsfield from the west and Mountcashel from the south. These three would create a stranglehold around Enniskillen. Berwick, still frustrated from the inactivity at Derry requested to lead a body of troops against the Inniskillingers. After attacks at Donegal on 21 June, he was reinforced giving him an overall strength of two regiments of horse, a force of dragoons and four battalions of infantry, a force of 3-4,000 men.

By July 1689 the infamous Galmoy had joined Mountcashel who had marched from Munster earlier in the month and formed a large army. Camped at Belturbet, they were joined by the northern Irish under Maguire. Some records speak of an army 7,000 strong, although this figure seems high and may have been based on a large amount of levies or recently conscripted troops of poor quality. More likely, Mountcashel had three to 4,000 men, of varying quality.

The plan to use three armies was simple in principle, yet difficult to implement under the conditions. Berwick, ignoring the plan, requested that Sarsfield ensure that English shipping could not enter Lough Erne by attacking Ballyshannon again. Berwick would attempt to join him later. Sarsfield camped five miles from Ballyshannon near Lough Melvin. Plans went awry, however, when despite his victory at Cornegrade in July, Berwick was recalled to intensify the blockade against English shipping that had been sighted in Lough Swilly, and the link up never took place. Sarsfield's characteristic optimism convinced him to stay where he was and urge Mountcashel in Cavan to march north and link up with Berwick when he was able to return. It must have been obvious to Mountcashel that the plan was beginning to fall apart, but he was ordered by James to advance on Enniskillen alone. Had Berwick's considerable force, with the morale boost of a recent victory, been available and able to link up with Mountcashel at the very least, the events that followed might have been very different. Mountcashel, however, following James's order, would face the Enniskilleners alone. He would not attempt to link up with Sarsfield. Enniskillen had held out long enough and he would force them to give battle.[1]

Anthony Hamilton and a regiment of dragoons reinforced Mountcashel. He was the older brother of Richard Hamilton, who was still at Londonderry. Anthony is best remembered as a writer rather than a professional soldier and was the author of the infamous *Memoires du Comte de Grammont*, which related the intrigues at the court of Charles II in the 1660s, and he is also recorded as having once been an actor. The third son of Sir George Hamilton, Governor of Nenagh, he was born at Roscrea Castle in Tipperary around 1645. His eldest brother James was a groom of the bedchamber of Charles II and was killed at sea, fighting the Dutch in 1679. Anthony accompanied his older brother George to the continent in 1667 to enter French service and served under Turenne in his brother's regiment. He served as a captain from 1672 alongside Justin MacCarthy and Patrick Sarsfield and under Luxembourg in 1676. As with so many of his contemporaries, his experience was based on his service on the continent. By 1685 he was a lieutenant colonel in Sir Thomas Newcomen's Regiment of Foot and a privy councillor in Ireland. Later he was to succeed Sir William King as Governor of Limerick and was given command of a regiment of dragoons, as recommended by Lord Clarendon, with a pension of 200 pounds a year. The same dragoons formed part of the Irish force sent to England in August 1688. His loyalty to the king meant that he left for France after 1688 and also returned to Ireland with James.[2]

The Jacobite strategy had now been considerably diluted in terms of its effectiveness. There were three key concerns. Firstly, James's ordering of a speedy resolution prevented a co-ordinated attack on the well-defended Enniskillen. Mountcashel did not have the troops or guns to lay siege to the town and was aware that he had to choose his battlefield if possible, and defeat the Inniskillingers in open battle. Secondly, the quality of the Jacobite troops was poor at best, although the cavalry was thought to be some of the best in Ireland at the time. Finally, leaving Sarsfield in his supposedly strong position at Ballyshannon still allowed a chance of taking that town and at least preventing shipping entering Lough Erne since the Inniskillingers would be busy dealing with Mountcashel's force. He would be effectively isolated, however. It is also important to consider that the Enniskillen troops' reputation and their own morale had been enhanced in the past months. Experienced English officers like Wolseley now joined 'heroic' figures such as Lloyd. Their reputation amongst the Jacobites had already given some cause for concern at earlier engagements. Mountcashel had additional concerns, however. He could no longer be reinforced quickly if in trouble, and he was now in unfamiliar territory, undertaking a plan which lacked co-ordination between his and other Jacobite forces. D'Avaux' general description related to decision making in the Irish army, is particularly poignant after the battle.

> It is very upsetting indeed that we should have so many difficulties in making decisions here, and that things are executed so badly once the decision has been taken.[3]

Mountcashel's Troops

Logistical problems and poor equipment prevented Mountcashel forming an effective force until 27 July. Looking at the numbers involved in the battle, there are some interesting points raised in the sources. Hamilton, MacCarmick and Story state that the Jacobite force numbered around 6,000. The *Jacobite Narrative* maintains that a 'flying camp' of horse and foot made up of 4,000 men comprised the force, while d'Avaux, the French Ambassador of the time, refers to three infantry battalions and sixteen troops of horse and dragoons together with four small-calibre cannon.[4] It seems unlikely that Mountcashel had a 6,000 strong army, although numbers may have been bolstered by untrained and unreliable levy troops. Mountcashel's troops were mainly composed of three infantry regiments/battalions:

Mountcashel's Regiment

Mountcashel's own regiment in 1689 is detailed in the *Jacobite Narrative*. This record was clearly made *before* Newtownbutler since a number of the officers captured after the battle (including Mountcashel) are still present. This is the only regiment in the French record that outlines the number of troops, and this in itself reveals some quite startling evidence. Despite the fact that many of the companies in the Jacobite army at this time were oversize, Mountcashel's Regiment appears to be low on numbers. Including officers for the regiment there are just over 400 men. This differs with the Ormond account from where Mountcashel's Regiment is noted at the start of July as having 650 men, 'well clad and very sightly'.[5]

Bophin's Regiment

John Burke, Lord Bophin, led Mountcashel's second regiment. His officers are recorded in the *Jacobite Narrative* but the number of troops are not. D'Avaux records that the regiment had 215 men in thirteen companies, again very low (though d'Avaux's records throughout appear to be twenty to fifty per cent less than those recorded in the *Narrative*). Again, though, it appears that the regiment was undermanned.[6]

Clare's Regiment

Lord Clare's (Daniel O'Brien's) infantry regiment is again recorded in the *Narrative* but numbers of troops are not given. Marigny, a French major from Champagne, was present with this regiment.[7]

Cotter's/Clare's Dragoons and Artillery

Cotter's dragoon regiment is recorded in the *Narrative* as having around 360 men, and in Ormond as 450. Clare's/O'Brien's Dragoons have officers recorded but numbers of troopers are not. It is likely, however, that they made up around six troops or 300 men. Anthony Hamilton and Cotter commanded dragoons at the battle. Additional cavalry that d'Avaux refers to then were either attached to Mountcashel's troops or were dragoons acting in a cavalry role, although d'Avaux records that nine troops of dragoons are included in Anthony Hamilton's detachment at Lisnaskea. He also records four small pieces of artillery in Mountcashel's forces with men of the king's troop manning the guns.[8]

Two of the three battalions in Mountcashel's force would at most have had 1,000 men between them, plus a likely total of five to 600 dragoons. This would mean that the additional infantry regiment plus cavalry (and possibly 'cannoneers') would have had to make up well over 2,000 men to reach the sizeable figures mentioned in other sources. It seems more likely that either Mountcashel's troops numbered around 2,000 to 3,000, or a large body of untrained and poorly equipped levies, whose effectiveness in battle would be questionable at best, had recently reinforced him.

O'Kelly refers to Mountcashel's men as 'raw and newly raised', again suggesting untrained levies. O'Callaghan also makes approximations as to Mountcashel's number; the three regiments of infantry (2,418 men), two regiments of dragoons (1,086 men) and ninety-six horse, for a total of 3,600 men with seven guns and one heavy iron piece, apparently by this stage the best-equipped Jacobite army in the field, despite the supply problems.[9] Although there is some disparity, it is likely that Mountcashel did not have the 6,000 men recorded in the Enniskillen sources.

Warfare in this Period

The conduct of war in the late seventeenth century was by no means standardised. In fact, methods and equipment differed tremendously across European borders and the very nature of land warfare was in a constant state of development. The reasons for this were based on tradition and technology. Much of the tactics that had been seen during the English Civil War of the 1640s were still 'fashionable', and the majority of infantry regiments still carried pikes for protection against enemy cavalry in addition to matchlock muskets. Technology, however, and the development of the more reliable flintlock musket, in combination with more deadly methods and tactics, signalled the start of methods of waging war that would see deadly effectiveness during the time of Marlborough and change little until the Napoleonic wars, over a hundred years later.

When compared with many of the larger European battles and numerous sieges of the period, early battles in Ireland were large skirmishes involving a few thousand troops. Most sources relate directly to the European battlefield of the period, concentrating on French, English and Swedish experiences. The concern here, however, is with small unit tactics on the Irish battlefield, for the most part using inexperienced levies, or at best poorly-drilled troops. It is also important to consider that although the quality and training of the troops may not have compared directly with English and continental armies, both commanders, and many of the officers, were professional soldiers. Mountcashel had obtained a solid reputation with the French military and William Wolseley was an experienced English officer.

The troops who would fight at Newtownbutler, however, were quite different in terms of experience and ability. The Inniskillingers were formed for the most part from ex-members of the militia with some experienced officers who had been sacked during Tyrconnel's purges (Gustavus Hamilton and Thomas Lloyd amongst them). Most of the armourers in Ireland were Protestants who had supplied the militia, and the Inniskillingers appear to have been able to easily repair broken weapons. As the 1689 campaign dragged on, the Enniskillen forces became better equipped through both raiding and re-supply. In contrast, the Jacobite forces were for the most part inexperienced and with the loss of the core of the officer class during the purges, ill-disciplined. Many of them had neither pike nor musket and were only armed with clubs or the infamous Irish *skein*, or 'half-pike'. This situation changed a little during 1689 due to limited French re-supply, and the general reduction in numbers carried out by Tyrconnel.[10] It is clear though that troops on both sides would not have had the experience or training that would enable them to fight in a manner similar to their French or English counterparts. The question is rather one of leadership and command. How far were the experienced commanders on each side able to train, control and effectively use the irregular forces under their command?

The end of the seventeenth century and the start of the eighteenth also marked a period of transition in terms of military thinking. The era that marked the rise of the standing army also saw the demise of the pike and the further development of flintlock and bayonet, but the changeover was a slow and expensive one. In most cases the tactics adopted were the best solution in terms of the limitations imposed by the weaponry in use. By 1689 most infantry regiments throughout Europe relied on the matchlock for firepower and the pike for defence against cavalry. The pike's numbers had dwindled so that firepower could be increased and the 'aggressive' use of the pike had all but disappeared. Its defensive use against cavalry was also limited, however, as the pikemen usually congregated in the centre of the battalion, providing little protection to the flanks.[11]

Various methods were in use in the French army in an attempt to spread the pike throughout the battalion's companies, but this saw little use outside continental Europe.

Musketeers could fire in a number of ways. The infantry 'countermarch' was one of the oldest methods of firing from matchlocks, dating back to the earliest use of the weapon. Normally this method required each rank of musketeers to fire and then move to the rear of the battalion while reloading. Successive ranks could either advance or retire and only one rank would fire at any one time. Another method used was firing 'by ranks', one or two ranks at a time. All methods required training and discipline, a luxury that few officers witnessed on the Irish battlefield of the time, until the arrival of foreign troops.

The matchlock was a cumbersome weapon which did not lend itself to use by 'green' or untrained troops. The ball was effective for about eighty yards, while the cumbersome loading procedure restricted rate of fire to about one shot per minute on the battlefield. Matchlocks meant slower reloading and thus 'thicker' battalions in order to achieve a good rate of fire from the rows of infantry. In battle, at least fifty per cent of fire could be ineffective even if troops were well drilled.[12]

The flintlock musket would prove more efficient and safe but would not be universally adopted until the turn of the century and beyond. Matchlock and pike were by far the most common combination even with well-armed troops in Ireland by 1689. The French themselves did not fully adopt the flintlock until the early 1690s.[13]

In 1689 the French supplied to Ireland 16,000 cavalry sabres, 3,000 swords, 5,000 matchlock muskets, 2,000 pistols, 500 carbines (for cavalry), 500 flintlock muskets (most likely supplied to dragoons) and 100,000 pounds of powder.[14]

On the Enniskillen side, General Kirke's supply to the Inniskillingers in July 1689 consisted of 600 'fire-locks' (flintlocks) and 1,000 'muskets', the distinction being made between flintlock for dragoons and matchlock for infantry. Reference is also made to the supply of 'match' (match-cord) for the troops, again indicating use of matchlocks.[15]

At this time the infantry battalion itself was normally made up of four to five 'ranks' deep and around 120 'files' wide (giving a rough average of 500-600 men, though this varied greatly). Two battalions would make up a regiment though this was not always possible in wartime and distinction between battalion and regiment is not always clear-cut in period sources. Generally officers would stand at the battalion's rear but sometimes in front when attacking. The files were separated for practical reasons. Each man using a matchlock held a burning match and had powder in his pockets or in a bandolier slung over his shoulder (the twelve 'apostles').

Loose powder and lit match was a lethal enough combination without keeping men tightly packed together. This meant that matchlock-armed troops had to maintain safe distances between ranks and files, typically six paces for ranks and one to three for files (one pace being roughly equal to two and a half feet). A fielded battalion could then be anything from 100 to 300 yards in width, though most likely the former if there were enemy cavalry about and the infantry felt the need to be closer to their pike elements. The nature of fire combat, and the unwieldy matchlock, meant that the battalion could only fire when halted. Protracted exchanges then took place at thirty to eighty yards until one side broke. The battalion would normally have twelve or thirteen companies of fifty to sixty men each, having a shot to pike ratio of 60–80 per cent, with ever-diminishing pike blocks as the latter years of the century progressed and more reliable musktry and training took hold.[16]

This type of combat was close, deadly, and strained the nerves of the troops to breaking point. It is easy to see why so much lay in the hands of the officer who had to encourage the men, keep their morale up and, most of all, keep steady and controlled volleys of fire going for as long as possible, all while attempting to avoid being shot from the saddle himself. It was no mean feat to attempt this with untrained levy and Mountcashel was experienced enough to realise that the battle would be decided quickly as protracted and orderly exchanges would not be the order of the day with the troops involved.

At Newtownbutler, the Inniskillingers deployed their infantry in two under-strength battalions of five to six companies and one main body of nine to eleven companies deployed as a reserve, each with several troops of cavalry to screen them. As the troops reached the town, companies of pikes and colours were left behind. MacCarmick also records that this comprised one-third of the total number of infantry. By implication then a number of points are evident. The Inniskillingers were operating in open country with vulnerable flanks: their best protection against enemy cavalry was their own cavalry and mounted dragoons. Pikes may have been seen as extra 'weight' in the advance, which could not be used effectively at close quarters. The leaving behind of the pike elements may also suggest that a flexible or 'skirmishing' formation was used in the advance. Although this would hamper the effects of co-ordinated fire, it is likely that firing was not carried out *en masse*. Henry is also keen to point out the skirmish nature of the Inniskillingers stating that his record, written in 1749, is based on the statements of some who were present at the battle.

> but Lloyd, who had but a few days before observed the effect of their impetuous courage – too great to be restrained within military rule – advised to let them proceed in their own way, whereupon they, scarce staying for their commanders, darted like lightning through all parts of the bog, attacked the enemy on the face of the hill, sword in hand, in a few minutes drove them from the field pieces ….

The impetuous nature of the Enniskillen troops and their lack of conventional 'drill' is clear and this type of fighting owes more to the reckless bravado of the attacker as well as the nerve of the defender. It is also interesting to note that the troops are described as having 'sword in hand'. The fact that the pikes formed one-third of each battalion also implies that the troops were not well equipped with matchlocks.[17]

Estimates for Jacobite numbers at Newtownbutler vary widely as we have seen: between 3,000 and 6,000, with the lesser number being more likely. There were clear motivations, however, both to exaggerate a victory and make light of a defeat when considering the important role of propaganda at the time and this may explain differences between sources.

Weaponry of the time may have been cumbersome, but poor quality troops made the situation worse. On the Jacobite side most of the primary sources agree that there were problems with the quality of training. Much stemmed from the nature of the standing forces that had existed in Ireland and their now revised composition. Disrespect for new officers, lack of discipline, together with lack of clear leadership had become a major problem within the Irish army by 1689. Competent and experienced officers such as Mountcashel were all too rare. The *Journal of John Stevens* echoes these same sentiments. Stevens, an English Jacobite points to the 'immorality of officers' and general 'thieving and drunkenness'.

> Our men were newly brought from the mountains, used to (living) in slavery without the use of any weapon : the most of them had never fired a musket in their lives
>
> ... so hard to be made sensible of the duty of a soldier or be brought to handle their arms aright, that it was difficult to make any of them understand the common words of command, much less to obey them.
>
> They will follow none but their own leaders, many of them men as rude, as ignorant, and as far from understanding of the rules of discipline as themselves.

Stevens is consistent in his view of the Jacobite troops (and their officers) as ill-disciplined, lacking qualification and experience and, in many cases, weapons. It is also interesting to note that he blames the poor performance of Mountcashel's troops at Newtownbutler on poor quality troops and officers;

> I observed that some of them never looked back till they came to Dublin ... I do not design this to have it thought the private men were not faulty, they have given us too many examples of their baseness and want of courage; but doubtless had their leaders been such as they ought, many enterprises had met with better success.[18]

Stevens also cites examples of corruption and desertion within the Irish army that cannot have helped discipline. Even with the reduction in numbers in April

1689, quality of troops and equipment remained poor.[19] The *Jacobite Narrative* draws similar conclusions, referring to internal problems within the Irish cause as a whole which did little to unite the army. These, as we have seen, are exemplified through the lack of planning prior to Newtownbutler, and the inability of the three Jacobite forces to link up. The Jacobite soldier is also seen as 'ignorant in the military art, as being debarred upon the account of their religion from posts of that mystery of a long time by the government'.

The *Narrative* is also clear on the potential of the enemy:

> And what is worse than this, they have a most potent enemy to deal with; for they are to stand against wealthy England, hardy Scotland, and the violent Protestants of Ireland.

Mountcashel understood the problems. He had served with English, French and Danish forces. He would undoubtedly have been aware of the difficulties with ill-disciplined and poorly-trained troops. The focus in both French and English armies was on training, both to increase the efficiency of troops and improve their morale in battle. In France the requirement for regular drill within individual regiments was seen as critical. It highlighted the importance of order, training and command within the battalion. Drill was also used to instil rules of movement into the troops so that they could manoeuvre, deploy and retire when necessary. The French ethos was more concerned with maintaining discipline, efficiency and order, since this could physically win battles before bloody close-range combat ever took place. Indeed the French felt that it took five or six years to create a good infantry regiment in comparison with one year for cavalry. Mountcashel did not underestimate the problems with training that his men had. His tactics and posture in the oncoming battle would have to be based on this. It is testament to his bravery that he stood at all.[20]

On the Enniskillen side, matters were quite different. The army had been organised by Protestants until the purges. Also, since the 1641 rebellion, Ulster Protestants had formed a well-armed militia. It is clear that the majority of male Protestants had been well armed and had probably received at least some training in the use of their muskets and pikes. The fact that the militia had to be disarmed prior to the start of the purges perhaps indicates their potential, at least to Tyrconnel. Large organised bands led by competent officers such as Hamilton and Lloyd could quickly reinforce Enniskillen.

They were not all professional soldiers by any means, but it would appear that they were at least skilled in the use of arms, had some training, and were to become expert in the use of hit-and-run tactics. Gustavus Hamilton had been one of the Protestant officers who had been expelled during the purge, as were many of his colleagues. With 7,000 Protestant soldiers dismissed between 1685 and 1688, many of whom stayed in Ireland, there must have been no shortage of able recruits. As we have seen, this collected experience seems to have been enough to drive off lesser-experienced Jacobite troops, without a fight in many cases. A combination of relative quality and the nature of small unit battles in Ireland made the Inniskillingers an effective force throughout the war.

D'Avaux, however, points out that neither side was very professional, and describes the Enniskillen men as 'ramshackle' . He also points to the poor quality of Jacobite troops as reason enough to be concerned as 'the enemy are not soldiers any more than we are ….'

O'Callaghan, though, also points to them as having belonged to a religious and political ascendancy and composed of 'yeomanry', as opposed to the raw levy potential of the Jacobites. Indeed, he singles out Mountcashel's own troops as the only Jacobite regiment at Newtownbutler above the level of recruit.[21]

Cavalry's primary function on the late-seventeenth-century battlefield was to defeat enemy cavalry, and then concentrate on infantry and guns. Although it could never replace infantry, its ability to charge home before heavy casualties could be inflicted was seen as a distinct advantage. Although by the War of the Grand Alliance, the cavalry sword was invariably used in the charge, some remnant of harassing fire from cavalry pistols may have been included (again showing the transitional nature of tactics at this time).

The Jacobite cavalry and dragoons in Ireland did not suffer from the same poor quality troops as the infantry. Jacobite cavalry regiments were thought to be some of the best in the country, and were well led with good mounts. They were represented by the social elite; indeed, the performance of the Jacobite cavalry at the Boyne in 1690 is notable and prevented a greater disaster.

Dragoons were also a major feature of the battlefield at this time, being part light cavalryman and part musketeer. They could serve as highly mobile infantry or be used to skirmish against exposed flanks, usually using flintlocks. Troops or companies of mounted troops were formed from thirty-five to sixty men. At Newtownbutler, the Inniskillingers fielded sixteen troops of cavalry and three of dragoons while Mountcashel had sixteen troops of both types.

The main projectile fired by the artillery of this period was solid shot, although grapeshot and canister were also used. The late-seventeenth-century artillery piece was invariably cumbersome and difficult to move once battle had commenced. The French system, as in other areas of its military establishment, suffered from a lack of standardisation and many different calibres were in use. Typical ranges on the seventeenth-century battlefield varied from 650 yards with a sixteen-pounder to 2000 yards with a twenty-four-pounder.

Artillery in this period was still in its infancy, in terms of its role as an active arm of the military, and it was frequently organised by authorities outside the army. The men handling the guns at this time could be a mixture of hired civilians, officers and infantrymen. Only small calibre field artillery pieces appear to have been in use in Ireland in 1689. A number of small calibre pieces were in use by the Jacobites at Newtownbutler. Problems with non-standard ammunition both for muskets and guns may also have been evident.

In terms of tactics, rigid rules were difficult to find for planning a battle, though choice of terrain and superiority in numbers were obviously critical considerations. Line of battle usually consisted of two main lines with 300 paces between each, with cavalry taking the flanks. Dragoons normally made up the second line or reserve if infantry was lacking. A reserve was sometimes kept as a third line. For artillery, the commander in the field preferred high ground giving the guns as large a field of fire as possible. On the attack, it was rare for one side not to break before contact was made.

The officers had their work cut out to maintain order in conditions where marching in cadence was not used and the battalion could be under fire. The nature of these conditions and mode of attack can be traced directly back to the firearms in use (this changed as firearms became more effective). When charged, and viscious mêlée was threatened, the defender could open fire at twenty to sixty paces, hoping to cause enough casualties to destroy the impetus of the charge and allow him to counter-charge. Even if the attacker pushed on, he could easily become disordered as the battalion crowded in on itself. The defender, if he held his position, could maintain good order for a counter-attack or stand. Such actions required good morale, well-trained and well-led troops. It should also be recognised that such tactics were still very much in development in 1689.

Without examining all the actions during the battle at this stage, it is evident that neither side can be described as a professional force. When assessing the relevance of the points made above to the Irish battlefield in 1689, it is clear that the battle was fought in an 'irregular' manner and based on motivation and morale rather than strict European-style guidelines and tactics. Troop quality had a bearing on the outcome of the battle. Both Mountcashel and Wolseley had similar problems on the day in that the troops had to be kept in order and 'stay the distance' both in attack and defence. With the time available prior to the battle it is unlikely that Mountcashel and his fellow commanders could have adequately drilled an undisciplined force. The best that they could do was to adopt a solid defensive position. Morale was still crucial in such situations. Untrained troops could break without receiving excessive casualties. French training in the attack relied heavily on this principle and on the psychological effect of large bodies of ordered troops advancing with good morale. The effect of this would usually be devastating on poorly drilled or untrained troops. The Inniskillingers appear to have had the edge on the day, perhaps through a combination of good morale, experienced command and the fact that they had faced Jacobite troops several times already in smaller engagements.

The matchlock also could have provided problems for both sides, especially since skirmish formation is at least implied. With an effective range of eighty yards or less, troops dispersed in hedges and cover would perhaps get one or two shots off at an approaching enemy. If this was dispersed and uncontrolled and not fired 'by ranks', the effect would be negligible and an approaching enemy would quickly close with the defender and decide the day through mêlée. Clearly then, the quality of the troops on both sides made a difference on the day, and the Irish battlefield in 1689 could be won on the basis of morale and 'staying power' rather than tactical outmanoeuvring and sophisticated fire control.[22]

The potential for irregular and poorly-trained troops to engage with each other in the battle that was to follow should not reduce its relative importance. This opportunity, for Mountcashel at least, presented a potential victory over a force whose very presence affected the morale of the raw Jacobite troops. Conversely, the Inniskillingers had a chance to inflict a major blow on the Jacobites, against one of their ablest commanders, and in their first large battle. The result would see a turning point in the war, whatever the outcome.

Crom Castle

James ordered Mountcashel to take Crom Castle initially, sixteen miles from Enniskillen. Taking Crom would prevent it becoming a rallying point and well defended garrison for the Enniskilleners, and would have left the surrounding population little hope of holding out should the town fall. James had considered going to Enniskillen himself but was dissuaded by D'Avaux.[23] A repeat of the debacle that instigated the siege of Londonderry could do little to help the Jacobite cause at this time. Crom Castle lies on the edge of Lough Erne, at the corner of a plain covered on two sides by water. It was vulnerable to attack by shot and cannon from a large hill across the river to the south and local tradition suggests that Galmoy placed his cannon there during the first siege (in a vain attempt to scare the garrison) and that Mountcashel may also have used the hill (although this is not mentioned in the sources).[24]

As d'Avaux indicates however, Mountcashel had four small calibre cannon and had little time for a protracted siege and would have had to use a more direct approach. D'Avaux indicates that the castle is overlooked on 'the Dublin side' by a hill and a lake at its foot. Interpreting the Dublin side as 'south' then this suggests 'Galmoy's hill' in Inishfendra Wood as the one in question, where there is also a small lake. This makes little sense, however, since Mountcashel would have had to cross water and this does not seem likely in the light of the latter account. It is more probable that d'Avaux is referring to an attack from the *easterly* direction (the Dublin *side* of Ireland). In this instance Lough Nalughoge and Ardandillure hill would more closely fit d'Avaux's version.[25]

The Enniskillen garrison at Crom had two companies of foot during Galmoy's attack in March. There is no evidence to suggest that it was reinforced, but it seems likely that it would have been, at least to some degree, to guard against future attack. The garrison had placed two forward encampments on either side of the hill (Henry suggests that an additional two companies were placed in these works), evidently to impede and thus warn of impending attack on the castle itself. The *Jacobite Narrative* describes the Enniskillen position in front of the castle as having earthworks although these may have been hastily constructed and could not have been held for long. It is also likely that the Enniskillen picquets had been observing Mountcashel's movements, since accurate intelligence and knowledge of the Jacobites' movements is a recurring theme in the sources. This is understandable, considering that the Enniskillen and Crom garrisons were mainly composed of locals who knew the countryside exceptionally well and who were able to stay one step ahead of the Jacobite forces in terms of intelligence.

Abraham Creighton, the garrison commander at Crom, on observing the Jacobite forces, sent despatches to Enniskillen, which arrived on the night of 28 July, informing the town that Mountcashel had arrived from Belturbet and had cannon with him. At the time, Gustavus Hamilton was ill with fever and the message came to Colonel William Wolseley who had been in command of the garrison for less than a week, having just arrived in Enniskillen as part of the English reinforcements.

On Sunday the 28th, the day that the despatch arrived in Enniskillen, Mountcashel's regiment attacked the Crom position on the left side of the hill while Bophin attacked on the right, Clare's regiment being kept in reserve. The garrison was quickly forced back and Mountcashel prepared to attack the castle itself. He had ordered his own regiment to reform at the encampment, while Bophin took Ardandillure hill in preparation for an attack on the castle's right. Mountcashel's Regiment had charged on, however, in some disorder, close enough to be in pistol range (an indication of their impetuous nature or an example of poor discipline amongst the troops). The Jacobites were forced to take cover around the walls of the castle, in what d'Avaux describes as 'huts', probably outbuildings near the castle walls. Mountcashel was now forced to bring forward his cannon to support his isolated regiment (the commitment of additional infantry would perhaps have made the situation worse, bearing in mind the quality of the troops). The subsequent fire was ineffective though, and three cannoneers of the King's

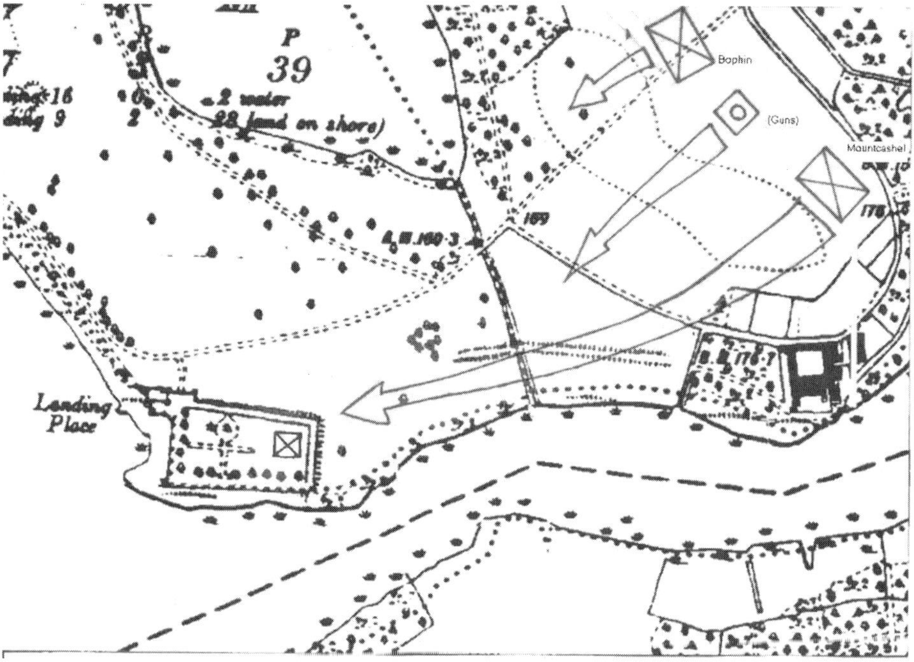

Mountcashel's assault on Crom Castle (using the later 1834 map as a basis).

Regiment were injured by counterfire. The guns were pulled back. Mountcashel could do little more during daylight and withdrew his own regiment.

He had lost around twenty men killed and sixty wounded (including his lieutenant colonel). He did not have the troops or siege cannon necessary for a continued assault. The only hope now lay in a night attack, perhaps using assaults against two of the walls simultaneously, thus dividing the defenders' fire. Creighton had meanwhile sent another message to Enniskillen (apparently easy to do despite the presence of the Jacobites in the surrounding countryside) recounting the day's events, this one arriving on the morning of Monday the 29th. This time Wolseley replied, assuring the besieged that he would relieve them within two days. He immediately gave orders for 400 to 500 men and some troops of horse to march to Enniskillen from Ballyshannon, leaving a small garrison there. The troops arrived on Tuesday the 30th at Enniskillen.[26]

Mountcashel was obviously aware of the activity since he postponed his night attack and pulled his troops out of the area. D'Avaux recounts that Mountcashel was aware of the Inniskillinger moves in his direction and, judging his position vulnerable, withdrew to Newtownbutler, a few miles north of Crom. Since the Inniskillingers did not advance until Tuesday, there seems no reason for Mountcashel to have postponed his night attack. He may have received early word from Sarsfield, however, of movement at Ballyshannon, though this seems unlikely considering the distances involved and the strong presence of Enniskillen scouts in the area. It is more likely that either the dates in the Enniskillen sources, related to despatches from Crom are inaccurate, or that Mountcashel's night attack was only suggested by d'Avaux, rather than having been seriously considered.

Lisnaskea

One source records that by the night of Monday the 29th Wolseley was aware that Mountcashel intended to send part of his force to Lisnaskea (ten miles south-east of Enniskillen) to garrison the castle there. Again, it is not clear whether there was a spy amongst Mountcashel's troops or the Enniskillen scouts had seen movement in the area. Mountcashel himself had by now withdrawn to Newtownbutler where the ground was more favourable for a static defence, and where he would have time to draw up a deception plan designed to draw the Inniskillingers into an ambush. Apparently aware of Wolseley's advance, Mountcashel seized the initiative and sent Anthony Hamilton ahead to Lisnaskea with thirteen troops of dragoons, (O'Callaghan records over 500 men). The *Jacobite Narrative* states that cavalry also formed part of Hamilton's force. He most likely set out on Tuesday the 30th, with orders to occupy a position on the road where advancing Enniskillen forces could be halted.[27]

The ruins of Crom Castle today.

It is not known whether Mountcashel had thoroughly scouted the area, but there was no shortage of suitable ambush sites on the roads leading to Newtownbutler, especially amongst the narrow passes on the Colebrooke river. In Enniskillen, Lieutenant Colonel Berry was ordered to make for Lisnaskea with around eight troops of horse, three companies of foot and two troops of dragoons, there to garrison Lisnaskea Castle or destroy it as required, in order to prevent it falling into Jacobite hands. Wolseley's concern after the siege of Crom was that Mountcashel sought to occupy the local fortifications, there perhaps to build strength and gain a foothold in the area in preparation for a larger co-ordinated attack. Berry was also ordered to determine the size of the enemy force if possible. Wolseley assured him that reinforcements would come if he requested them. Berry set out on the morning of Tuesday the 30th. Arriving at Lisnaskea, he found the castle in such disrepair that he considered it of little consequence (probably due to Galmoy's sacking of the area earlier in the year), his men camping in the surrounding fields that night.[28]

By the morning of Wednesday the 31st Berry moved forward, mounted troops scouting ahead with orders not to engage the enemy if spotted but to retreat until better ground could be found. The scouts moved along the old Donagh road, the main force following closely behind. Anthony Hamilton was just six miles away and had marched his dragoons along the same road. Berry's scouts went forward another two miles (near Donagh), before encountering Hamilton's forward elements. The scouts immediately reported a large force of dragoons, foot and horse moving on their position. As the French sources record that the force was composed of dragoons and possibly some cavalry, it is likely that that some of the 'foot' were actually dismounted dragoons.

Berry began to retreat back to Lisnaskea. As he retreated, he observed the size of the Jacobite force from rising ground, estimating them at twice his number (perhaps an exaggeration). He continued to pull back until he could find a more easily defended position and avoid a risky fight in the open. As he retreated, he sent word to Wolseley at Enniskillen, informing him of the situation and urging him to hurry with reinforcements. Berry was not prepared to be caught in the open. With more professional forces at his disposal, perhaps he would have handled matters differently, but the ambush and subterfuge of the actions that followed again highlights the nature of the fight. Guile and manoeuvre were the order of the day in Ireland. Hamilton pursued closely on the tails of the retreating Inniskillinger column and Berry had to repeatedly use his faster cavalry to double back and protect his rear in order to prevent the retreat becoming a rout. Some of Hamilton's chasing dragoons were mounted and could easily close with the slower Enniskillen infantry elements.

Though it is likely that Hamilton had to take some care to avoid ambush himself, and thus move cautiously, he pressed hard and was only prevented from routing the retreating Enniskillen force by Berry's timely rearguard actions with his cavalry force. D'Avaux also records that Hamilton's force pushed four or five cavalry companies forward and pursued for five miles without support. Both sides were now dangerously isolated from potential reinforcements. Berry and Hamilton, the field lieutenants of Wolseley and Mountcashel, would make the opening move, and set the scene for the larger battle to follow.[29]

By now it was around nine in the morning. Passing through Lisnaskea again with Hamilton close behind, Berry had the choice of the old or new road to Enniskillen. Choosing the newer road, closer to Lough Erne (and apparently using local knowledge), Berry retreated a mile out of Lisnaskea across a small river to a pass, where surrounding bogland turned the road into a narrow causeway. This was the only passable route for an attack and thus made an ideal ambush position. At the end of the causeway Berry deployed, hoping to defend the pass until relieved by Wolseley. MacCarmick describes the forces: Captain Malcolm Cathcart with 120 foot and Captain Martin Armstrong who had to rally his cavalry, which had seen some action while protecting the rear of the column. MacCarmick refers to his lack of support at Cornagrade earlier in the month, and he records that Cathcart sought assurances that the cavalry would support him on this occasion. He then placed an ambush of twenty men on the road in cover on the other side of the river, with orders to hold until the main body opened fire. The balance of the foot was in cover on the opposite bank with cavalry in reserve. The Enniskillen force was being hard pressed by the pursuing dragoons and the hasty ambush was perhaps being prepared out of necessity in order to prevent already weary troops breaking and fleeing.

Another Enniskillen source records that this ambush was actually set by Berry who had the troops in cover at the end of the causeway, within musket range of the opposite end while d'Avaux records that Anthony Hamilton met two battalions in cover with cavalry on the left and right! It is not clear where the balance of the Enniskillen force was during this time but the fact that there was time to set up such an ambush may indicate that other Enniskillen troops were attempting to delay Hamilton's men before pulling back across the river. Whatever version is accepted, it is clear that by the time Hamilton's Jacobite troops had arrived at the causeway, the Inniskillingers were in ambush and defensive positions. Leading his own troops from the front, Hamilton dismounted and began to advance with a regiment of dragoons to within forty yards of the river, his troops firing as they inched forward, later moving along the causeway. The Inniskillingers returned fire, killing several dragoons and wounding Anthony Hamilton in the leg; the flank ambush also fired, causing additional casualties amongst the Jacobites. Hamilton retreated, sending another officer forward in his place who was subsequently killed.[30]

What happened next differs depending on the account. D'Avaux claims that the first volley routed the dismounted dragoons and they fled as far as Mountcashel's camp at Newtownbutler. The *Jacobite Narrative*, however, records that Anthony Hamilton sent word to Captain Lavallin to wheel the men to the left – as if to rejoin Mountcashel! Lavallin ordered 'to the left about' (left turn), to which the men turned and marched off initially before fleeing. Still more enlightening is MacCarmick's account, where the dragoons were ordered to face 'to the *right* about', in order to bring them out of range. The similarity between the sources is striking, bearing in mind that Hamilton's 'left' was Berry's 'right'. On facing, the troops fled.

Another Enniskillen account is simpler, and the dragoons' advance faltered and turned into a retreat after seeing Anthony Hamilton's replacement killed. Inniskillinger pursuit across the bog with infantry and with cavalry on the causeway then created a rout amongst the remaining Jacobites. The *Narrative* and MacCarmick's account (a Jacobite and an Enniskillen source) are too similar to be ignored. Also interesting is the fact that the only officer named Lavallin in Mountcashel's army was an ensign belonging to Mountcashel's Regiment (see Appendix A) and there is no record of such a captain amongst the dragoons. This could be ascribed as irrelevant or inaccurate were it not for the fact that the *Narrative* considers this rout as undermining Mountcashel's edge in numbers and forcing him to subsequently act defensively at Newtownbutler.

Three weeks after the action, it records that 'Captain' Lavallin and Anthony Hamilton were both present at a court martial in Dublin where Hamilton was acquitted and Lavallin condemned to death. He protested that he had delivered the order as Hamilton had given it, which many believed since he was a 'gentleman of good estate' from Cork. When Ensign Lavallin became a captain, and why he was present at Lisnaskea is not clear, although it is interesting to note that one Enniskillen source records the presence of infantry in Hamilton's Jacobite force. What is clear is that he got the blame.

Returning to the battle, the Inniskillingers now charged across the bog and over the river, catching the dismounted dragoons quickly and slaughtering many of the routed troops. The remainder were pursued back through Lisnaskea and for a mile beyond. Berry's force was halted, however, when his scouts made him aware that part of Mountcashel's main force had been spotted advancing towards him. He retreated back to Lisnaskea, having killed or wounded about 200 men and having captured thirty prisoners, who were quickly sent back to Enniskillen. Throughout the encounter, Berry's troops were able to put local area knowledge to good use while Anthony Hamilton had to exhibit some caution in his approach. Nevertheless, Hamilton's pursuit was relentless enough that it proved to be his undoing. Another important consideration in the Lisnaskea skirmish is the causeway through the swampy bog, a feature that characterises so much of the Lough Erne countryside. Passable to infantry, it severely limited the use of cavalry and mounted dragoons, a factor which becomes critical later at Newtownbutler.[31]

Newtownbutler

The skirmish at Lisnaskea had taken place at around nine o'clock on the morning of 31 July. By eleven Berry still held the pass beyond Lisnaskea and received word from Wolseley who would meet him north of the town. The new colonel had marched along the old road from Enniskillen, leaving the new road about a mile to his right. Wolseley arrived with reinforcements and Berry was thanked for his 'morning's work'.

The Inniskillingers had not eaten since leaving and had moved quickly, with little time to bring adequate provisions. Wolseley was in a dangerous position. The men under his command were made up of militia and volunteers, not seasoned professionals. Morale was an important factor considering that the Enniskillen force had to inflict a quick and decisive blow on the Jacobite troops. The fact that Mountcashel's army was so close probably convinced many of the men to stay and fight, the chase through Lisnaskea being fresh in the minds of Berry's men at least. The proximity of such forces to Enniskillen itself, and thus the families of the militia, must also have been a concern. Wolseley assembled his officers. A decision would be required and though perhaps we should recognise the sense in Wolseley making a considered move rather than a rash one it is important to remember that he had not seen the Inniskillingers fight, and had little knowledge of their methods. Preserving morale was important. The officers, many of whom had arrived with Wolseley, wanted to go on, but the question would also be put to the men. The troops, perhaps influenced by the morning's victory, agreed (reputedly with a cry of 'no popery'), and the matter was decided.

D'Avaux is also quite clear on the matter, believing that the rout of Anthony Hamilton's dragoons encouraged the Inniskillingers to attack Mountcashel on the same day. The Lisnaskea skirmish had given the Inniskillingers the confidence that they needed, and no doubt calmed some of the fears that the English officers present must have had.

Wolseley took four men out of each cavalry and dragoon troop to form his scouting party. The Enniskillen force now consisted of sixteen troops of horse, three troops of dragoons and twenty-one companies of foot, approximately 2,000 men. The scouts moved about half a mile ahead of the main body and Wolseley organised his remaining troops, Tiffin's battalion with five to six companies of foot plus some dragoons under Wynne, Colonel Thomas Lloyds's battalion of foot, similarly organised, Wolseley's foot (the main body) with eleven infantry companies and the cavalry of Lieutenant Colonel Berry and Major Stone, comprising sixteen troops of horse. The officers were briefed to the extent that Lloyd's foot would take the left and Tiffin's the right, with Wolseley's main body in reserve if an attack was required. The horse would take the wings while the dragoons would protect the infantry's flanks. Clearly, the Inniskillingers were in the presence of an experienced soldier and Wolseley was taking no chances.[32]

The Enniskillen force-marched from Lisnaskea and a further two miles through the village of Donagh and thus towards Mountcashel. Aware that the main battle was now unavoidable and he would have to fight outside the town, Mountcashel changed his position and placed his cannon beyond it, guarded by his dragoons. MacCarmick records him as 'advantageously' posted between Newtownbutler and Wattlebridge farther south, with his cannon positioned in a 'lane' facing a narrow pass through a bog. Again, if we take the sources literally, both sides seem aware of the enemy's movements, perhaps due to cavalry picquets and scouts, but clearly hindsight is a powerful tool for each of the writers. The Inniskillingers had marched less than half a mile from Donagh when the scouts spotted a forward element from the Jacobite army. Mountcashel's forces retreated and Wolseley advanced until the Jacobites stopped about a half mile before Newtownbutler, on a steep hill through which the road lead. A large Jacobite force was formed up on the hill.

The approach was dominated by a large expanse of bogland, with only a narrow 'causeway' or raised road leading to it, a feature so typical of much of the surrounding townlands. Wolseley again consulted with his officers to determine the best method of approach against the good defensive position that Mountcashel's forward elements now occupied. He ordered Tiffin to take the right flank and Lloyd to take the left, as per his earlier deployment, and to move both foot battalions across the bog. The dragoons would be divided, sending half with each foot battalion. Berry's cavalry would advance along the causeway (the bog being too soft for horse) while Wolseley would keep the balance of the force as reserve ready to commit as required. As the Enniskillen troops deployed, Mountcashel's troops opened fire, the volume intensifying until the advance was made. The Inniskillingers fired two or three vollies in response to the Jacobite fire. Before the Enniskillen foot could reach the Jacobite positions, however, they withdrew in good order towards Newtownbutler, which had by then been set alight.

The officers now had considerable difficulty in preventing the Enniskillen troops from pursuing and becoming dispersed. Mountcashel had anticipated the potential of the Enniskillen troops to break order and chase his men through Newtownbutler. This was a sensible plan, whereby their attacking battalions could be broken up and attacked further to the south by the Jacobite horse in a piecemeal manner, the infantry's formal order and close lines having been disrupted. Had the plan been successful, Mountcashel's ambush could have used his cavalry elements in the role for which they were designed, and he would therefore not have to rely on the weaker elements in his army, his poorly trained and ill-disciplined infantry. Pursuing infantry passing through Newtownbutler could not be easily supported by their own cavalry, leaving them even more exposed.

Wolseley, however, was no fool. He had seen the Jacobites retreat in good order and believed the action either a feint prior to an ambush or a movement designed to gain better ground. He sent orders to Tiffin and Lloyd to the extent that 'no man should go out of his rank' and that 'pursuit should be carried out in good order' until it was certain that the Jacobite troops were indeed retreating. The Enniskillen foot complied and advanced in good order past the burning village, still taking some matchlock fire from the retreating Jacobites who now headed towards their main body south of the village. Mountcashel's initial plan had failed. The Jacobite retreat was understood as an attempt to provoke disorder or to draw the troops into ambush but the officers had been hard pressed to keep the Inniskillingers from pursuing. Indeed, one Enniskillen source records that it is Colonel Wolseley and his fellow officers who:

> from a height opposite to the place where the enemy was posted saw them go off in so good order that they believed it was either to draw our men into an ambush, or bring them to some place of better advantage for the enemy.

And that, 'no man should go out of his rank, but pursue them in good order until they were certain that they were flying ... .'

On the English side, it is interesting to note that a 1690 revision to the *English Abridgement of Military Discipline* notes the importance of troops taking no action until 'the last word of command be fully delivered', this in turn based on the experiences of troops during the 1689 Irish campaign, a reference perhaps to the impetuous nature of the less experienced men involved and highlighting the importance of order and control within the battalion.[33]

Mountcashel had received reports from the fleeing dragoons of a much larger enemy force than actually existed, in common with most sightings of the Enniskillen forces. His troops' brief action north of Newtownbutler, and the proximity of the Inniskillingers, meant that any retreat to Belturbet would not be possible without a fight. He formed a strong defensive position south of the town. On leaving Newtownbutler and nearly a mile past it, the Inniskillingers came to the edge of a vast expanse of bog 'half an Irish mile over' (an Irish mile being 2,240 yards), with only a narrow 'causeway' leading through it. Again, the particular geography of the Fermanagh countryside would dictate the nature of the fight. Mountcashel had formed his troops on a hill opposite the bog with his cannon placed at the end of the causeway.

MacCarmick gives us a little more description recording that Mountcashel had placed his cannon in a 'lane' facing a narrow pass through a bog, a more elaborate description of the causeway. His foot were positioned on the right and left of the lane all under cover so that only the men around the guns could be seen. His horse was then on the extreme right, on a hill. The *Jacobite Narrative* also refers to his position as 'on a pass, which was a causeway, on each side of a morass'. Mountcashel had put some small cannon at the end of the raised road, and his horse behind this. On each side of this position he put his foot and dragoons. O'Callaghan puts Mountcashel's numbers at this stage at 2,348 infantry, 543 dragoons and ninety-six horse (this including losses at Lisnaskea), a total of 2,987 men. These are of course a little too exact to be taken literally, but are comparable with other sources.[34]

MacCarmick talks of the advantageous position which McCarthy held on the hill south of Newtownbutler, the main body of his men behind cover. Troops deployed in line as per French military doctrine, with ranks four or five deep, could not hope to hide in cover, but the battalion deployed *en masse* had its benefits in terms of morale. Mountcashel had most likely deployed some of his men in a skirmish formation, certainly not a standard deployment with regular troops, but more adaptable with any levies which were present. The disadvantage with this approach was that these men were not likely to hold their position if attacked. There was no effective 'body' of troops, which could be commanded by officers, or cajoled by sergeants. They were more likely therefore to rout if charged by a determined enemy.

A number of key points emerge. Mountcashel may have deployed troops during the main battle in skirmish order. Considering the effects on volley fire, the number of untrained soldiers and poor fire control, with resulting effects on morale, this would have been a mistake in any European engagement, although this may have been his only option since many of these companies were made up from those moving back from the initial exchanges, and time may not have been available to order troops properly. His French training would also have made him aware of any diversity of ammunition or musketry. Mountcashel had terrain and numbers in his favour. His choice of terrain perhaps was an indication that he knew that the troops were of poor quality and he was undoubtedly aware that Inniskillinger morale benefited from the recent defeat of Hamilton at Lisnaskea.

> Lieut.Gen. Mac-Carty hearing of our approach, drew off his men and cannon from Crum-Castle, near to a place called Newtown-Butler ... .where he posted them very advantagiously; his cannon in a lane, facing a narrow pass through a bog, ... his foot upon the right and left of the lane, all under covert, that not a man of them could be seen save those that were about the cannon.

Wolseley ordered the Inniskillingers to advance across the bog as they had done north of the town: the approach was as before, with Tiffin on the right, Lloyd on the left, Wynne's dragoons supporting, and Berry with the horse on the causeway. MacCarmick records, however, that, in this case, the pikes and colours, one-third of each foot battalion, were left behind as the musketeers advanced. As the horse began their approach along the causeway the Jacobite cannon fired, stopping the cavalry in its tracks. The narrowness of the road, the enemy cannon, and the bog prevented the horse supporting the infantry. The Inniskillingers could afford to leave pikes behind in their approach since the nature of the ground would also deny the Jacobite cavalry an opportunity to attack the Enniskillen foot. A loose 'skirmish' formation is also suggested.

D'Avaux records that they attacked with three 'ramshackle' battalions, perhaps indicating that Wolseley also threw in the reserve, or even that he could control them no longer. As they approached the hill, the Jacobites fired from their positions in cover and the Inniskillingers returned fire.

> When our foot were advanced through the bog, the enemy fired extream thick upon our men, notwithstanding we could not see a man of them; but when we came close upon them, we fell a firing where we saw their smoke rise.[35]

The Jacobite fire appears to have had little effect. Without having had time to reload their cumbersome matchlocks, however, the Jacobites had lost the initiative. The advancing Enniskillen foot quickly covered the remaining distance to the Jacobite position. The day would be decided in a savage infantry mêlée. Training and drill would matter little now as man-against-man, the Inniskillingers and Jacobites fought hand-to-hand. The Inniskillingers quickly got the upper hand and seized the cannon on the causeway, killing the gunners. The remaining Enniskillen foot now advanced up the hill to the Jacobite positions. Mountcashel's forces had apparently remained in their defensive positions hoping that the Enniskillen advance would be broken by additional musket volleys. Seeing the cannon seized, the Enniskillen cavalry raced along the causeway. Mountcashel still had hopes that a fatal volley of musketry, slicing through the charging Enniskillen infantry, would decide the day. But it was not to be.

The charge of the Enniskillen infantry had captured the guns, and they were now to be supported by the rapidly approaching cavalry. This created an infectious panic in the Jacobite ranks. To Mountcashel's horror, his cavalry and dragoons (perhaps still demoralised from their earlier defeat at Lisnaskea) wheeled about and fled towards Wattlebridge, leaving the foot battalions to fend for themselves. According to d'Avaux, they fled without firing a shot, many of them discarding weapons and coats, and even their tired horses in order to move faster.

The Jacobite foot stood for a time, perhaps firing unco-ordinated volleys, but in vain. Many must have realised that the situation was hopeless without the support of their horse and guns. Dispersed as some of them were, and perhaps ill-equipped with pike to defend against the reckless charge of the Inniskillingers, the outlook was bleak. The Enniskillen foot was soon among them and again Jacobite volleys appear to have been unco-ordinated or ineffective since mêlée occurred very quickly. D'Avaux records that Mountcashel's Regiment performed well, while Clare's and Bophin's fared poorly. Mountcashel remained mounted, in the thick of the mêlée until his horse was shot from under him and he was captured. Major Marigny of Clare's Regiment, and formerly a captain in France, also performed well leading the battalion himself for a time after the lieutenant colonel fled. The regiment did not effectively support him though, and he was reputedly shot three times in the face and killed.

What of Lord Mountcashel? Had he been wounded and captured during the battle as d'Avaux states? The Enniskillen sources this time record a more colourful chain of events. Mountcashel and a number of his officers had hidden in a wood near their former artillery position, which was now guarded by Captain George Cooper, and a number of Enniskillen troops. Mountcashel, now apparently resigned to his fate, courageously charged the men guarding the guns. Cooper initially believed the mounted troops to be Enniskillen cavalry falling back and could only stare in disbelief as Mountcashel opened fire with his pistol. The Enniskillen foot returned fire, wounding him in several places (MacCarmick records him being wounded in thigh, lower back and groin, his life being saved by his pocket watch). As he fell from his horse, the Enniskillen foot advanced to club him to death with their muskets, until one of the Jacobite officers shouted his identity. Quarter was given to him and his officers.

When asked about the attack, Mountcashel replied that he felt James's cause lost since his troops had been the 'best' in Ireland and he had not wished to survive the day! His recorded statement in this case seems a little unlikely.

There also appears to be some confusion as to events occurring during the battle.

The *Jacobite Narrative* states that the Enniskillen troops actually performed a flanking move after being fired on by the artillery, passing through a wood and attacking from the rear of the Irish position.

> At this they drew back and passed through a wood that was at one end of the said morass, and marched unperceived against the rear of the Irish, who seeing the foe coming surprisingly upon them in that posture, took their retreat towards Derry.

Story also records that the command error noted earlier at Lisnaskea actually occurred at the hill at Newtownbutler at the critical point of the Inniskillinger attack.

> This story seemed at first to me incredible; but I was told it partly happened by a fatal mistake in the word of command amongst the Irish; for the Enniskillen men charged the Irish right wing very smartly, which Mackarty perceiving, ordered some of his men to face to the right, and march to relieve their friends; the officer that received the orders, mistook, and commanded the men, instead of facing to the right, to face to the right about and so march;

The rear ranks immediately panicked in this account and broke. This would explain the apparent rout of so many troops so quickly and would make the presence of Captain Lavallin more plausible, but the *Jacobite Narrative*'s record of Anthony Hamilton's court martial lends credence to the Lisnaskea version of the order. MacCarmick is also certain that the mistaken order occurred at Lisnaskea. It may be reasonable to assume that mistaken orders were given on both occasions but this seems unlikely. It is more probable that confusion rests with the writer in this case.[36]

By now the Jacobite foot was routed and fleeing. In the confusion, amidst the smoke and screams of the dying, most of the infantry made an error that would prove fatal. Leaving the hill, many fled to the west, towards Lough Erne and the vast steaming bogland 'full of bogs pools and loughs', dropping their weapons as they ran. The Enniskillen foot pursued and slaughtered many of them as they floundered in the marshland. Some of the infantry headed south towards Wattlebridge, but to no avail. The Enniskillen horse had pursued the fleeing Jacobite horse over the 'narrow way' where the cannon had been placed. They had passed through Wattlebridge, where some horse was left to guard the bridge over the Erne.

Reaching a meadow near the area the slower Jacobite foot tried to force their way across but were beaten back by the cavalry. The Enniskillen foot in turn pursued around 500 Jacobites into a wood near Lough Erne. They tried to escape across the lough but all were cut down, save one! That night, the Inniskillingers searched the bushes and surrounding countryside for surviving Jacobites, the English officers by now having little control over them. MacCarmick reports that by morning, some of the troops found in hiding had been given quarter but hundreds had been killed.

D'Avaux disputes these events to some degree, claiming that the Inniskillingers did not pursue effectively, although he admits that many Jacobites were lost. Interestingly, d'Avaux also points to the fact that, if the Jacobite cavalry had returned at this critical juncture, they could have made a great difference.[37] This makes sense when we consider that the cavalry could have attacked the pursuing infantry, letting the Jacobite infantry escape, rather than be slaughtered. Tradition still records the flight of the 'Yellow Dragoons' from the battle, so called because of their facing colour on their uniforms. These were Clare's Dragoons and tradition records that no one dared attempt to stop the flight of the yellow dragoons, for fear of being trampled.[38]

The Aftermath

D'Avaux records that in the aftermath of Newtownbutler, 'terror' had settled in amongst the Jacobite troops because of the numbers killed, the quantity of arms lost and the growing reputation of the Inniskillingers. He feared that the town's garrison could now defeat both Berwick and Sarsfield in turn, and both he and James saw great risk in wasting further time around the town. Efforts would now be devoted to defence. Londonderry had not been taken, more English troops would inevitably arrive to reinforce Wolseley and Schomberg's Williamite army was ready to cross the Irish Sea. Three weeks after the battle, Anthony Hamilton and Captain Lavallin were brought before a court martial in Dublin, presided over by Rosen, the French commander. Hamilton was acquitted and Lavallin condemned to death. It seems that Anthony Hamilton had 'friends in high places' in Dublin Castle.[39]

The wounded Mountcashel was taken to Enniskillen on the night of the battle. Fewer than twenty Enniskilleners had been killed. Their sources also record that 6,000 Jacobites had faced 2,000 Enniskilleners and that 2,000 Jacobites had been killed with 4,000 prisoners brought to Enniskillen! These figures make little sense when compared with earlier investigation. It is more likely that 500–700 were killed and that Mountcashel's force numbered around 3,000. This is of course speculative but makes more sense in the light of earlier evidence. MacCarmick also records that the Inniskillingers had captured cannon, powder, colours and muskets. A letter was found on Mountcashel. Written by Sarsfield two or three days earlier, this detailed Sarsfield's position at Bundroose, awaiting orders. Berwick was also apparently near Enniskillen and Sarsfield added that if Mountcashel and Berwick would attack on the east he would attack the west, but it was all too late now for valiant strategy. Mountcashel was defeated. The Inniskillingers felt compelled to return home quickly though, in case Mountcashel's action had actually been a diversion.

The troops reached Enniskillen on Thursday 1 August. Based on the content of the letter found earlier on Mountcashel, the Enniskilleners had marched on Sarsfield, nearing Ballyshannon on Friday 2 August. They received a message from Captain Folliot reporting that Sarsfield had left Bundroose and returned to Sligo (reputedly on hearing word of Mountcashel's defeat) and that arms and

The old road to Donagh, viewed from the north.

ammunition from General Kirke had arrived at Ballyshannon. Tiffin and Gore were sent to the town with a party of horse and foot both to reinforce it against Sarsfield's possible return and to later escort the arms and ammunition back to Enniskillen. The rest of the troops returned home.

Wolseley then sent a troop of horse after Sarsfield to ensure his retreat, but the Jacobites were indeed pulling back. By 4 August, Enniskillen had received the news from Londonderry: the siege had ended and the Jacobites had marched well past Omagh. Berwick and Sarsfield had gone, as had any plans for attacking Enniskillen. Schomberg had landed at Carrickfergus and by 7 August, 500 horse and 200 foot from Enniskillen were asked to accompany Kirke's force to join him. 200 Jacobite prisoners were also sent to Londonderry to help unload supply ships. In the same month, Sarsfield evacuated Sligo through Gore's deception. In September most of the Inniskillingers were ordered to Schomberg's camp at Dundalk while Lloyd was ordered to secure Sligo, but Sarsfield quickly recaptured it by splitting Lloyd's force.[40]

But what of Mountcashel? The letter found on him, although appearing unlikely when reading the Enniskillen account, is made more credible by a similar letter written by Berwick and sent to Sarsfield, on 31 July, in relation to a co-ordinated attack on Ballyshannon;

> Deare Notorius
>
> This is to give you notice that Marechal Rosen or I will march within three or four days from this place to Ballyshannon, so that if you looke sharp this way, you see us laying on these rebelly and cowring rogues;

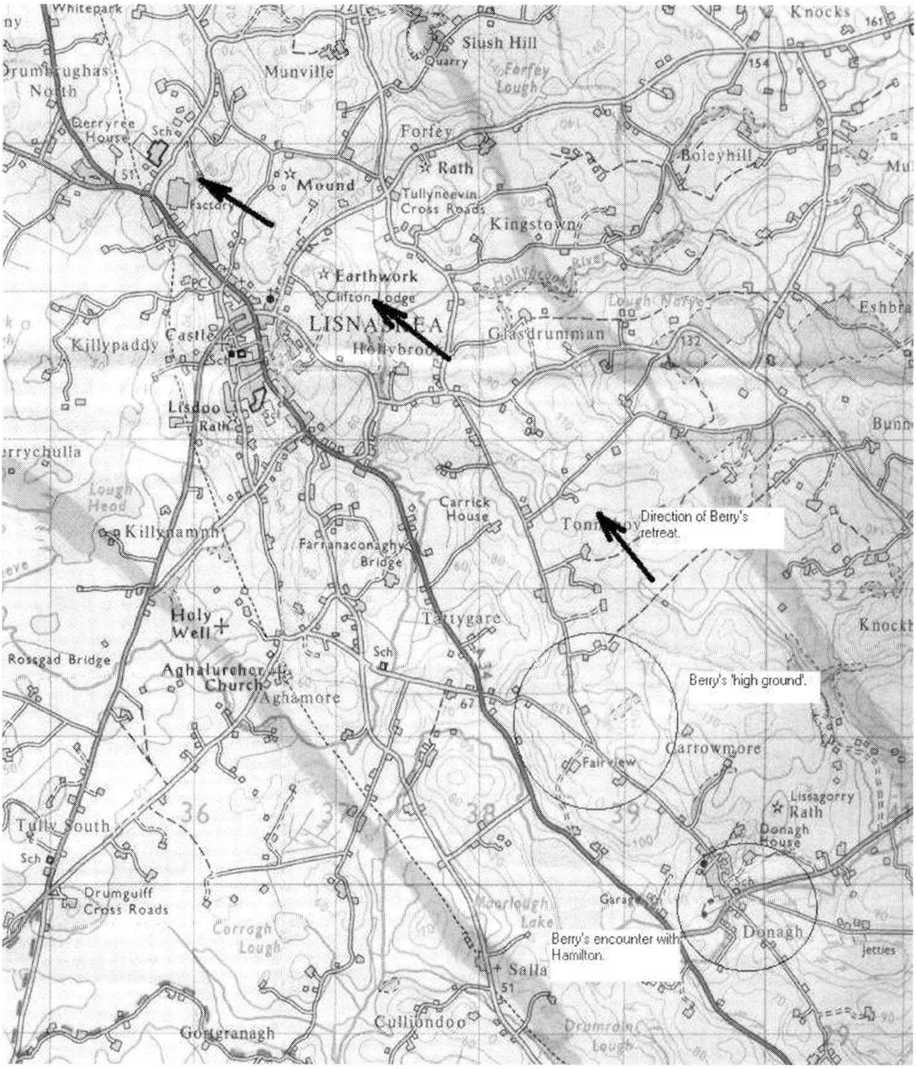

Berry's retreat on the OS map.

which may give you also an opportunity of attacking on that side of the water to make a divertion. I am afread the siege of Derry will be raised, and I thank god that I have not nor ever will give my consent unto it. I will say no more of this till I meet you at Balishanon in the meanewhile I remain Deare Notorius

Your kind Friend and servant
Berwick

For Brigadier Genll Sarsfield
Endorsed Duke of Berwick to Sarsfield
July 31 1689

Taken in context with the message found on Mountcashel, a Jacobite plan does again emerge but, as we have seen, action was taken too late to prevent Mountcashel's defeat and the rout of his army.[41]

Where is the Battlefield?

The story of Mountcashel's defeat at Newtownbutler could end at this point were it not for the mystery that still surrounds the battle. It is fascinating to determine the modern location of the battlefields of this era, not simply because there can be a scarcity of relevant sources, but such research allows the author (and ultimately the reader) to travel the path of the generals and troops. Landscapes change and industrialisation alters so much of the modern landscape that developing a wholly accurate picture remains difficult, but some aspects of many historical battlefields remain undisturbed. There have been many changes to the surrounding landscape at Newtownbutler, not least of which is the extensive drainage of the bog, which has created farmland and pasture from the swamp. The key features that determine the events on the historical battlefield, if we recall the tactical importance of respective rivers, hills and roadways, should remain relatively unchanged.

The following account relies heavily on combining the research gathered from the primary sources, with an interpretation based on Mountcashel's likely actions where there is some dispute in the accounts, together with an appreciation of the geography in terms of both older maps and current Ordnance Survey material. It is unfortunate that seventeenth-century maps and source materials for the area were destroyed in a fire at Crom Castle in 1764. Maps still in existence in the British Library do not give the required detail for the time, although there are some interesting maps of Enniskillen showing the relative indefensibility in comparison with Londonderry. The oldest available set of maps of the Newtownbutler area was drawn up in 1834–5 and revised in 1909. There is also a useful collection of local writing made in the early eighteenth century, referring both to the battle and the condition of the area. Finally, there is a broad spectrum of local knowledge both traditional and based on local investigation. One thing is clear, however: the landscape has changed dramatically in the last 300 years and not all of this has been recorded. The changes have mainly been due to an attempt to solve the drainage problems in the bogland areas through land reclamation. This predominantly occurred during the nineteenth century, and many causeways and traditional paths have been removed. No clear evidence of the original causeway systems exists on the nineteenth-century maps.[42]

A recurring theme in the primary sources describes the use of causeways and paths that the troops on both sides would have used and it is worthwhile to examine these. Trimble describes the use of the word 'causeway' as incorrect, and the term is actually 'causey', a local term describing a path raised over a boggy or marshy area, a causeway being more indicative of a paved street. Bagwell also mentions the causeways discussed at Lisnaskea and Newtownbutler, indicating that many of these have disappeared and cannot be traced, drainage work at Belleek having done much to 'dry' the surrounding countryside.

In order to discover the location of Mountcashel's last battle in Ireland then, it is necessary to examine the sources again, in terms of local tradition and landscape characteristics. The area around Crom Castle, as it relates to Mountcashel's siege, can be traced by examining the 1835 map. Having established that Ardandillure hill and Lough Nalughoage more closely resemble d'Avaux's account, Mountcashel's assault westward can be determined. The advantage that the researcher has at Crom is that much of the landscape in this instance is unaffected by drainage. It is also possible, standing atop Ardandillure hill, to see Crom in the distance, changed little from the day that Mountcashel surveyed the ground that he would attack across. The castle itself has fallen into disrepair and been partially rebuilt on at least three occasions. Many of the key features in terms of landscape are still present and there is no reliance on the presence of causeways. With Lisnaskea and Newtownbutler this becomes more difficult.

The Lisnaskea skirmish is characterised by two main routes, the 'new road' which Berry takes, where the forces first met, and the boggy pass to the north where the skirmish with Hamilton's dragoons took place. Berry's troops first encountered Anthony Hamilton's scouts near Donagh, but it is not clear which road this was on. On modern maps the road through the village of Donagh can still be seen in high ground. The route of this road has remained apparently unchanged. This would agree with Hamilton's description of rising ground used by Berry. This is also borne out by the 1835 map. The main road through low fenny ground (now the A34) to Newtownbutler also exists on the 1835 map, and this would appear to be an easier approach. There is no record of the use of this road prior to 1835, however, but, bearing in mind that the bogs have been considerably drained in the last 200 years, it is likely that this road did not exist in 1689 and local tradition bears this out. This makes Berry's use of the hill road towards Donagh his only option. Hamilton and MacCarmick also describe the 'new' road, closer to Lough Erne, which Berry takes. They are quite specific about the location of the Lisnaskea skirmish. Andrew Hamilton writes of the pass:

> this new road, which turns off from the old at the end of the town of Lisnaskea, and marched in good order, ... till he came about a mile distant from Lisnaskea to a bog with a narrow causeway through it ... .

MacCarmick is more specific, 'but our horse getting through a river below one Mrs. Lenards, about a mile from Lisnaskea, toward Enniskillen, at a very boggy deep pass ... .'

Graham also comments on the traditional choice of route:

> Of two roads leading to Enniskillen from Lisnaskea, Berry took that which had a short time before been made through bogs and low grounds nearer Lough Erne than the old way, as being more secure and having several passes on it much easier to defend than the other ....[43]

The 'new' road is implied on both modern and 1835 maps as joining the older at a junction about a mile above Lisnaskea. There is no record prior to 1835 of a different road and so it must be assumed that the route taken by Berry is that running closer to Lough Erne. Local tradition suggests that the skirmish took place at Ballindaragh, near the bridge where the Colebrooke river crosses the road, though this area is over two miles north on the new road from Lisnaskea. It is more likely that the skirmish took place just above the Derryree area where a tributary of the river crosses the road and the area lies between two areas of high ground – a 'narrow pass' over boggy ground, as is stated in the sources.

It should also be noted that only MacCarmick mentions the river and the Derryree area makes more sense considering this reference, since the area concerned is on the same level as the surrounding lowland, and thus boggy marshland. No clear causeway is shown on the new road but it is apparent that the nature of the routes in much of this area would, of necessity, create causeways or raised roads, and land may have been reclaimed in subsequent years. Bagwell also refers to this, implying that investigations in the early part of this century could not accurately identify the location of Berry's causeway.[44]

Tracing Berry's route north from Lisnaskea along the 'old' road, and adjusting for distances, the observer finds two tributaries crossing the road, and there is little evidence to suggest that one is more reliable than the other. However, the southerly river is approximately one mile north of Lisnaskea.

An analysis of the Newtownbutler battlefield becomes more complicated since local tradition and information gleaned from the primary sources is not always compatible. Although the battle has been discussed from the point of view of the primary sources, local knowledge raises some key questions. To this end a degree of investigation into Mountcashel's tactics is required.

The battle started with Mountcashel's delaying action outside the village. Again referring to Hamilton and MacCarmick:

> We advanced after them till we came within about half a mile from Newtownbutler, where there is a steep hill that the road leads through; and before you come to the hill there is a bog with a causeway through it, where only two men at most can ride in a-breast.
>
> When we had marched within half a mile of Newtownbutler, we discovered some of the enemy drawn up on a hill before us; so that the foot upon both wings marched through the bog to come in with the enemy; the horse was forced to keep to the causeway, which was but narrow;

The main road through Newtownbutler has certainly remained unchanged in location since 1835, and even referring back to the earlier conclusions regarding the Donagh road, this actually leads onto the main road running into Newtownbutler. This is now a junction but may have formerly been part of the main road from Donagh and would certainly explain Berry's earlier use of it. Before that, there is little evidence but, since the primary sources in this case indicate that the road leads straight through the hill, it seems obvious that the imposing hill that lies before Newtownbutler is the single most effective defensive position for a delaying Jacobite force. At this point local tradition begins to raise questions however. Piper's Hill, shown on the 1835 map which lies a further half mile to the north is the traditional location for this skirmish and is reputedly named after it! This hill, however, is more than a mile to the north of the town and lies to the west of the road. Upon examination moreover, its position makes little tactical sense. The hill does not straddle the main road, and thus defending troops would not have their backs to the town, allowing them to become outflanked or even encircled. The main road hill also lies partially to the west and this may have added to the confusion over the years.[45]

The main focus of local tradition in the area, however, is with the main battle itself. The primary sources used so far are referred to by many historians without, it seems, forming any conclusions as to the location of the final battle. Referring again to Hamilton, MacCarmick and d'Avaux.

> Our men ... advanced after the enemy, keeping their ranks, and the enemy still faced about in their rear, firing at us until we went through the town of Newtownbutler, and near a mile past it. And thus in very good order they retreated and we advanced till they came to a bog on the road, near half an Irish mile over, with a narrow causeway through the middle of it, by which we must pass to them. As soon as ever the front of our men came to the bog-side, they saw the enemy all drawn up on the hill opposite to

> them at the other side of the bog, having their cannon placed at the end of the causeway ....
>
> Lieutenant General MacCarthy hearing of our approach, drew off his men and cannon from Crum Castle, near to a place called Newtownbutler, betwixt it and Wattle-bridge, where he posted them very advantageously; his cannon in a lane facing a narrow pass through a bog, that not above one horse could come abreast; his foot upon the right and left of the lane, all under covert, that not a man of them could be seen save those that were about the cannon; his horse upon the right of all, drawn up upon a hill.

D'Avaux also gives some indication of the location of the battle;

> This deed [Lisnaskea] gave the rebels so much encouragement that they came to attack Mylord Monkassel [Mountcashel] the same day; as he heard that they were coming after him, he changed position and placed his cannon on the main road, guarded by dragoons; ....[46]

It is clear then that the road in question sat almost a mile past the town, to the south, and half a mile 'over'. It is not clear whether this indicates the width, or an additional half mile to the south. The bog straddles the road with a narrow causeway giving passage. This may imply that the main road narrows to a causeway, or the causeway is 'off' the main road. Mountcashel was drawn up on a hill opposite the bog, with his cannon placed at the end of the causeway, or alternatively in a 'lane' facing a narrow pass through a bog. His men were drawn up on the hill (Hamilton) or beside the 'lane' with cavalry on the hill (MacCarmick). The causeway was narrow, only allowing passage of one or two horses at a time. All secondary sources cite either MacCarmick or Hamilton. Although some sources cite d'Avaux, the *Jacobite Narrative* and O'Kelly, their locations are vague. Hamilton is the only source which gives an indication of the distance beyond Newtownbutler, to which the Inniskillingers advanced. Mountcashel had small-calibre cannon. Point-blank range (meaning unelevated barrel for artillery) for such pieces was up to 260 paces (217 yards) and maximum range (at 45 degrees) could be 1,200 paces or more (1,000 yards), although long-range firing would invariably be inaccurate and ineffective.[47]

The sources indicate, however, that accurate firing on the causeway kept the Enniskillen horse at bay, so we are dealing perhaps with a very 'short' battlefield, and this would be borne out by the speed with which the Enniskillen troops on foot were able to reach Mountcashel's lines.

Local knowledge and 'legend' surrounding the battle also play an important part in the investigation of events. There are three versions of events supported by local knowledge. In each case, the presence of a local road known as 'MacCarthy's Road' and a well ('MacCarthy's Well') are important. The road, according to some, was levelled in the eighteenth century in a local land reclamation scheme and no longer exists but other opinions suggest that the route followed, at least in part, the line of the main road and some existing farm tracks. The well was also reputedly filled in, in the early part of the twentieth century, but is shown in the revised 1909 version of the 1835 map. Despite the degree of local knowledge which exists, the OS map is marked with a battlefield symbol near the centre of the village, in a position which bears no relevance to any research evidence or tradition, but is placed for convenience. There are no battlefield monuments to mark the site.

Locally there are three versions of the story of the battle. In the first, 'MacCarthy's Well' marks the approximate position of 'MacCarthy's Road', no longer in existence, but which ran off the main road and near the well, and on to a position near farm buildings shown at Kilgarret Hill. Mountcashel's artillery was positioned at the base of the hill on this lane, facing the road. Another version of the same story states that 'MacCarthy's Well' marks the point where woodland once stood. This is where Mountcashel emerged from later in the battle to attack the Inniskillingers guarding the guns.

In the second version of events, 'MacCarthy's Road' has now been covered by the main road running across Kilgarret Hill. The main road is the causeway and the well is so named because this was part of Mountcashel's defensive position.

In the third and final scenario, it is suggested that Kilgarret Hill did not play any part in the battle. Instead, the battle took place in Sandholes townland,[48] at the hill just south-west of Kilgarret. A lane running south from the main road onto the hill was 'MacCarthy's Road'. This was removed during the land reclamation schemes in the late eighteenth century. The main road that is used today did not exist or was little more than a track. This version of events agrees in some respects with the first option, since 'MacCarthy's Well' again marks the original position of 'MacCarthy's Road', although Mountcashel's defensive position in this case is farther south.[49]

Each version seems valid since the evidence is minimal. There are several facts that focus further analysis however. Kilgarret Hill dominates the surrounding area and is a natural defensive position affording the most advantageous view of the enemy advancing south. The main road travelling south still sits high on the surrounding bogland, in the manner of a causeway. The 1835 map of the area shows causeway markings on the main road's approach to the hill. Since there is no record of the parish in 1689, it must be assumed that a narrow causeway supported part of the road. This route is still indicated as a causeway on the 1909 map. It is unlikely on initial investigation that Mountcashel could have ignored Kilgarret.

It also seems unlikely that he would have positioned his forces away from a line facing the main road, against the most likely avenue of approach, due to the poor terrain present on each side of the road. It would also not make sense to position the cannon away from the road where they could be more easily outflanked. Mountcashel's battle lines would have run perpendicular to the road, on a hill which he could defend more easily than any other ground in the area. He had no reason to choose another position since the enemy would come to him. He knew that his troops were in the main of poor quality but he no doubt hoped that his position would make up for this. He had no reason to take unnecessary risks. The facing of Mountcashel's troops does not seem in doubt, however, based on their actions when routed:

> they being strangers in the country, fled all to the right hand, through a great bog above a mile long, which leads towards Lough Erne, most of them all throwing away their arms into turf-pits.[50]

Fleeing to the right flank of the Inniskillinger attack runs perpendicular to the main road leading directly to Lough Erne.

Kilgarret fits the requirement in all respects, save one. Kilgarret Hill is approximately half a mile south of the centre of the village. This disagrees with Andrew Hamilton's account, which states that the Inniskillingers passed through the town and onwards for approximately one mile before arriving at a bog half-a-mile 'over' with Mountcashel's troops facing them on a hill on the other side. No other source is so specific as to the location of the bog and the hill. Although the use of the term 'approximately' is open to interpretation, Kilgarret is too close to the village.

At this stage the investigation must look further for the remnants of causeways. The map does indicate that a track or road existed leading to the position running past 'MacCarthy's Well'. The track in this area leads west from the main road, then turns sharply south-west as if a road had previously existed north of this position. The well has been filled in and the upper part of the road removed but the track south of it still exists in some parts and in others has become little more than a well-trodden path. It is, however, raised well above the level of the surrounding bogland and has been obviously modernised and raised in some parts. This route leads to Sandholes Hill from the 'back' of Kilgarret Hill. Again it affords a commanding view of the surrounding area, but the view of the village itself is partially blocked by Kilgarret Hill. It is immediately apparent that the position would allow the Inniskillingers to be partially obscured on their approach and would seem unsuitable as a defensive position. It is, however, just over one mile from the centre of Newtownbutler and fits Hamilton's account.

Why would Mountcashel allow the enemy to approach in this manner? There are perhaps other factors to consider. Firstly, the extent of 'soft cover' that existed on both hills at the time is unknown, since the landscape has changed significantly, Sandholes may have offered more cover for Mountcashel's raw troops. Secondly, it should be remembered that Mountcashel's delaying force harassed the Inniskillingers during their advance and could have reported on numbers and direction of approach on returning to their own lines, making their degree of hidden movement irrelevant. Finally, Kilgarret Hill obscured Mountcashel's own position until the last moment, in theory preventing him being quickly outflanked and potentially drawing the Inniskillingers into a 'close-range' volley. The position may have been chosen to make retreat easier, should this be required. In practice this did not work. There is no modern archaeological evidence to suggest this location, but an analysis of the 1835 *Ordnance Survey Memoirs* for the area indicates that several bodies were 'raised' in the Sandholes area in the early part of the nineteenth century as a result of drainage. There is no additional evidence in Irish archaeological records to support these findings yet the location would appear to support the Sandholes theory. A final testament to the validity of the Sandholes argument is the verbal record of the local landowners, some of whom remember the removal of a very old causeway, running directly towards the hill, in the early part of the twentieth century.

Clearly then, the location of the battlefield is in some doubt but evidence suggests that the hill at Sandholes is the most likely defensive position. It is backed up by Hamilton's account and the presence and direction of tracks in the area. It should also be added that this location is the preferred one amongst the local population, and the 1989 're-enactment' of the battle took place on Sandholes Hill. This account has more support in the town based on its age. Of all the versions it is remembered as being passed down in local tradition and stories, at least since the early part of the twentieth century. This type of story cannot be ignored, although it must be backed up by research and in this case Hamilton's account would lead to the conclusion that Mountcashel's last battle in Ireland was most likely lost at Sandholes Hill.

One of the traditional sites associated with the slaughter of the Jacobites after the battle is the 'Bloody Pass'. This area is part of Lough Erne and is thought to be one of the points at which the Inniskillingers caught up with the remnants of the fleeing Jacobite foot. Local legend also has it that many of the Jacobite dead were interred here. Wattlebridge still exists, although it has changed significantly. The bridge has been rebuilt several times and the river itself is much smaller than it had been 300 years ago, again due to the number of drainage schemes in the intervening years. The *Ordnance Survey Memoirs* for the area also quote local tradition of the time in suggesting that many of the bodies were buried at Kilgarret Hill after the battle. It is not clear whether this means the townland or the hill, although this may account for some of the confusion as to the location of the battlefield. As with the Bloody Pass, there is no archaeological evidence to support this, and the only record of bodies having been 'unearthed' remains in the Sandholes area.[51]

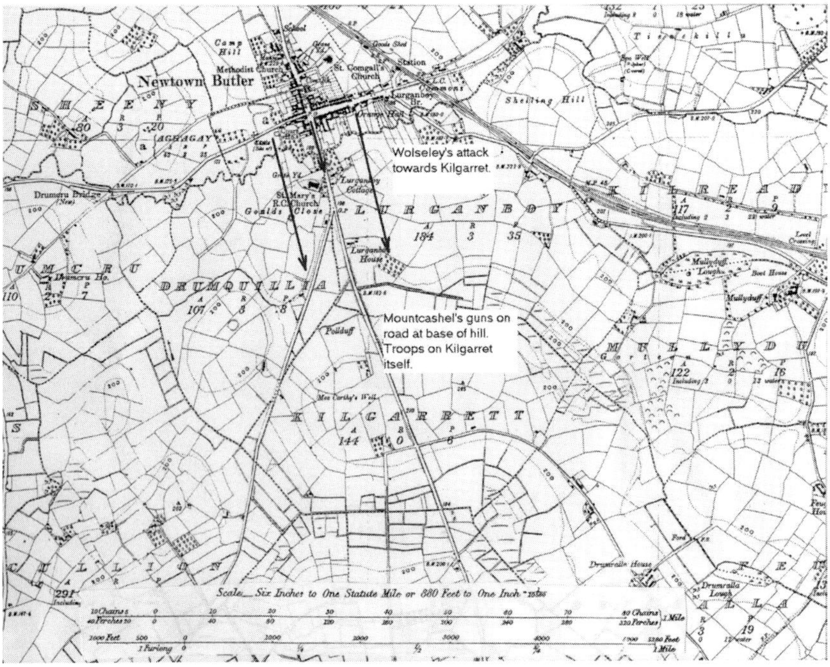

The 'Kilgarret Hill' scenario at Newtownbutler.

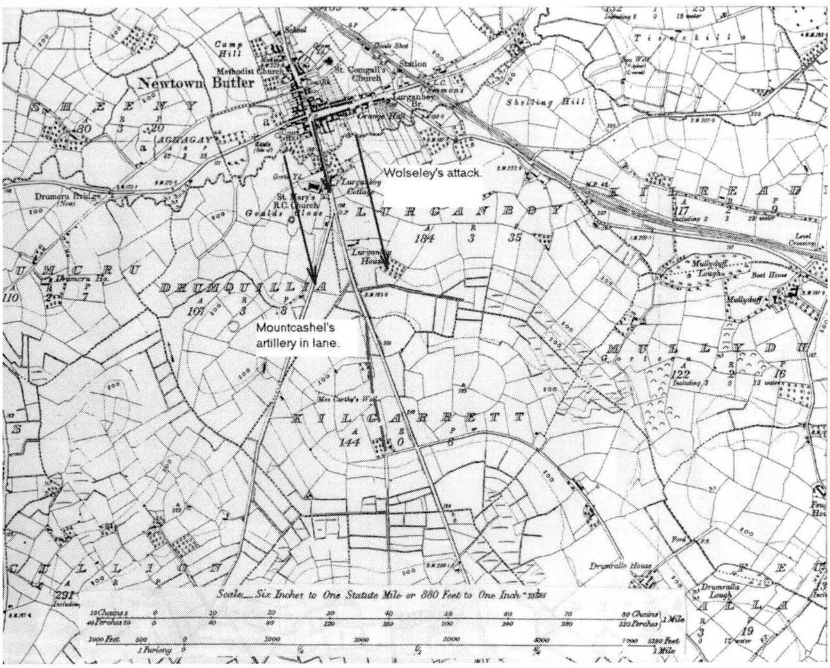

The 'MacCarthy's Well' scenario.

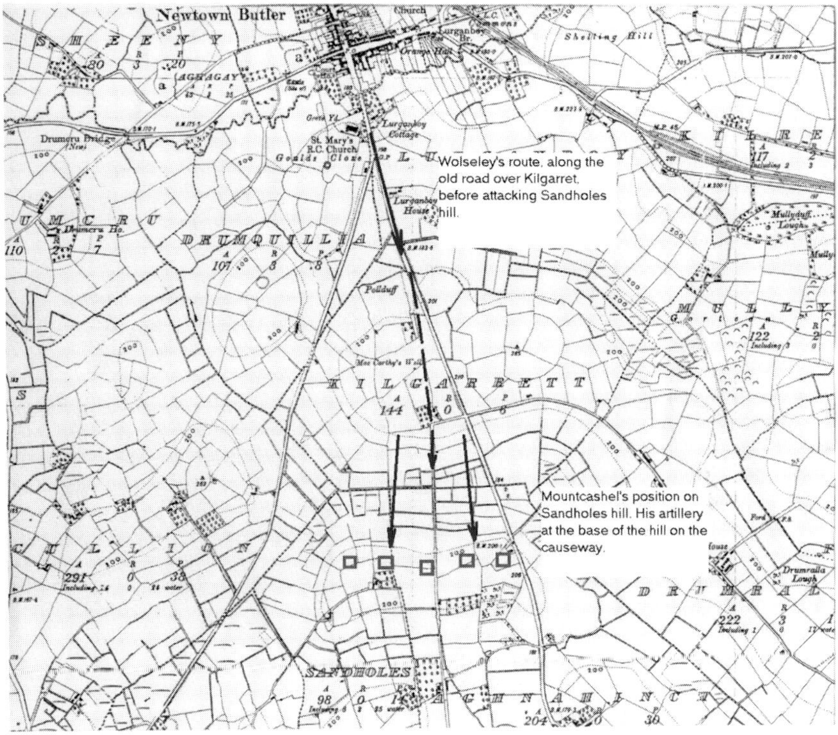

The 'Sandholes' option – focusing on the more likely location of Newtownbutler battlefield.

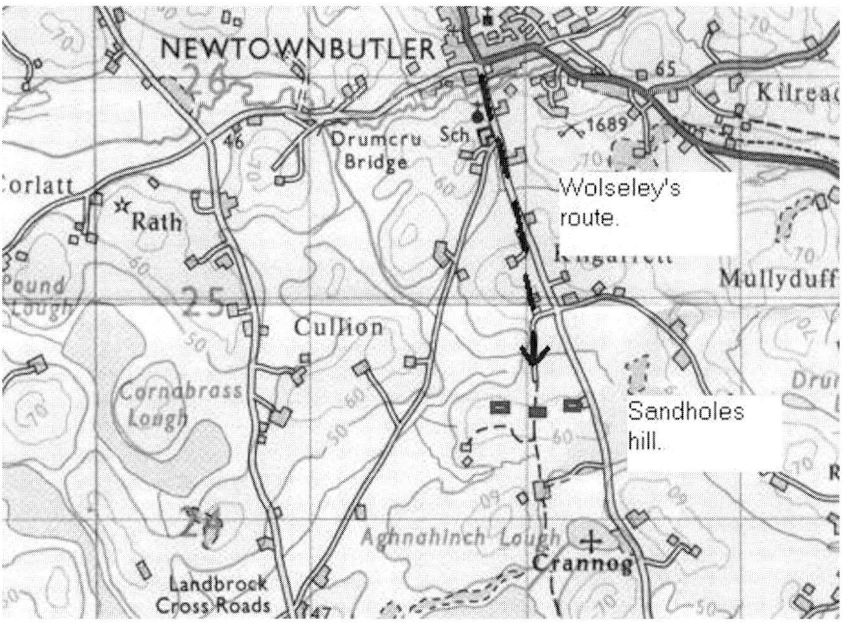

The 'Sandholes' option – focusing on the more likely location of Newtownbutler battlefield.

Sandholes Hill today.

Wattle bridge and the 'Bloody Pass'. The area has been significantly drained, though a fairly wide river still exists.

Wattle bridge and the 'Bloody Pass'. The area has been significantly drained, though a fairly wide river still exists.

Chapter VIII

Escape from Enniskillen

Lord Mountcashel had been defeated by a well-led, although somewhat irregular, force of Enniskillen militia. His men had been routed and in many cases indiscriminately killed by the pursuing troops who were, to all intents and purposes, out of control. It is clear though that the Enniskillen troops genuinely feared for their lives at this time, and the lives of their families, should the Jacobites emerge victorious. In addition, such a massacre might have been frowned upon in the professional military of the time but would not have been entirely unexpected. Of course such acts paled in comparison with the atrocities carried out by both sides during the confederate wars of the 1640s, and Galmoy's and other Jacobite officers' actions in this regard did not help matters. Such analysis does not excuse the activity, but merely helps us to understand its context.

D'Avaux wrote to Louis after the battle, alluding once more to the confused Jacobite strategy:

> His Britannic Majesty is impatiently expecting news from the Duke of Berwick. He had ordered him, a while ago, to join Colonel Sarsfield and to help disperse the rebels lying between the sea and Inniskillin. This plan was broken because we heard about the Duke of Berwick's troops and the King wished to go back to the first plan. This can be very advantageous if it succeeds, but I fear very much that he will have all his troops destroyed to such an extent that not enough of them might arrive in time in Dublin to help us when the enemy arrives. If that is the case, the King of England will find himself with 6 battalions who have never seen a shot fired and who are poorly armed. The troops from the siege of Derry have come back completely destroyed. Those commanded by my Lord Mountcashel were beaten and routed in such a way that bodes ill for such troops. Those from Iniskillin came in total confusion but very bravely attacked my Lord Mountcashel. The cavalry and the dragoons fled without firing a shot and later most of them, having exhausted their horses in their flight, dismounted and continued on foot. They threw away arms, swords and even their doublets in order to run faster. My Lord Mountcashel remained at the head of the infantry, who also did very badly. To be fair to his battalion, he was wounded, his horse killed and he was taken prisoner. As he

> was abandoned by everyone, he was believed dead but he is in Iniskillin and well looked after. The rebels are already asking for my Lord Monjoye in exchange.[1]

Clearly there was hope even at this stage of getting Mountcashel back. An exchange for Lord Mountjoy, held in the Bastille since Tyrconnel's deception in 1688, was already being discussed. It is also interesting to note that Mountcashel's courageous, if foolhardy, assault to reclaim his guns is recorded only in the Enniskillen sources. D'Avaux attributes Mountcashel's wounds only to the battle itself without recounting his gallant though futile charge. Wounded he was, however, as undoubtedly were some of his officers. The captured men were moved back to Enniskillen itself, via water, no doubt making for a more comfortable journey for the wounded Mountcashel. The captured private soldiers would have to march to Enniskillen; no such luxury for them. The town had not been under siege and had not suffered the starvation that had occurred at Derry. There were severe shortages though, despite the number of sheep and cattle that had been obtained through Lloyd's raiding. Bread and wine were in especially short supply. To this end, and giving an indication of the reasonable treatment that Mountcashel was to receive, he was permitted to inform James as to his plight and the nature of his wounds. James, even at this stage and despite their disagreements, must have been hopeful that some means could be found to return Mountcashel to the Jacobite fold. He sent Doctor Connor, one of the royal physicians, and Mr Huben, one of his surgeons, to Enniskillen, along with money, provisions and wine for Mountcashel and the officers.[2]

Recalling the battle, Mountcashel had been wounded in his thigh, lower back and groin, his life saved only by his pocket watch. When we consider that the calibre of musket balls of the time was around three-quarters of an inch, we must assume that, at the very least, Mountcashel would not have been able to walk, even if the wounds had merely been caused by ricochets or the musket-balls had not penetrated. His wounds were severe and he became weaker. D'Avaux writes again to Louis in September, almost two months after the battle:

> Eight days ago Sir, begged by Milord Mountcashel, the King had the Secretary of State write to M. de Schomberg, to tell him that he requested to be released on parole in order to go to Dublin to be treated, promising to return to jail as soon as he could walk.[3]

He had clearly been severely wounded. The letter also alludes, however, to his attempts to gain his parole. Two weeks after the battle, the Marshal Duke of Schomberg had landed in Carrickfergus. The arrival of William's foreign professionals had begun and the Jacobites would remain on the defensive until the end of the war. It is unclear how much of the conduct of the war Mountcashel was aware of, but he was keen to return to Dublin on some form of parole at least, in order to recover, before returning to Enniskillen (thus preserving his honour). He wrote to the Representative for Cork, Sir Richard Nagle, the Irish Attorney-General and Secretary of State, an old colleague who, Mountcashel believed, could negotiate with Schomberg and thus secure his release. Nagle was determined to help.

An Irish cornet (second lieutenant) was immediately dispatched in order to approach Schomberg's army with a letter proposing Mountcashel's immediate conditional release. The army was marching south towards Newry when the cornet was intercepted and the letter brought to Schomberg's secretary. Schomberg would not receive the communication, however. Nagle had addressed it to Marshal Schomberg, and the Duke of Schomberg, as William's greatest general was now entitled, would not recognise his old French title.

This requires a degree of explanation. Schomberg had been a marshal in the French army of Louis XIV, but he was also a Huguenot, a French Protestant. With Louis's revocation of the Edict of Nantes in 1685, his attempt to eradicate organised Protestantism in France had begun. Schomberg had fled to Holland to fight for William and was now being addressed as if he still belonged to Louis's forces.

Perhaps Nagle should have known better in light of the context of his plea. On the other hand, there is perhaps an element of both practicality and pomposity in Schomberg's action. He had no compunction to see the release of a French-trained Jacobite Geneal who could end up fighting against him if parole was broken. In either event Mountcashel's request would remain unfulfilled.[4]

He was, however, to have a second chance and from the most unlikely of sources. He was not the only noble prisoner of war, although the conditions of his imprisonment seem to have been somewhat better than those of Lord Mountjoy. Mountjoy had been imprisoned in the Bastille since late 1688 through treachery, after having been sent by Tyrconnel on a false errand to Louis XIV. William, recognising Mountjoy's son's plea for his release, considered the possibility of an exchange since Mountcashel was the only senior Jacobite officer in Williamite hands. Hopes of release were to prove ill-founded. The French felt that Mountjoy was a prisoner of the state, after his having had some discussion with the very Huguenots whom Louis was trying to subdue although it is unclear whether there was any substance to the accusation. D'Avaux communicated the events to Louis.

> Since I have written this letter, the King of England has received a telegram from my Lord Moncassel, who brought a letter from Cork, in which he was saying to my Lord Moncassel, begged by the son of my Lord

> Montjoye, that King William was willing to agree to the exchange of this my Lord against my Lord Moncassel. As soon as we know that my Lord Moncassel is free, we will also free my Lord Mountjoye and he will be allowed to go to Antrim or any other town close to M. de Schomberg, as soon as King James has given his consent for the exchange to take place.
>
> The King of England testified to my Lord Tirconnel and myself that he was very embarrassed by this arrangement because my Lord Montjoye was a state prisoner and that he had a lot of influence amongst the Irish Protestants. However he added that all those who relied on him, and were in the North, were already armed. Moreover it would seem very harsh that he should refuse an exchange that would free my Lord Moncassel and therefore he gave his consent. He had already replied to the person that came on M. Moncassel's behalf that he readily agreed to the exchange so long as I was not opposed to it. The reason, sir, that His Britannic Majesty said I could object to it was that my Lord Montjoye has had dealings with French Protestants against your Majesty's service and if that were the case he would not ask your Majesty to release him. As I have not received any orders from your Majesty on this matter, I did not think I could object to this exchange.
>
> The King of England wrote to my Lord Moncassel that he agreed. Thus my Lord Moncassel will be allowed to travel to some town closer to M. de Schomberg. In the meanwhile, I am honoured to await your Majesty's orders.[5]

The exchange would not take place. Instead, further discussion would be the order of the day as the opposing gentry dithered over the release. Mountcashel remained incapacitated in Enniskillen. There were rumours of a rescue attempt by Berwick but the balance of power had shifted in Ulster and the Jacobites did not have the resources to mount such an effort. By October 1689 Mountcashel had given up all hope of a successful exchange with Mountjoy and once more took matters into his own hands. He wrote to Major General Percy Kirke, the English officer who had sent Wolseley and his men to Enniskillen. Kirke had provided for Mountcashel to some extent during his incarceration and had ensured both that he had a degree of freedom in Enniskillen itself, and that he was not simply left to die from his wounds. Mountcashel again requested his release and asked Kirke to speak to the Earl of Shrewsbury for him. Shrewsbury was the English Secretary of State, and he would remember the young Justin MacCarthy from his time in England many years before.

Kirke was assured by Shrewsbury that Mountcashel was a man of honour and a man of his word and, should parole be granted, would return to Enniskillen or adhere to any form of restriction that might be enforced. The politics of the situation were against him, however. Despite the positive light in which Kirke later portrayed him, little headway was made. Mountcashel had been turned into a political pawn and, worse, it seemed that he was now being forgotten about, his political importance diminished in light of the war. By this stage he was sickened by his plight and could see for himself how futile appealing to his friends and playing with politics had become. In a move so characteristic of the man's resolve, and in light of the uncertainty of the situation, Mountcashel determined to make his own escape from Enniskillen.

D'Avaux records this intention in a letter to Louvois in December, also alluding to his continued preference for Mountcashel in France (and his reputed short sightedness). It was also clear that he was still in communication with James over any attempt. This perhaps indicates that he would need his aid (through Berwick?) to make his way south from Enniskillen should the escape attempt succeed.

> Milord Moncassel proposed to the King of England two methods, which he feels quite safe to escape from Inniskilling. I talked to the man he sent and in seven or eight days from now, we will attempt one or the other. If it succeeds Sir, I beg you to ask his Majesty to agree that he should command the Irish troops travelling to France. I know that his strong wish to serve makes him risk everything; although his short-sightedness will prevent him from ever becoming a Marshal, I can assure you that he will be very useful in getting rid of a great many bad officers and in recruiting others to keep the Irish troops dutiful and disciplined.[6]

His previous correspondence and good relationship with Kirke had meant that the guard had been removed from his quarters in Enniskillen. He had the freedom of the town and by now must have become known to a large section of the populace. He must also have made acquaintances of a sort, perhaps amongst the militia and soldiers who had been guarding him, perhaps even amongst the civilians. Although he had decided to make his escape, he was still motivated by the concepts of honour, a driving force at the time, especially amongst those who had been trained in the French military where the concept of personal *gloire* held sway over almost all military precepts. He would not, therefore, break the conditions of the parole that had been granted by Kirke. Instead, he made it obvious, perhaps through the locals that he knew, that he meant to escape from the town.

There was no doubt that the Governor, Gustavus Hamilton, would hear of the plan, since the populace's first loyalty was to their own town, no matter what they thought of Mountcashel; the planned escape of a defeated Jacobite, who had six months before meant to capture Enniskillen, would have been hard to keep quiet. This was part of Mountcashel's plan, however, and his only way out of the desperate situation in which he found himself. The guard was quickly replaced at his quarters, and some of his privileges removed. He felt compelled to at least make it plain to Kirke that he had no wish to betray the kindness that he had shown him and the replacing of the guard indicated to Mountcashel at least that, if he did now escape, the sophisticated requirements of military honour would be served.

Fate it seemed had played into Mountcashel's hands. By November he was still quartered in a house on the very edge of Lough Erne, perhaps moved there by Kirke to facilitate his recovery. In hindsight this was perhaps the most inappropriate location to keep a prisoner who had professed his intention to escape! Although the house may have been granted under the auspices of Mountcashel's parole, the situation had now changed. He had bribed an Inniskillinger sergeant called Acheson. It is likely that he formed part of the militia guard that had been re-instated at his quarters. Believing now that he would not be marked with dishonour, Mountcashel had arranged with Acheson to provide two small boats (known locally as cots). The sergeant had agreed to accompany Mountcashel, guiding him to Lough Erne and freedom.

The same man may even have been the individual referred to in d'Avaux's letter. On a cold November night, the two got safely away, accompanied by two of Mountcashel's officers. It is not known what route they then took, or even if friendly troops were waiting for them at the edge of the lake, though it is tempting to think that a form of plan after his escape must have been made and perhaps Berwick did become involved after all. Indeed, d'Avaux's letter suggests that some arrangement existed. The fate of Acheson is known, however. He fatefully returned to Enniskillen, the records say to leave a letter, but perhaps due to a change of heart. He was captured and later tried and shot as a traitor. Lord Mountcashel, however, had escaped.[7]

By December Mountcashel had successfully made his way to Dublin. His arrival was turned into a public event. Twenty carriages and several hundred horsemen, officers and locals led the procession. James himself received him at Dublin Castle and, that night, bonfires were lit all over Dublin in celebration. Celebrations were also held in Cork and throughout Justin's home province of Munster when the news was received. His wife Arabella, who had waited in Dublin for six months, also received the husband whom she must have feared that she might never see again. Only Tyrconnel was unhappy to see Mountcashel. As expected, Schomberg held his escape as a violation of parole, declaring that he would know what honour to expect of the Irish in future. The Jacobite rejoicing would be shortlived; Mountcashel would help form the Irish Brigade for service in France. D'Avaux at least was happy:

> Sir, as you did me the honour from the start, to tell me that the King was asking Sir Makarty to command his troops and you have had the courtesy to write since that His Majesty was no longer thinking of having Makarty because he was convinced that he was the prisoner of the Prince of Orange under the name of Montcassel, I thought that Makarty having escaped from prison, his Majesty intended me to execute the orders given concerning Makarty. Although he had undertaken to escape in order to serve in France, that alone would not have convinced me, Sir, if I had not believed that it was important to have a man so liked in his Majesty's service, so loved and influential in Ireland that he could keep dutiful the Irish troops in France.

James however was still seen as somewhat of an impedence.

> If the King of England would give permission to all those who wanted to follow him, you would have the best officers in the army; but his Britannic Majesty is far from consenting to this
>
> ... Makarty has done what he could to remove the bad lieutenant colonels and majors; but he has not been able to succeed. He reckons that in the last resort they should be removed from office on arrival in France and thinks that it will not have any adverse effect in this country. If we did not have a man of such authority, we could not do such a thing without upsetting everyone here. He claims, Sir, that he will be able to replace these discharged officers with a few Irish who are serving at present in France in the German regiments. But I believe that his Majesty thinks that these officers are already his and would want some other sent from Ireland. What I wanted to say, Sir, is that without the help of Milord Montcassel, I would have had difficulties in setting up things here.[8]

And of Mountcashel's Regiment:

> Milord Moncassel did not want to surrender himself or these regiments. He will be happy to do whatever you will judge appropriate. He is working on gathering a good regiment, the King has given him permission to take what is left of the one he commands, and that is the best regiment in the kingdom.[9]

The Irish were regaining an experienced general only to lose him again. Without Mountcashel, however, French hopes of obtaining suitable troops would have been hampered if not blighted altogether. For his part, Mountcashel had pinned all his hopes on French service and his loyalty would not be found wanting.

Not all of the captured officers were so lucky. Captain William Bourke of Clare's Regiment, who was also captured at Newtownbutler, was to be found petitioning for his release from a Londonderry jail more than two years later.

After Anthony Hamilton's escape from Newtownbutler, and his successful acquittal, he was present at the Boyne in 1690 but was not at Aughrim in 1691. He accompanied James yet again to France, although it is not clear exactly when. He remained in France until 1706 when he accompanied the 'Old Pretender' on his abortive expedition. Returning to St Germain, he died there in April 1719.

The Enniskillen request for experienced officers had brought William Wolseley to Enniskillen and the Battle of Newtownbutler. Wolseley's campaign in Ireland was far from over after the battle. In February 1690 he defeated Berwick at Cavan and a few weeks later was severely wounded. He was back on his feet again by the summer and fought at the Boyne where a curious, or familiar, incident occurred. A mistake in the word of command faced his troops in the wrong direction, and they were routed by Richard Hamilton's (Anthony's brother who had co-ordinated the siege of Derry) cavalry, with only the intervention of Dutch cavalry saving further loss. Wolseley was also present at Aughrim and, by August 1692, he had been appointed Master General of the Ordnance in Ireland, a position similar to that offered to Mountcashel in the Irish army some years before. In March 1693 he was made brigadier general of all horse and in 1696 he was appointed one of the lords justices in Ireland. He died unmarried in December 1697, eight years after his victory at Newtownbutler. Lieutenant Colonel Berry, who had accompanied William Wolseley to Enniskillen, served with the Inniskillingers for the remainder of the war.[10]

Chapter IX

A Return to France

Mountcashel's Reputation with the French

On a cursory examination of the events that occurred at Newtownbutler, the reader is left with the impression that Mountcashel was outmanoeuvred and overcome by the ferocity of the troops under Wolseley. Further analysis, as we have seen, shows the weaknesses in Mountcashel's troops, however, and the general lack of cohesion within the Jacobite strategy. The extent to which Mountcashel can be blamed in isolation for the failure of the short campaign is therefore somewhat debatable. Amongst the French only Fumeron, a commissary, blamed Mountcashel for the defeat. Mountcashel was still favoured amongst the leading Frenchmen of the day, at least in Ireland at that time, and also by Louis himself.

The reasons behind this should not be lessened by events at Newtownbutler. There were other leading Jacobite generals, and an examination of Mountcashel's distinct qualities as far as the French were concerned is necessary before a fuller understanding of French motives can be reached. Mountcashel himself was keen to command the troops destined for France as early as February 1689 and he had written to the French war department in this regard.[1]

This would suggest that the concept was partly instigated by Mountcashel in conversation with those in the French military with whom he had formerly served and in part by the French need to have well-commanded Irish troops. That is not to say that he felt that the Irish cause was lost as his later communication with Sarsfield tends to refute this argument.[2]

His preferred destiny lay with the French army, however. This is again clearly indicated by his actions after James's landing in Kinsale. At this time Mountcashel sought assurances from the French that his acceptance of the position of Master of Artillery in the Irish Army would not complicate, or otherwise jeopardise, his wish to lead the Irish Brigade in France, his actions motivated by his desire to appeal directly to the French with regard to their continued assistance with the Irish cause.[3]

Louis's Irish diversion may have been a way of playing for time on the European stage but Mountcashel, at least, still believed that the French king would support

Ireland. For Louis's part, his communication clearly indicated the course of action. Both Louis and Louvois preferred Mountcashel.

His future in terms of his career was secure, however. D'Avaux also saw him as the only eligible general, with little competition it seemed. James's hope that Berwick was a suitable candidate held little water with d'Avaux:

> I have found out Sir, that the King of England intended to have the Irish troops go to France led by the Duke of Berwick. I cannot help telling you that, although he is a respectable man, so they say, he is a bad officer and he lacks common sense. I replied, when I was told that he was not Irish, that I believed the King wished the commanding officer and all the corps to be of the same nationality.[4]

Unkind words from the French ambassador, but d'Avaux was not in the business of 'brown-nosing' with Louis's allies. Berwick's English heritage and his father's struggle, albeit diversionary in Louis's view, could not have helped matters.

Then there were the Hamiltons. Both Richard (the commander at Derry) and Anthony (who had fared so poorly at Newtownbutler) were held with barely concealed contempt by the French court. Louvois, the French minister of war, had stated that not only was the command not to be considered for either of the brothers, but neither was to be given a colonelship in any of the regiments, if nothing else creating a negative bias with regard to their military careers. Louvois's letters to d'Avaux give evidence of the degree of contempt with which the brothers were held in France:

> His Majesty [Louis] is asking you to train the best officers and as far as possible people that the King could trust and whose change of mood, so common in that nation, he should not fear, noting also that he does not want any of the Hamiltons.
>
> I must inform you through this note, that His Majesty does not want Messrs Hamilton who served in France, the last of which was a colonel in an infantry regiment. This last Hamilton has left to lead the Irish troops due to come out of service and is not even one of the colonels. His Majesty would be grateful if you explained this as late as possible and only if absolutely necessary. This would be only to inform the King of England in particular and to ask him not to mention it to anyone.

Patrick Sarsfield, Mountcashel's friend and fellow officer from their days in France and England, fared somewhat better in the eyes of d'Avaux who described him as 'not of such noble birth' as Mountcashel but 'brave, honourable and of a never failing honesty', who had distinguished himself through his own merit in the war so far. Sarsfield had also served in France and had not Mountcashel escaped might well have led the first brigade there, being the only alternative in French eyes. D'Avaux, ever enterprising, attempted to get both. James would have none of it.[5]

Mountcashel had made a positive impression with all the French observers, despite his defeat and subsequent capture at Newtownbutler, where as we have seen, d'Avaux blamed the poorly-trained Irish troops rather than their general.

> Although he managed to escape to then serve in France. This alone Sir, would not have led me to agree, if I had not believed that it was absolutely necessary for the King to have a man so devoted to his service and so liked and of such reputation in Ireland, as to keep the Irish dutiful in France and to raise recruits in this country, and even as many fresh troops as you wish. If the King of England [James] wished to give permission to all those who want to follow him, you would have all the best officers in the army.[6]

He also recognised sound leadership qualities in terms of earning the respect, and thus potentially ensuring the bravery, of his men, as well as his ability to recognise good leaders amongst the officer class. Mountcashel was seen as a professional French-style officer, whose qualities had been honed through his early experience and training, yet these same qualities appeared to be lacking amongst his contemporaries. Who else then but this Irish gentleman to organise and lead the apparently undisciplined Irish regiments for Louis? D'Avaux understood and, perhaps having had some experience with foreign troops in French service, must have been fully aware of how important it was for such troops not only to be properly led, but also to have a leader who both appreciated and embraced the French way of war.

Foreign officers rarely rose to high rank, however. Indeed the French system was designed to prevent such eventualities. D'Avaux states that Mountcashel's short sightedness would prevent his becoming a great general or French marshal. This statement was perhaps designed to protect him in the early years, and to alleviate fears amongst potential French rivals for higher military office. Of course, recent events at Enniskillen had left Mountcashel little choice in terms of where his future lay. James was reluctant to lose him but the nature of his escape opened up the question of his honour, despite Mountcashel's attempts to avoid such a prospect. If he was captured again, the Williamites could shoot him out of hand. This must have provided further inducement, should any be required, to strive for the command of the brigade. Tyrconnel too seemed content with Mountcashel's leaving for France. The two would never meet again.[7]

Foreign Troops in French Service

The idea of foreign troops serving in the French army was nothing new. The concept of both foreign mercenaries and foreign regiments within the army had been in use since the previous century. The seventeenth century and Louis XIV's reign saw a renewed interest in the idea and Irish units had fought for the French in the 1640s and 1650s. During the Dutch war in the 1670s, the French army contained twenty-six foreign infantry regiments, nineteen per cent of the Army. By the War of the Grand Alliance, this had risen to forty-eight regiments. All foreign troops received French arms and French training and effectively became working battalions and brigades within the army. Louis had little choice in his pursuit of such regiments. The French economy had suffered greatly and this was the third of Louis's major wars in Europe. His aggressive defence against the Grand Alliance would cost millions of livres and, although the war would solve little in the short term, France would pay dearly. In light of this, it was felt that Louis's Irish diversion should be extended for as long as possible.[8]

As we have already seen, the Irish situation was not specifically designed to put James back on the throne of England, but to convince William that such an event was possible, thus drawing valuable Williamite military resources from mainland Europe. The diversion worked, albeit for a short period, and William's forces were committed in Ireland until October 1691 and the Treaty of Limerick. By summer 1689 and Newtownbutler, d'Avaux echoed James's thoughts in terms of the urgent requirement for experienced French troops to shore up the ailing Jacobite army. Louis agreed, but there would be a price to pay. 6,000 French troops would be sent, but 6,000 Irish would return to fight in France.

The exchange was never to be without conditions. Louis was not so naïve as to effectively give away his finest regiments. They were under orders to support the Irish but not to become involved in battle to the extent that they would suffer excessive casualties. At the Boyne in 1690 the French troops kept the route of escape for the Jacobites open, and even shot at elements within the fleeing troops in order to prevent the retreat becoming a rout, thus retaining a large part of the army rather than allowing it to become scattered. This was the only part they played in the battle, however. The French were more than a show of force but still less than an effective addition to the ailing Irish army and Louis knew, even if James did not, that once his diversion and Ireland's usefulness had come to an end the troops would be coming home. He would reap greater benefits from Ireland, however, as by the end of the war he would receive much of the displaced Irish troops.

Irish Regiments for France

This was in the future. For now there were regiments to form. The French requested that 6,000 men be recruited to replace the men that Louis was sending to Ireland. The French wanted five regiments. Compliance with the French requirement, however, would be a different matter. The Irish army was in disarray. The besiegers at Derry had fled from Ulster. Mountcashel's Newtownbutler force had been mostly scattered, captured or killed. The French would arrive in March in preparation for the Williamite assault in the summer. Mountcashel was set an enormous challenge and would have to establish and organise the Irish brigade within a very short time.[9]

Attempting to comply with the French requirements as far as possible, the Irish initially tried to raise four regiments. James, in an effort to gain men of some quality (and also to allow him to keep those experienced officers that he had), appealed to the noble Irish families, who would send a son along with the regiment to command overseas. The O'Neills could not raise any troops and Lord Clanrickarde had little intention of sending his men anywhere. Lord Dillon would, however, have a regiment available and ready, under the command of his son Arthur.

Mountcashel had to re-establish his own regiment that had been to all intents and purposes destroyed at Newtownbutler. By January he had 300 men in arms, hardly an auspicious start. The following weeks, however, were to see something of a resurgence in his popularity and his ranks swelled to 1,200 troops. This stands as a testament to the man's popularity by this stage, and his escape from Enniskillen seems to have turned him into a 'folk hero'. It is easy to see then why the French held him in such regard, if such was his effect on the men. It would not be so easy to raise the troops for other regiments however. D'Avaux commented to Louvois:

> I have nothing further to ask you concerning the state of the troops, but I think it is necessary to tell you again today, what I have had the honour of saying so often: there is little effort made to satisfy the promise made to the King to send Irish troops; there are only eight hundred men ready to embark for France at the time of my writing, except for Moncassel's regiment.
>
> Regarding this regiment, there are twelve hundred good men; there were hardly four hundred when Mylord Moncassel arrived in Dublin after his release from jail, and he increased the regiment to the level I relate within three weeks, although he was give no help, on the contrary many hurdles were put in his way.[10]

Mountcashel then used his influence to help his fellow colonels. Colonel Robert Fielding was an Englishman who had joined the Jacobite cause after James's flight, and had also married Mary Ulick, the widow of Cormac MacCarthy, Mountcashel's older brother. Justin now came to his aid, helping him raise sufficient numbers to form a regiment. Mountcashel's was not the only regiment that had been re-formed after Newtownbutler. Clare's Regiment had also been recruiting and was able to raise men for France. Again, however, the popularity of the regiment's colonel was to play a significant part. D'Avaux would have scathing comments:

> Concerning O'Brien's regiment, Mylord Claire's son, we have found only seven hundred and forty eight men in the thirteen old companies of the regiment plus the three new ones, and some of them will be rejected. Mylord Claire has so little purpose in organising this regiment to go to France that he has not informed any captain to raise his company to one hundred men; moreover, there are only three captains in this regiment with royal commissions, all the other ones are lieutenants or ensigns, most of them insignificant and without presence, whom he picked up to replace those who were killed, left the services or were taken prisoner at Enniskillen. He has not yet decided which one of his children or nephew would lead the regiment; there is no lieutenant colonel or major.[11]

Lord Clare had not intended to send his son to command the regiment. The men declared, however, that they would disband if not led by an O'Brien. Lord Clare relented and named his son Daniel as colonel. Lord Galmoy, the man who had first besieged Crom, and who is conspicuously absent from the later events at Newtownbutler (despite his presence with the northern Irish a few days before) also raised a regiment. This could not have been difficult since his lack of attendance at the earlier battle would have left the bulk of his troops intact.[12]

By March 1690 then, in preparation for the arrival of French troops from Brest, Mountcashel had formed five regiments, his own, Dillon's, O'Brien's, Butler's and Fielding's. The brigade as a whole formed around 5,800 men. These would fight for France – the conditions of service left little doubt as to their allegiance. They would fight for Louis against his enemies, indeed, whosoever he would command them to fight, except James II, the only clause in their 'contract'. Soldiers' pay had also been agreed prior to the troops leaving Ireland, the rates being at least familiar to Mountcashel since they dated back to the arrangements made for George Hamilton's Regiment of Foot in French service in 1671. The rates also corresponded to James's preference for Jacobite troops in Ireland. A captain received five livres (francs) per day, a lieutenant two francs and twenty-five cents and an ensign one franc and eighty cents. Common infantry soldiers received nine francs per month, but deductions were made from the common soldier's pay for the colonel of the regiment, in addition to his pay of around 2,700 francs per year.

The Irish troops would certainly not become rich through their service, though differences between the Irish and the French troops were marginal.[13]

French troops arrived on 20 March at Cork. The Comte de Lauzun, who was to replace Marshal Rosen as the French commander in Ireland, commanded them. If the Irish that remained thought that this boded well for their cause, they were mistaken. Lauzun was a courtier, and not fit for such a high level of command or responsibility. He would, however, ensure that as per Louis's command, the French troops would remain relatively uncommitted and intact.[14]

Irish troops now stood ready to embark for Brest in France, and would leave on 7 April. The men had been recruited quickly and, although numbers were adequate, Mountcashel was to be plagued once more by the quality of his troops. Many of the men had never fired a musket or seen military service, and Mountcashel must have hoped that the French would see potential in many of the recruits rather than their relative inadequacies. Indeed, we can presume that the numbers quoted were inflated through last-minute recruitment in a desperate bid to impress the French. The troops were in bad condition, even prior to embarking, and many were clothed in rags. The situation with regard to arms and training was something that Mountcashel hoped that French aid would quickly overcome.

There had been some disagreement between d'Avaux and Louvois over the matter, even prior to the Irish Brigade being formed. D'Avaux had insisted that 6,000 to 7,000 good troops could be recruited in Ireland. Louvois, the French War Minister, had wanted quality over quantity and would accept 4,000 of the experienced Irish with good officers rather than an untrained rabble. Louvois was to have his way.

Arriving at Brest by 23 April, the Irish reached France. Mountcashel was summoned before Louis at Versailles, where he was well received. He was presented with 4,000 *ecus* in order to equip the brigade and an annual pension of the same sum, in addition to his colonel's salary. He would certainly benefit from his stay in France. Mountcashel also submitted himself to a French court martial in order to clear his name, at least in French eyes, with regard to his escape from the island town of Enniskillen. He was pronounced innocent of having breached the terms of his parole. The French military and Louis would certainly not hold these actions against the commander of the Irish. Mountcashel must also have been relieved that the whole affair was now over and he could put Newtownbutler and Enniskillen behind him at last.

The French were still concerned in one respect, however, that being the quality of the troops that they had received from Ireland. They had insisted that, as far as possible, each regiment should consist of sixteen companies of 100 men each, a challenge, even if there had been a surplus of experienced troops in Ireland at the time. The immediate decision taken by the French was to reduce the complement from five regiments to three. The Butler and Fielding Regiments would be broken up, and the useable troops dispersed to the other units. A surplus of around 700 men was shipped back to Ireland almost immediately. Over the course of the following weeks, additional men were weeded out until the French had obtained their three regiments with 1,600 men each.

Even with the reduction in numbers, Mountcashel's men were in a sorry state. They had brought no arms from Ireland and were clothed for the most part in rags. A French record of the time speaks of them being 'shirtless, shoeless, hatless and afflicted with vermin'. This opinion must be taken in context with a number of other factors. The native French were little used to seeing Irishmen, let alone those who had just emerged from an active campaign across the sea. A little intolerance is not unexpected, especially in an age where its use was the rule rather than the exception. At least one source records that French troops were in a similar state upon their return from Ireland in 1691. Irish weather and conditions are nothing if not consistent.[15]

Mountcashel's men were in need of arms and uniforms, however, and it had never been intended that they should arrive as a fighting force ready for battle. Louvois had already implied that the Irish would be quickly 'fitted out':

> I must also add that His Majesty [James] should not worry about clothing these soldiers, on the contrary, it would be better that whatever little material is left in Ireland, should stay there for the purpose of clothing the king of England's troops, rather than the Irish, who will find far better materials in France than those: this will be more advantageous to the Irish colonels who will come, since the uniforms of their soldiers, dressed with better cloths, will last at least two years.[16]

Despite their initial shock, the French army took stock and set to work to outfit the new regiments. It is interesting to note that, despite being initially issued with grey coats (there was a surplus of grey material in this regard as evidenced by the amount supplied to Ireland at this time), the Irish clamoured for red. Many of the regiments in Ireland wore red, in a similar manner to English regiments of the time. The Enniskillen records refer to troops of the town taking the red coats from captured Jacobites prior to the Battle of Newtownbutler. Clearly then, the Irish had no qualms over wearing the red coat and this may be explained, albeit in a strange manner, by their need to express their identity. Individual regiments within the vast French army remained for the most part indistinguishable when deployed *en masse*. Only guards' regiments and, perhaps more importantly, some of the foreign regiments (such as the Swiss) were characterised by their unique uniform colours.

This perhaps is where the Irish yearning to look different from their French counterparts had emerged. The Irish troops had no idea if they would ever see their native land again, even if they did survive French service. Standing out from the mass of French infantry gave them an identity and symbolised their nationality. The colour of the uniform was not so important as the fact that it was not distinctly French. In an age where uniforms were so closely tied to regimental identity, morale and esprit de corps, it is not surprising that insistence on wearing French grey would create serious questions amongst the Irish. Initially at least, however, there seemed little choice, and the matter was not settled until Mountcashel had gained assurances that the next uniform issue (in the field) would be red. It is not clear when in fact this did occur, though the Irish regiments recorded in French service throughout the 1700s, wore red.

The flag of the brigade had a Saint George's cross with a lion in gold under a golden crown. Although seemingly English in style rather than Irish, this was a rather typical flag of the period. The cross device was used in the majority of French and English flags at this time and typically 'Irish' symbols had not as yet appeared. The regiments had been clothed and armed and were ready to march. Encamped at Nantes, Mountcashel had been made a Lieutenant General of France and by the start of June had been commissioned as Colonel of the Mountcashel Regiment. As O'Callaghan notes, he had held both positions in England and Ireland and now in France.

The Irish troops had been formed into three regiments: Mountcashel's, Clare's and Dillon's. Daniel O'Brien, the fourth Viscount Clare, was the young colonel of Clare's Regiment. His father, who had intended not to send his son with the regiment until pressurised, had gone into exile with Charles II and had been rewarded with considerable tracts of land in County Clare in 1662, shortly after the restoration. O'Brien had again remained loyal to the king upon James's flight and by 1689 sat in the Irish parliament in Dublin, was Lord Lieutenant of County Clare and had raised a regiment of dragoons and two regiments of infantry for service. These troops had fared poorly at Newtownbutler if d'Avaux's report of the plight of Captain Marigny is to be believed, and the flight of Clare's dragoons had not been forgotten. James had also selected the young Daniel O'Brien and his regiment for French service. Whether the action at Newtownbutler had motivated this decision is unclear, but Lord Clare would have to work hard to remould the regiment's reputation.

Arthur Dillon commanded the third regiment of foot and similarly represented one of the noble Irish houses. During the English Civil War, and the subsequent wars in Ireland, Dillons had fought abroad in Spain and France, commanding Irish regiments. The seventh Viscount, Theobald Dillon, had gained the title in 1682. He was by 1685 a lieutenant colonel in the Earl of Clanricarde's Irish Guards, and himself raised two regiments of foot for James. Dillon's two sons, Henry and the younger Arthur, commanded these troops. Arthur's regiment was selected for French service, and he was only twenty years of age when he landed in France.

The original aim had been for the Irish regiments to fight under Noailles on the Catalonian border but the war was not proceeding as Louis had planned, and the situation in the Savoy region of northern Italy meant that reinforcements were needed quickly. By the end of July, the Irish Regiments had received their orders to fight under Saint Ruth and Marshal Catinat in Savoy.[17]

It is useful at this stage to set the participation of the Irish troops in context. This was not the first of Louis XIV's wars; neither was it the most successful for France. In fact the war would almost bankrupt the country. It is important therefore to establish the reasoning behind Louis's employment of the Irish and the massive front that he had to defend. The war had its roots in the earlier part of the century, a time when Louis's lust for power and glory was insatiable. The French concept of *gloire* at this time meant that manhood was tested in combat and battle and this suited the young Louis's personality and direction.

The French saw *gloire* as essential for any young nobleman. What better way to promote oneself but to bathe in the glory of conquered territories? In this respect, Louis would portray the very essence of French nobility. Despite his position and the popular opinion that we now have of the Sun King, the young Louis was present at most of the major battles and sieges and ensured that he was trained by the best French generals of the time. His need for personal achievement would effectively dictate French foreign policy for many years.

The War of the Grand Alliance

It is not necessary within this work to outline the details of Louis's reign, but it is important at least to determine the nature of the conflict within which Mountcashel had become embroiled. Louis XIV came to the throne in 1643 at the age of four and France was already at war. It was as an adult, however, that the king, finally able and keen to make his own decisions, would start five major wars in Europe, ending only with the War of the Spanish Succession (1701-14) where John Churchill, first Duke of Marlborough, would gain such notoriety. The young king began his conquest in 1661, in an attempt to conquer new territories for France.

For so long in the shadow of Spain, France saw Spanish power diminishing, and eyes were slowly turning to the Spanish Netherlands in northern Europe. The great commander Turenne backed Louis as did many of the important French nobles, despite the warnings of the young Louvois. As a pretext for war, Louis could always fall back on the absence of dowry payment, promised by Spain as part of the Treaty of the Pyrenees earlier in the century. When Philip IV, King of Spain, died in 1665 the stage was set for Louis to make his move.

Louis had not counted on the Dutch, however. The French and Dutch had allied against Spain in the sixteenth and early seventeenth centuries, a move that had ensured that limits were placed on Spanish expansionism. The Dutch United Provinces had secured their independence from Spain in 1648, an independence that could easily be threatened by the wrong alliance. History was repeating itself. French moves in the Spanish Netherlands were a little too close to home for the Dutch and, concerned over French expansion this time, they formed an alliance with England and Sweden as a deterrent to French aims. The Dutch were by now a sea power and wielded great commercial influence, they and the French now being business rivals. They were understandably concerned over having the French on their doorstep. Louis's moves may not have been motivated by concern over trade, but Dutch resistance to French power was certainly motivated by the potential loss of such bargaining power. Louis had to be satisfied with gaining twelve fortified towns on the French border, but his eyes were still on the Spanish Netherlands. He soon realised that the once friendly Dutch were now a problem. For the Dutch came the slow realisation that the ascending French were a much bigger problem than Spain had ever been.

Louis would not be denied. He had been flouted at the beginning of his career by Dutch independence. He would use the French army to force his will. He had faithfully supported the Dutch and they repaid him with disdain. By 1672 French plotting had ensured that a war with the Dutch was inevitable. Louis's armies under Turenne and Condé crossed the Rhine into Flanders, initially with rapid progress. But Louis was now facing the young William of Orange, the new Dutch Stadtholder, who, rather than surrender after substantial French gains in the south, flooded the lowlying countryside, preventing further French movement. It was the first time that Louis and William had faced each other, but the Dutch war had sparked off the enmity that would plunge Europe into war and force kings from their thrones as the two men sought to outwit one another.

The Dutch War had also seen the death of Turenne and the retirement of Condé, two of Louis's best marshals. Men such as Louvois, the Minister for War, and Vauban advised Louis now. Although not directly responsible for Louis's use of defensive operations in the coming year, the loss of such men and rebuff in Flanders can not have given Louis the feeling that French might was unstoppable. It clearly could be stopped or at least held at bay, and William had gained many allies through his resistance. Spain, the Holy Roman Empire and other German states had rallied behind the young Prince of Orange. The Treaty of Nijmegen ended the Dutch War in 1678. Louis had made some gains, adding some cities and a province to his borders, but had by now realised that the prize of the Spanish Netherlands would not come easily, nor would it come through the use of brute force alone.

By the late 1670s Louis's attitude towards France and his personal *gloire* had changed from that of a conquering nation under an aggressive king to that of an absolutist monarchy guarding the delicate borders of the nation. France was a greater power geographically but could little afford further costly wars. It would still fight if necessary, however. The alliances against Louis in the late seventeenth century would take their toll, not helped by the defeat of the Turks by the Habsburgs, allowing the Holy Roman Empire to ally with the smaller European nations against France. Louis regarded these fledgling German states as a real enemy and acted defensively, in his view, by conquering many of the large cities on his eastern frontier in the 1680s. His seizure of Strasbourg in 1681 and Luxembourg (through legal machinations and the language of treaty), allowed him to control many of the vital river crossings across the Rhine. Europe could not ignore the fact that Louis was still acting aggressively, no matter how much the French king felt that he was protecting his own borders. He may well have felt that his attitude to Europe had changed but he could not advertise the fact. Louis could not admit that his policy and attitude had altered, and Europe could only believe that the Louis of old had returned. The language of treaties and the political activity of false wars continued long into the 1680s, further opening the gulf between Louis and his European neighbours. By 1688 Louis's seizure of Phillipsburg on the Rhine in Alsace was the final straw, not only amongst the Grand Alliance, but amongst the Dutch who now gave support to William's appeals to allow him to take action in England before that kingdom became a strong ally of France.[18] As we have seen, Louis's actions would have dire implications for both Ireland and Lord Mountcashel.

Chapter X

The Wild Geese

Louis's Irish favourite was now in France and there was a war to fight. By June 1690 the Irish regiments were ready for battle. Mountcashel had received a royal commission from Louis allowing him to command the Irish troops in French service. In addition he had, for the third time, been commissioned as a lieutenant general, a rank he had previously held both in Ireland and England under James II. Louis also awarded him the Colonelship of his own (Mountcashel's) regiment, perhaps a formality by this stage but important nonetheless in terms of morale, especially for any troops who had been with Mountcashel for a long time. By 1690 Louis had deployed four armies, in Flanders under Marshal Luxembourg, one on the Rhine at Villeroi, in Catalonia under Noailles and in Savoy and Piedmont under Marshal Catinat.

The Savoy theatre of war had emerged during a troubled year for Louis. The Savoy-Piedmont region lay sandwiched between southern France and Milan, a dominion of the Habsburgs. The region had a troubled past and Duke Victor-Amadeus, the head of state, had a reputation for playing political games with the more powerful factions around him. He had little choice. His troubles in part stemmed from Louis's revocation of the Edict of Nantes in 1685 when French religious intolerance for the Huguenot Protestants finally spilt over. The Huguenots were not the only group upon which Louis would vent his wrath. The Vaudois represented a small Protestant community in Piedmont on the border of the French region of Savoy. So that the flight of Huguenots to this region might be stopped, something that Louis was determined to do, he decided that French might would fall hard on the mountain people. Penalties were harsh for those Huguenots caught fleeing the country but in this instance, Louis would send a message to those powerless communities who sought to shelter them.

The Vaudois, or 'Barbets' as the French called them, lived in the Alpine valleys to the south-west of Turin, and they had been persecuted before, by the Inquisition and the Savoyard government, and through their labours had become an implacable foe when necessary. William also knew this and would ply them with English gold in the years to come. Ever the efficient king, Louis delegated the matter and ordered that Victor Amadeus, the Duke of Savoy-Piedmont, do something about the Vaudois. The duke, a young man of twenty, and married to a French princess, was not easily intimidated, but the presence of the nearby French fortress of

Pinerolo in central Piedmont meant that the French garrison could either be used to aid the duke, or against him, as Louis decreed. The French king then ordered the Marquis d'Arcy, the local ambassador, to force the duke's hand in the matter, and deny tolerance to the Protestant subjects of his dominion.

The duke protested and used the stalling tactics and political games in which he would have to excel in later years. He preferred more subtle measures but Louis would have none of it, insisting that French troops would be used to 'aid' the duke should his actions prove fruitless. Louvois, the French war minister, saw Victor Amadeus as a vassal of France. The sending of French troops onto his land was a mere formality. By January 1686 the pressure brought to bear by Louis's political ranting and the presence of French troops in the nearby fortress had done the trick and the duke gave in. The episode did nothing to endear the French to the duke, however, and at this stage it is easy to imagine him entertaining thoughts of joining William and the new Grand Alliance. That would come later. Now, he would convert his subjects to Catholicism, by force if necessary, and with French help if the situation demanded it. Victor Amadeus decreed intolerance and issued his declaration. His troops marched into the valleys of the Vaudois but it was not enough. By February d'Arcy was petitioning Louis for French troops. Marshal Catinat, a man whose destiny would become entwined with the region, marched to Turin with five infantry regiments and ten squadrons of French cavalry.

After some discussion with the duke, the French force moved on to the fortress at Pinerolo. Despite a last-minute attempt by the Swiss to allow the Vaudois to leave peacefully, the mountain people resolved to stay and fight, a brave decision in the face of French military might and the implacable will of Louis XIV. Victor Amadeus, with little choice as to what would happen next, gave the Vaudois a final chance in April 1686. If the rebels would lay down their arms and return home, he would grant an amnesty for those who had fought back. Their refusal would mean that troops would be used after a delay of eight days. The Vaudois stubbornly refused to negotiate and the combined French-Piedmontese operation, with around 7,000 men, began. Troops moved simultaneously from the French fortress and the Piedmontese town of Bricherásio.

The Vaudois were irregular troops, and were outnumbered two to one. They did have the advantage of knowing the terrain but would be no match in open warfare for the professional troops sent against them. They attacked the French lines of communication but were driven back by French reinforcements from the fort, with heavy casualties. The mountain people would not make the same mistake again and from then on chose guerrilla tactics over direct contact with their pursuers. The French-Piedmontese force began to occupy the now empty Vaudois towns and villages, collecting non-combatants as they went. Over 5,000 men, women and children were now prisoners of the French.

As the year wore on the Vaudois learned to fight as irregular troops. They ambushed the French and Piedmontese troops and columns, used hit-and-run tactics, and became an annoyance to the regular force that pursued them in their mountain strongholds. Catinat responded by using small irregular units of his own to root out the pockets of resistance. Those rebels who were caught were executed and the French war machine needed but little time to end the insurrection. The countryside was desolated and the mountain people killed or captured. Those who did try to escape across the Alps were mostly captured also. By June Victor Amadeus held over 8,000 Barbets prisoner; the total would reach 12,000 by the end of the campaign. Louis and even Catinat made it clear in their correspondence that they would like to see the end of the mountain people once and for all and, with the echoes of the atrocities of the thirty years war, only half a century before, the Vaudois could expect little quarter. They were held in Piedmont, in concentration camps, where some died through inadequate food and water, while most died from disease, certainly a despicable chapter in French history, though at least consistent with many of the actions of the time. By December 1686 only 5,000 Vaudois remained. The Swiss, whose offers of assistance had been ignored in preference to resisting the French, now helped to re-settle the survivors in Protestant areas of Germany. But this was not the end of the mountain people. In the years to come, many of the Vaudois would return to their valleys and mountains and this time they would be aided by William. William did not see the region as secondary in terms of its military importance, as did the French. Instead, he saw an opportunity to attack France along its south-eastern borders, potentially also generating rebellion amongst the Huguenot populations of the region. Louis had not eradicated the Vaudois as he had hoped and the stage would be set for a clash with the Irish troops now fighting for France.

By 1690 the situation had changed. Not only was there an active war, but Victor Amadeus II, Duke of Savoy, had changed allegiance and joined the alliance against Louis. He was still under both political and military pressure, sandwiched as his kingdom was between the Dauphiné region of France and Habsburg Milan. His lands would be hotly contested in any European conflict. Within his territories, encompassing coastal Nice, mountainous Savoy and the Piedmont region, treaty obligations had allowed Louis to hold the vital fortresses of Pinerolo and Casale, where Marshal Catinat was governor, both well inside the duke's borders. The situation gave Louis vital political and military leverage even before the war had started. At the start of the year Victor Amadeus was still on reasonable terms with Louis. His insistence that the duke hand over Turin to the French, however, was enough to convince Victor Amadeus that it was time to change sides.

The war began in the region in earnest in June when the duke had French residents of Turin arrested. Louis must have known that Victor Amadeus had been communicating in secret with William's League of Augsberg, the Grand Alliance against the French. His response was immediate, ordering troops to the south-east of France. Saint-Ruth, who would a year later lead the Irish at Aughrim, was ordered to command in the region, but he would be delayed. In the interim Louis needed troops in the area fast. The Marquis de Larré would lead 10,000 militia and 200 cavalry, while Catinat commanded 12,000 French troops. He began by taxing the town of Carmagnola 50,000 livres, then demanding over one million livres from Turin. Such was the custom of the time, an effective method of reducing the ability of towns and cities to support the enemy. Hardly 'scorched earth', yet ultimately effective as Catinat could ensure that the twin fortresses at least would remain well supplied. He was able to send as much grain and animals to the fortress as he could, vital at this stage since the French did not fully control the region.

The duke, however, was not out of the fight and had two cards still to play. Firstly, and vital to any fighting that he would have to do in the region, he had made amends with the Vaudois, the mountain fighters whom he had once sent to their deaths. Now reconciled with their former oppressor, and eager to have their revenge on the French, many of the Vaudois had returned to their valleys and taken up arms. This practically guaranteed a savage, brutal war, characterised by atrocity and massacre as the Vaudois and the French indulged in their respective hatred of one another. The duke also had received reinforcements in the form of Spanish troops and with the promise of German troops to follow under the command of Prince Eugene of Savoy, a brilliant young commander who had sought French service and been turned away, only to become a thorn in Louis's side in this war (and the wars to come).

It was the summer of 1690 and the Irish regiments now marched toward the Savoy region of France. The defeat of the Turks had indeed created the situation where numerous Imperial troops could be freed for service against the French on the Italian border. Louis's fears had been realised and the French needed reinforcements in Savoy, and quickly. Enter the Irish, arriving in late July, in an attempt to boost the numbers of the French army on the Italian border under Marshal Catinat. The troops were vital since Catinat fully realised that he did not have enough men to lay siege to Turin itself. He therefore attempted to control as much of the duke's land as possible, feeding his men off the small towns, grain and available herds.

Catinat had advanced into the Po river valley, leaving his second in command, the Marquis de Larré, to deal with the Vaudois in northern Savoy and to keep open the vital lines of supply and communication. Though militarily weak in a conventional sense, the Vaudois, or *Barbets*, were now infamous through their prowess in guerilla fighting and could close the French army supply routes if de Larré moved, but Catinat was now facing increasing numbers of Imperial troops.[1]

It is not clear exactly when news of James's defeat at the Boyne would have reached Mountcashel, perhaps as he marched, or upon arrival. It was clear, however, that he could do little save protect the honour of his own regiment and show France how the Irish exiles could fight. Perhaps Mountcashel still believed that creating a good impression with the French and, more especially, Louis would create the correct conditions for Louis to send more direct help to Ireland in the form of additional French troops. His later communication with Sarsfield would certainly support this argument.

Mountcashel was not just an Irish general fighting for the French, he was still a patriot and an Irishman and despite his European obligations he retained a strong interest in the changes in the Irish situation. After their defeat at the Boyne on 1 July (Old Style), the Irish troops retreated to the lines of the Shannon river. The battle had shown the weaknesses in the poorly-equipped and poorly-trained Jacobite infantry. The elite Jacobite cavalry had however prevented a disorderly affair becoming a slaughter. James, however, had once more lost his nerve and returned to Kinsale and then to France, leaving the responsibility for the rapidly deteriorating situation with Tyrconnel, Berwick and Patrick Sarsfield. He would never set foot in Ireland again. The effects of the rout spread like wildfire. The surrender of the garrison at Drogheda shortly after the battle precipitated a collapse that would rapidly gain momentum. Small Jacobite garrisons fell or fled, at Wexford, Duncannon and Waterford, at the approach of William's forces. Many of the Williamites were thus convinced that there was little fight left in the Irish army.

On 17 July, William's troops laid siege to Athlone. The Jacobites would make a stand – a strategic necessity since the town commanded many of the crossings across the river, one of the few natural defences that acted in the Jacobites' favour. The siege proved difficult for the Williamite forces and was quickly given up in preference to a pursuit toward Limerick and the rest of the Irish army. Tyrconnel had reached Limerick on 6 July, the same day that William had entered Dublin. The disorganised and poorly equipped remnants of the Irish army would have to be re-organised. William, by now fully aware of the time and resources that the Irish war was consuming, opted for a rapid strike against the regrouping Irish troops. His decisive blow would fall at Limerick and by the beginning of August he had started to move his troops. William was being forced to waste valuable time on the Irish affair, time that Louis knew he could use to his advantage in mainland Europe. The Irish diversion was working.

As William had met with success at the Boyne, the French at the Battle of Fleurus had defeated his allied army in Flanders. Louis's navy had also won a victory at Beachy Head. The news forced William to return to Dublin with the intention of returning to England. The French successes, as so often occurred in this deadlocked and indecisive European conflict, were not adequately followed up, however. William finally made his decision, changed his mind once more, and continued toward Limerick with his army.

His decision and ultimate intention of defeating the Irish remnants, rather than serving to bolster the defence of the town and thus unite the Irish factions through an understanding of what was coming, only served to further divide them. Berwick in particular cited that 'The place had no fortification but a wall without ramparts, and some miserable little towers without ditches'. Tyrconnel also questioned the prospects of holding the town. Only Sarsfield seemed hopeful, being of the opinion that Limerick must be held since otherwise all was lost.

The French, now under the Duc de Lauzun, who had been ordered by Louvois not to risk valuable French lives, marched to Galway just before William's arrival at Limerick. Boisseleau, who had landed at Kinsale with James and had since governed Munster with an iron hand, was appointed by Tyrconnel to command. He, at least, knew the character of the poorly-equipped and demoralised troops now under him. Over 10,000 men were concentrated at Limerick and well over half had no equipment. Most of the Irish cavalry, however, were still surprisingly effective and numbered over 3,000 strong. These were rapidly encamped on the banks of the Shannon within six miles of Limerick in order to prevent an encirclement of the city, a feat that the Williamites would not accomplish on this occasion.

The siege began on 7th August. Sarsfield, however, in an act of considerable daring, attacked and effectively destroyed the Williamite artillery at Ballyneety, removing the army's ability to conduct successful sieges. William would not be daunted, however, and launched an assault on the town with his infantry. Without the benefit of artillery the assault faltered, suffering 1,500 casualties. The siege was called off by the end of the month and William returned to England in September. The Irish war would have to be finished without him. If the Irish were to put up such a fight then he could scarcely waste time and thus play into Louis's hands. He would leave matters in the care of Solmes, and later Ginkel, in the hope that attrition and manoeuvre would gain a rapid victory and release the allied troops for Europe. There would be some good news, at least in the south of the country, when Cork and Kinsale fell to Marlborough by October – shattering Jacobite hopes of French relief from southern ports.

The successful defence of Athlone and Limerick however, had meant that the lines of the Shannon had held. There was little cause for celebration though. The restraining authority of James had to some extent held back the squabbles and intrigues of the Jacobites. His absence meant that such wasted efforts still remained. Many of the native Irish were now committed not only to the pursuit of French protection but the creation of a separate Irish state. The old English, however, saw the blossoming of agreement with William. To this end, the native Irish saw French security as the only means to end the land question, religious freedom and even their remaining in Ireland; their best troops and perhaps their best general were currently in France after all. The French troops who had served in Ireland waited at Galway for the arrival of the transports that would return them home. The Irish would have no such respite. Tyrconnel would travel with the French, in the hope of securing more direct aid in the court of Louis. He handed control of affairs over to Berwick.[2]

More than ever both Mountcashel and the troops serving under him had to show how disciplined and well-armed Irish soldiers could fight, and die if necessary. Catinat, Mountcashel's new commander, was the son of a French magistrate and had reached his rank through merit rather than wealth or family connections. He was a good soldier and favoured by Louis, although he had a reputation for being cautious in the field. He could also be ruthless and brutal as the situation demanded, ably demonstrated by his treatment of the Vaudois to date.

He now faced numerically superior Imperial forces, but his plea for reinforcements had at least been answered, in the shape of 5,000 able Irishmen under Lord Mountcashel, enabling him to continue the 1690 campaign in Upper Savoy. Catinat's main adversaries were the Duke of Savoy and the young Prince Eugene, who had greatly distinguished himself against the Turks. (Catinat and Eugene would meet again in the War of the Spanish Succession in a decade. Eugene would get the better of his old adversary on that occasion, however). Imperial troops on the defensive also had the advantage of the countryside and the nature of the terrain. Mountains dominated the region and many of the Imperial strongholds were characterised by inaccessible and thus easily defended approaches. It also held the Barbets, Vaudois Protestants, well used to both the mountains and the nature of warfare in the inhospitable terrain.

Catinat and the other French officers, having little knowledge of the Irish, must have had some reservations, especially since the task ahead seemed so difficult. These were untested regiments and, although some of the officers spoke French, few of the men did. Many of the French officers must have looked upon the Irish as, at best, second-rate troops and, at worst, untrained levies. They had not been trained in the French school of military discipline, had not been constantly drilled until orders became second nature and movement in battalion became fluid. French fears would not be realised, but Catinat was no fool, and appointed a trusted officer to command one of the regiments. Andrew Lee (or André Lee), Marquis de Lee, had left Ireland and joined Sir George Hamilton's Regiment as an ensign. After the demise of that regiment, Lee remained in France, obtaining a commission as a lieutenant in the Furstenburg Regiment. He had served with much distinction in

France thus far, becoming a lieutenant colonel in the Greder Regiment, and so was placed as second in command of the Clare Regiment, joining it at Vienne.

Lee was trusted and the Irish were not, as yet. He would be a link between the French staff officers and the rough-edged Irish, and would become a source of information, effectively allowing the Irish to be closely monitored. The French in the field must still have had some doubts. How would these rough Irish exiles fare in a real battle? Though Lee could not have known it at the time, his future lay with the Irish regiments.

Catinat's task was difficult and the question of the Irish would be answered soon enough. He had already advanced as far as the Po valley, leaving some troops under Lieutenant de Larray in Upper Savoy to protect lines of communication and supply against the Vaudois. Advancing into Piedmont, however, Catinat was faced with a larger Imperial army, which was slowly being reinforced. He had to reinforce and summoned the troops from Upper Savoy. This left the lines of supply dangerously isolated to Vaudois attack, and additional reinforcements would be required to plug the gap and prevent the threat to Catinat's rear. He had little choice then but to use the untested Irish. Mountcashel's troops reached their destination by the end of July, and joined the French army near Chambéry, the capital of Savoy. St Ruth had also arrived with his new command. Though his ultimate fate would be connected with the Irish at Aughrim, St Ruth was an experienced soldier, having served Louis since 1667 in Holland, Flanders and Germany. By 1688 he had been promoted to lieutenant general with the army of Moselle. His orders in June 1690 had changed matters, and he made for the Dauphiné region of France.

Catinat's difficulties had extended the campaigning season. The lateness of the summer meant that quick decisive action had to be taken. Catinat's difficulty with lack of troops had prolonged matters, and the late arrival of both St Ruth and the Irish meant that a campaign based on long sieges or attrition was out of the question. St Ruth had a strategy in mind, however. He ordered the Marquis de Varennes to march against Chambéry via les Echelles (the ladders), an obviously mountainous and rugged patch of the inhospitable terrain, while St Ruth with the balance of the force (including the Irish) would approach via Champarluen. Though the aggressive approach of the French hampered Vaudois operations, there were still fears of a long siege.

Count de Bernix, the governor of Chambéry, who garrisoned a well-fortified position in a town which could have held out until Imperial forces arrived, decided that the situation was futile and opted to withdraw, citing that he had too few men to man the works. St Ruth reached the town by 12 August, and garrisoned it with 800 Irish troops under the Marquis de Thùoy. Imperial troops in the town of Annecy also fled but, as French troops reached Rumilly, the duke had decided to make a fight of it. Rumilly was well fortified when compared with other towns in the region and the French assaulted the works, overcoming what defenders there were. The campaign it seemed was going St Ruth's way. The duke it seemed had attempted to defend too many towns with too few men despite the degree of reinforcements that were available. Aggressive French moves were paying dividends for St Ruth.

Success continued. The passage to the Ruè river was defended only by 2,000 to 3,000 militia and 500 troops. French pressure dispersed most of the troops, the balance surrendering. This action allowed the French advances to roll through the areas of Chablais, Fausilly, Iserentaise and the area around Geneva, moving to the borders of the Calvanistic Republic of Geneva itself. Victor Amadeus could only now occupy the sparse regions of Montmelian, Moutiers and the higher Alps. The terrain was becoming more difficult to master, however; indeed the duke must have counted on this, hoping to draw the French into a costly war of attrition in the Vaudois mountains.

O'Conor most accurately describes this:

> The Piedmontese troops, commanded by the Count de Bernix and M. de Salles, evacuated the Duchy, retreating by the valley of Maurienne, and afterwards crossing the mountains that separate it from the valley of the Isere. That river, rising at the foot of Mount-Iseran, and collecting the cascades and rivulets that flow from the inexhaustible glaciers of the Graian Alps, turns to the north at the foot of the little St Bernard, and forces its foaming course through a chain of mountains, winding round projecting rocks, that present admirable positions for the defence of this great pass into Italy. The mountains forming its boundaries rear their snowy tops to the skies, and in many places descend almost perpendicularly to the river, narrowing its channel to a few hundred feet, and deepening it so as to be unfordable. No trees or shrubs facilitate the ascent; impending rocks, whose adhesion is often dissolved by the summer sun, threaten destruction, and fragments and loose stones, as slippery as the glaciers, endanger, at every step, the bold adventurer who dares to climb these precipitous steeps; gloom, barrenness, desolation, the thunder of avalanches, the roaring to cataracts, the colour of the waters, as dark as Cocytus, and the solitude of these dreary abodes, unnerve the arm and appal the heart. Wildness and grandeur characterize this defile through an extent of forty miles.[3]

Victor Amadeus and the Piedmontese knew that the difficult country would hamper French efforts. This, combined with the irregular activity of the Vaudois, would make the rest of the campaign difficult for Catinat and St Ruth. The Duke of Savoy was not having an easy war, however. His troops had been pushed back to the borders of Italy. The Imperial troops were divided into two armies, one under the Marquis de Salles and one under the Count de Bernix, who had fled Chambéry. The retreating Piedmontese and Imperial troops were now in a powerful position, defending mountainous passes that they were readily familiar with. They eluded all French pursuit, evading the advancing troops in the mountainous regions of the country. They eventually found two easily defended positions on the Isere river, where the mountain passes led into Italy, at the Little St Bernard and Mont Cenis. On this occasion well-defended passes and the implacable Vaudois would act in the duke's favour. He did not, however, count on the equally implacable Irish.

St Ruth had had enough of the fruitless pursuit. He now needed results. What better way to test his new Irish troops. The nature of the French marshal's profession was ruthlessness, and St Ruth certainly would have had no qualms over using the Irish as 'shock troops' in preference to wasting French lives in what could still prove to be a fruitless assault against a well prepared enemy. St Ruth may also have calculated on the Irish troops' readiness to prove their ability and their determination in the inhospitable terrain. De Thùoy and the 800 Irish garrisoned at Chambéry were immediately ordered to march towards St Ruth's position. The Marquis de Vins, with the balance of the Irish troops, three regiments of dragoons and some cavalry, was simultaneously ordered to march from Annecy. The reinforcements, together with some light artillery, would join St Ruth with two infantry battalions and a cavalry regiment on the banks of the Isere river. O'Conor again gives an excellent description of the terrain's defensive bias:

> The village of Cintran, on the right bank above Moutiers, retains the name and revives the memory of the *hominess intensi et inculti* who opposed, in this very defile, the march of Caesar to the conquest of Gaul. At Moutiers the valley becomes enlarged, less savage, and has an appearance of industry and civilization, but still bounded by barrenness and desolation. Escaping from this spot of momentary tranquillity, the river again rushes into a defile, precipitating its waters over ledges and rocks into deep chasms, through which it foams on in a lengthened and furious rapid, and after another expansion above Aigue Blanche, rushes through the rocks of La Batie, which it nearly surrounds, and forms a natural, and almost impassable moat, rendering the position of that fortress as impregnable as any that military science could devise. Lower down it enters the Iserentaise – the Davantasia of the ancients. Here it maintains its original impetuosity, and runs rapidly through a defile equally savage, narrow, and tortuous, where a handful of resolute men, by precipitating loosened rocks and avalanches, might arrest the career of armies, however

> numerous, though guided by the genius of a Hannibal or a Napoleon. In Caesar's time the unarmed and undisciplined barbarians opposed him in vain from the high grounds, not daring to encounter in the valley underneath the disciplined valour of the legions. These same passes, guarded by great bravery, by military science, and all the improved implements of war, were forced by the valour of the Irish, and generalship of St Ruth.

St Ruth's force now assembled, he entered the Isere valley using a scouting element of 300 picked men to reconnoitre the land ahead, and to spring an ambush without allowing full battalions to be rapidly destroyed in close infighting where French drill and musketry could make little difference to the outcome. The scouts were probably dragoons or similar light troops for this very reason.

De Salles and his troops were discovered in the lower part of the valley. He had his 1,200 men ensconced on a rocky plateau (O'Conor and his contemporaries describe this simply as a 'rock'), fronted by the river and suitably flanked by mountainous terrain, its difficulty for the attacker further enhanced by the presence of defensive works and *abattis*. De Salles was in no hurry to be shifted on this occasion. St Ruth, however, was equally determined that the opportunity for victory should not slip away once more. On the night of 11 September 1690 he ordered de Thùoy to the foot of the mountain with the Bretagne dragoons and 100 of the Irish troops. These troops would prevent De Salles men easily escaping, should he change his mind about staying. St Ruth had spent enough time chasing the duke's armies. De Salles, however, would not attempt to escape and spent the time available reinforcing his position using felled trees and additional *abattis* to further slow the French forces that would undoubtedly attempt to carry the position by assault. Rugged defiles and easily defended passes characterised the approach and St Ruth at this stage can have been in little doubt as to the degree of slaughter that would be the inevitable outcome of having to assault the position.

His reconnaissance, probably using part of his dragoons and hand-picked infantry, had made him aware of de Salles' defences, no doubt giving an indication of where these were weak and where the most advantageous approaches were located. In light of the actual events, this seems more likely. St Ruth chose to assault the position at three different points. Firstly, the Marquis de Vins would lead a dragoon force along the river ascending the plateau downstream. St Ruth would also be present with these troops. Then, his cavalry force, presumably dismounted and acting as a feint or diversion, would assault the centre, climbing the 'rock' itself in a bold yet dangerous move. Finally, Mountcashel at the head of his own regiment with de Thùoy, would march along the mountain through a narrow gorge or defile and thus gain access to the plateau and assault the position. St Ruth was obviously using only a fraction of the troops at his disposal.

This perhaps illustrates that he had little hope of success, at least in the first foray. He must have believed that it would take several assaults and he was saving his troops for a hard fight. Mountcashel, however, would be in the vanguard, with his Irishmen in their first fight since Newtownbutler. In all aspects of the attack, the defenders must have had each point of access well defended. The results of the action would indicate that St Ruth had found a flaw in the defences, however. The frontal assault, no doubt planned to draw attention away from the flanking moves, could not have been fully carried through (the cavalry perhaps recognising their role as cannon fodder!) since French casualties were relatively light.

The records that are available with regard to the action speak mainly of Mountcashel's role. Despite their defensive position, it is clear that a determined charge was able to dislodge de Salles's troops. We can speculate that St Ruth had indeed found a poorly defended pass for Mountcashel and his men to arrive through, giving the Imperial troops with matchlocks little time to defend against a charge (echoes of Newtownbutler). The defenders were rooted out of their works by Mountcashel and his regiment and pursued into the mountains, with around 150 killed. In the mêlée, de Salles's lieutenant colonel was killed beside him. De Salles took cover in the undergrowth but was discovered and taken prisoner. French records speak of St Ruth losing only ten to fifteen men in the entire action, three of these Irish, with two Irish wounded. This seems incredibly light. Mountcashel, however, had also been hit by musketfire while leading the charge. Some French records state that this was not a serious wound, though this may have been made light of based on his importance. Other sources talk of Mountcashel being badly wounded. Dangeau for instance notes that 'St Ruth reports that in the late battle of Savoy the Irish troops had performed marvellously'. He also reports, however, that Lord Mountcashel had been 'dangerously wounded' by a musket ball in his chest.

O'Callaghan relates the event from both French and Imperial sources.

> Three Irish killed, and two wounded, with Milord Moncassel slightly, by a musket-shot, in the left breast; having been very much distinguished; as well as those of his nation.
>
> The Irish, commanded by Milord Moncassel, who were present at this encounter, fought exceedingly well, and having seen how their chief was wounded, they refused to abandon the pursuit of their enemies, till they should have taken the Comte de Sales, who commanded them. They led him in triumph to Lord Moncassel, in order to console him for the wound which he had received.

A number of points are clear from these sources. The Irish had performed well, having carried the position and conducted a pursuit, suggesting that their morale had been high and they had remained a cohesive force. Mountcashel's men had purged the ghost of Newtownbutler, a recent defeat which must still have haunted the survivors. Mountcashel had also proven that he could lead his men in battle and they would fight well for the French. The suggestion that de Salles had to be brought back to Mountcashel suggests that his wound at the very least prohibited him from continuing the pursuit with his men, and certainly makes it sound more serious than the French suggested at the time. He had been previously hurt at Newtownbutler just over a year before. Combining the relative severity of his wounds with the fact that he was now almost fifty, relatively old for the period, he was lucky to be alive.[4]

After the battle St Ruth was reinforced once more in the form of O'Brien's Regiment and some additional cavalry. The force moved higher into the Alps towards the source of the Isere along the Little St Bernard and Mont Cenis river valley. The Count de Bernix was entrenched in another well-defended position with 400 men. Again, the duke's men had used the natural defensive features of the local countryside to their advantage, and Bernix's position lay in a narrow defile flanked by apparently inaccessible mountains and the river itself. Andrew Lee, then in command of the O'Brien Regiment, was tasked with finding a way through the mountain. Perhaps using local knowledge, but certainly relying on the determination of his Irish troops, Lee found a pass which would enable him to emerge at a position behind the enemy defences. Little expecting an attack from the rear, Bernix's troops fled, leaving their positions, artillery and stores, and escaping across the river bridges towards Italy via the Aosta valley. French forces pursued the retreating troops in order to prevent their rallying, but it seemed that St Ruth's late-summer campaign was becoming more successful by the day.

The Irish contribution was fully recognised and St Ruth distributed the captured provisions and spoils of the enemy, mainly to the Irish troops, who enjoyed the bread and wine that had been captured. St Ruth also allowed the Irish to seize the flocks of sheep that were available on the mountain.

The French advances and incredible successes had created a climate of fear in the surrounding towns and villages to the extent that, on the night of Lee's victory, St Ruth received officials from the town of Montiers, accepting its keys from the archbishop and magistrates the following day. Two days later, the French troops had marched to Morienne, where a similar surrender was arranged. Brisansonnet also fell, and the army encamped, ready for the onset of the colder months.

Mountcashel and 3,000 Irish troops would garrison Chambéry through the winter. In Savoy only Montmelian remained defiant against the French and St Ruth blockaded the town, bombarding where possible. The amount of captured land in Savoy would now yield sizable revenue for the French. It had been an important and wholly successful campaign for St Ruth, but greater still for the Irish exiles who were beginning to establish their reputation.

Catinat had not been idle during the period of St Ruth's triumphs. The use of Irish reinforcements had allowed him to successfully detach from the main force. What would these troops be able to accomplish, however? A siege of Turin was beyond the scope of the numbers involved, but with his lines of supply and communication secure, he ordered Antoine de Pas, the Marquis de Feuquières, to tax, or where necessary, burn the enemy held towns and strongholds. These undertakings would not be easy, however, and at Luserna the marquis suffered 600 casualties from his 1,200 troops, after being forced to abandon the town through enemy counter-attack. Victor Amadeus now seized his opportunity. He had been securely defending Villafranca until the opportunity to attack a weakened Catinat emerged.

He would not miss this chance. Catinat, his forces bolstered with French militia, moved south to Saluzzo. The two armies clashed on 18 August at the Battle of Staffarde. Near Saluzzo the battlefield was characterised by marshland and hedges, making reconnaissance and movement difficult. The duke's army was defeated however, suffering 2,800 casualties and losing 1,200 prisoners and eleven of their twelve cannon. Catinat's casualties numbered 1,000 killed and wounded. Saluzzo quickly fell and the duke fled once more to Turin. Catinat wasted no time after breaking the enemy and taxed Cerisoles and Autrives amongst others. Towards the end of the campaign, the duke attempted to defend the route to Susa, but he was outmanoeuvred by Catinat, who captured the town on 13 September.

The French troops wintered in Savoy, Dauphiné and Provence at the end of a well-conducted campaign. For Louis the unexpected victory was the only notable success amongst a series of stalemates in the other theatres of the war. A small number of troops, including French regulars and militia and the previously unknown quality of the Irish troops, had combined with brilliant generalship to outclass and outmanoeuvre an implacable foe. For the Irish it was just the beginning.

The 1691 Campaign

The relative successes of the individual regiments within Mountcashel's Brigade would in a way become its undoing, as the regiments would be split up for the 1691 campaign. Some of the Irish would fight in Catalonia on the Spanish border while the rest would remain in Savoy. St Ruth, the French marshal who had helped secure Savoy for Louis, would hand command over to the Marquis de la Hoguette, who had returned from Ireland with Lauzun. St Ruth would take his place, leading the Jacobites at the Battle of Aughrim in July 1691, where his career would be savagely cut short and he was decapitated by a cannonball. An unjust end for the victor of Savoy perhaps, but clearly indicative of the dangers that senior officers faced at this time. As Hoguette took charge in Savoy in autumn 1690, the citadel of Montmelian, although besieged not in strictly seventeenth-century terms was blockaded via trench lines and redoubts in the hope of provoking surrender through starvation. The methods of the French siege expert, Vauban, though tried and tested, were manpower intensive, and numbers were not a luxury that was available. By February 1691 French guns were close enough to bombard the town, causing damage to the grain stores. Surrender seemed far from the mind of the defenders, however, as the besieged troops continued to make forays against the French lines. The summer would eventually see the opening of more traditional siege lines against the town, after operations to secure the area against enemy reinforcements. Montmelian surrendered in August, though the citadel within the town held out until the end of the year.

Mountcashel had been in close communication with Sarsfield earlier in the year. Sarsfield had high hopes of continued success after the Williamite debacle at Limerick. As ever, the request for French aid in terms of arms and equipment was prominent. He also requested that Mountcashel encourage Irish interests in the French court. The divisions had not been healed and it was clear that Limerick had indeed been a turning point, but for all the wrong reasons. The representatives of the native Irish 'party', including the Bishop of Cork and the Luttrell brothers, travelled to France in order to make their case and to denigrate and thus undermine Tyrconnel. Sarsfield would further write to Mountcashel denying that such activity represented a split, citing its purpose as representing the Irish army, their aim to oppose those who would deal with William and thus deliver Ireland to him. Mountcashel wholeheartedly backed the Irish faction.

In his next move he was not only motivated by patriotism but hoped to use some of the goodwill that he had generated with Louis. He wrote to the French king in August declaring his support for the Irish faction and with characteristic frankness declaring that French aid had been wasted in Ireland to date. James's dismissal of the Irish should not therefore signal that Louis should do the same. Mountcashel was clearly aware at least of the dangers in ignoring the situation, obviously still believing that the French saw more in Ireland than a simple sideshow to prevent Williamite concentration in Europe. With his usual candour, he warned of the imminent defeat that would occur without intervention.

Tyrconnel had also journeyed to France in a bid to set the record straight as to the Irish and the state of French backing. Despite rumour of his growing apathy with the situation and matters of Irish defence, French promises once more inspired his will to resist. He did, however, make clear his objection to both Mountcashel's and others alleged distortion of the facts in terms of his intent. The feuding between the two would continue. Tyrconnel was asked to raise more troops for French service on his return to Ireland. It would of course have been difficult under the circumstances to give troops away, though Tyrconnel's subsequent procrastination was blamed on other factors. He claimed that few would want to serve under Mountcashel, an excuse which even the French found hard to stomach since the general's popularity did not seem in question. Louvois would have none of the deception, warning Tyrconnel that his quarrel with Mountcashel should not be 'prejudiced against the service of the King who is trying so hard to maintain you, you should therefore overcome your petty grievance against my Lord Mountcashel'.[5]

It appeared that the French would not stand to see their Irish commander rebuked by the wily Tyrconnel.

Savoy was but a memory for Mountcashel and his regiment by April 1691. He was ordered to Catalonia on the Spanish border with Arthur Dillon and 1,000 picked Irish troops, a largely experienced force by now, which Mountcashel must have wished had accompanied him to Newtownbutler two years earlier! The previous 1690 campaign in Italy stood in stark contrast to the events of that year on the French-Spanish border. The Marquis de Noailles led around 12,000 troops in this region facing 13,000 Spanish troops commanded by Villahermosa. One aspect of the campaign, however, was similar to that of Italy, in that local irregular troops, who were familiar with and comfortable in the mountainous regions of the country, were present. In contrast to the Vaudois, however, these mountain people or 'Miquelets' fought for both sides. In 1690 Noailles conducted a defensive campaign against the Spanish troops facing him and there was little movement. For the 1691 campaign, and under increasing pressure from Versailles, Noailles would go on the offensive. In common with Savoy, the terrain in the area was rocky, mountainous and unforgiving, favouring the defender and irregular troops and requiring the use of explosives to move artillery in many instances.

By late May Noailles had 10,000 men in fourteen battalions, with eight squadrons of cavalry and some miquelets. He would initially move against the town of Urgell. Again, as with the Savoy campaign, lines of communication and supply were dangerously open to attack at the hands of irregular troops who could simply fade away. In addition, the French had to repair the roads ahead of their advance. Noailles established his camp at the town of Bellver, garrisoned with the 1,000 Irish troops. The heavy artillery had to be brought across the dangerous mountains, the troops literally blasting a path as they advanced. The Marquis de Quinson would command siege operations at Urgel and digging commenced on 5 June. By the 10th the vital artillery had arrived and was emplaced, the bombardment commencing the following day.

Within a few hours the Spanish governor of the town had surrendered with 1,000 troops and 1,200 irregulars. Urgel's fortifications were demolished and Bellver was further strengthened against enemy attack. In order to strengthen his position still further, Noailles moved a detachment under Chaseron toward Barcelona, ostensibly on a foraging expedition. Although the Irish troops remained in garrison, protecting the newly fortified Bellver, Mountcashel accompanied the expedition. The detachment of troops, however, was also able to capture several fortified towns and castles and put the Spanish to flight wherever they were encountered. The towns of Valence, Boy and Soor were quickly captured. Mountcashel was present at the operations around Valence and Boy. Although there is little record of his activities during these operations, it is likely that his presence and leadership helped the French cause. The Spanish, although slow to react to the incursion, were now alerted.

The Duke of Medina Sidonia advanced towards Noailles's position at Bellver. Noailles had received some reinforcements in the form of the Roussillon militia to supplement his small force. The fortifications and the reinforcements acted in his favour, however, and Medina Sidonia, arriving on 15 August, opted against a siege or assault, moving swiftly west to lay siege to Prats-de-Mollo. Acting upon the opportunity to take decisive action, Noailles assembled his troops and pursued the Spanish force, relieving the town and forcing the withdrawal of the enemy. Both French and Spanish troops now went into winter quarters and the campaign ended for the year. There had been little fighting for the Irish; the 1,000 troops had effectively been used as camp guards, though Mountcashel had seen some of the limited action in this theatre. In the two years of fighting,the Savoy campaign had taken the most toll on the 6,000 Irish who had landed at Brest. Louvois's letter to Tyrconnel in spring 1691 requested a further 1,200 men to fill the ranks of the Irish regiments. Many of these men had been lost toward the end of the campaign at the costly siege of Montmelian. The Irish had re-acquired their reputation as professional troops, but at a terrible cost.[6]

Even at this late stage Mountcashel believed that the Irish cause was not lost. French relief could stop the Williamites. Mountcashel once more wrote to Louis and the French court. He again spoke of French resources having been wasted to date; St Ruth's death had been ill fated, but conduct under his guidance had shown how the Irish army could fight. The troops at the very least should be paid and another good general, together with continued French support, could still rescue the situation. He also believed that Limerick could stand another siege provided that the French engineers there adequately provided for defence. Although Mountcashel did not wish to leave French service, he would gladly return there to muster more recruits for his regiment. It was already too late, however. By October 1691 the number of Irish recruits available for service in the French army would no longer be a problem. Limerick had fallen after a second siege and 15,000 Irish exiles would sail to France to fight for Louis under the conditions of the Treaty of Limerick. Tyrconnel had died prior to the siege, along with many of the Irish hopes.

1692–1694

Mountcashel spent 1692 on the Catalonian border. The year to follow would prove decisive. By the end of it the French king desired peace but was in no way sure how he could achieve it. William had similar thoughts since the war was now becoming difficult to pursue both militarily and economically. With no solution in sight, however, and keen not to see retreats, Louis raised even more troops, increasing the size of the French army to 400,000 men. The war had become an end unto itself, with little dramatic victory and stalemates in most theatres. Gone were the heady days of glorious French victories under Turenne and Luxembourg, both long dead. The 1693 campaign would see Mountcashel serve with the Army of Germany on the Rhine, under Lieutenant General Marshal de Lorge. Clare's (O'Brien's) Regiment still served in Piedmont. The fourth Viscount Clare would die at Pignerol this year from wounds received at the Battle of Marsaglia. Andrew Lee would replace him. Dillon remained with Noailles.

It would be a tragic year for the Irish, and Sarsfield, Mountcashel's dearest friend would also fall at Neerwinden. For Mountcashel a new theatre of war loomed. The war in Germany had, in a similar fashion to Italy, moved to and fro with little real progress. The war had started when French forces crossed the Rhine in 1688, seizing Phillipsburg and other large towns. Despite early successes, Louis's attempt to create a line of defensive fortresses and his resultant scorched-earth policy created a tide of resentment in Germany, where the atrocities of the Thirty Years' War had not been forgotten.

In 1689 the French had been surprised by the degree of German resistance, led mainly by Charles, Duke of Lorraine. The long siege of Mainz lasted from July until September when the French ultimately took the town. This victory was tempered by losses in the theatre, however. The front stagnated in 1690 with little activity. By 1691 the threat of French offensive action prompted the release of Dutch reinforcements to the allied forces, holding the French in check, and prolonging the stalemate. By now the French Marshal de Lorge commanded the army of the Rhine and by 1692, heavily outnumbered by the allied army, complex manoeuvre and decisive battles seemed as distant as ever. By 1693 the theatre would remain in intractable stalemate unless decisive action was taken.

It was to this area that Mountcashel and his regiment were ordered. Mountcashel would serve as a lieutenant general commanding his own regiment (now of three battalions) and the regiments of Charlemont and the Marine, around 6,000 men, many of whom had arrived in 1691 after the Treaty of Limerick. The Irish element of the French army now numbered over 16,000 men. Many of the men who had landed in 1691 were rejected in a manner similar to those of Mountcashel's men who had been sent home.

De Lorges joined the army in early May and immediately attacked Heidelberg. He then crossed the Rhine at Phillipsburg and split his forces, the larger part moving toward the Germans under the Prince of Baden at Heilbronn, while the smaller force attacked Heidelberg, laying siege on 21 May.

The garrison surrendered on the following day. Louis, seeing at the very least movement and potential victory on this uneventful front, despatched reinforcements to de Lorges, increasing his strength to twenty-seven infantry battalions and forty-five squadrons of cavalry by mid-July. Baden had by now withdrawn across the Neckar river. De Lorges joined with additional French troops to form an army of 45,000 men. Baden, however, could not be drawn out of the defensive position that he now held, though small actions were fought, including the reduction of Besigheim where Mountcashel's grenadiers joined with the French grenadiers of the Picardy and Auvergne regiments in the assault. The Irish force and Mountcashel were also present in the reduction of Heidelburg, Wingemburg, Eppenheim and Darmstadt. There had been a remarkable degree of movement in 1693 in the German theatre, but only in comparison with previous years, and in real terms the stalemate was becoming worse.[7]

Abroad, the year had not been a good one for Mountcashel. The Williamites had defeated the Jacobites in Ireland, and many more of the Wild Geese had since left to fight under the French flag. The Irish Parliament of 1689, along with its policies, now stood redundant, and those senior Jacobites who survived, including Mountcashel, now became 'attainted' in a similar manner to those Protestants who had been listed as rebels in 1689 during the Irish Parliament. The land that Mountcashel had accumulated in Munster was now confiscated, but worse was to come. The town of Bandon, where Mountcashel had ultimately shown mercy, demanded reparation from those lands. These were fairly large and the Bandonians now requested that the £1,500 that they had paid as their pardon be paid out of the value of the seized estates. Ironically, William Wolseley had helped endorse the Bandonians' requests. What was left of the estates was granted to the Earl of Romney, later to be sold on.[8]

Mountcashel had also made his will during the year. Trouble with his wounds had perhaps perturbed him and indicated that he only had a short time left. Having lost his estates, however, he only had his name and title to give. As he and Arabella had no children, he gave the title to his third cousin Florence Callaghan MacCarthy of Carrignavar. He insisted that the young man should attempt to regain the lands taken by the Williamites and to give continued service to both the Stuart dynasty and the King of France, his legitimate sovereigns. Even at this stage, the divided loyalties of the Irish that had been their undoing were highlighted.[9]

Mountcashel's suggestion of loyalty to the Stuarts in 1693 is questionable. James's last act in which Mountcashel would be involved unfolded with the erstwhile king's declaration that he would now uphold the Act of Settlement in Ireland. His obvious attempt at winning back English support was treated with contempt by the Irish faction, despite James's promise of recompense to those Irish who had remained loyal to him. Events had now come full circle since those heady days of the 1689 Irish Parliament. Mountcashel, in particular, protested strongly over James's reversals and was answered by the Earl of Middleton, James's Protestant 'Secretary of State' in June:

> The King was pleased to declare, yesterday, that his declaration had been dispersed, by his order, in England. I suppose none will be surprised to hear, that the people of England should have so just a value for the Kingdom of Ireland, as never to be induced to resign the interest they had in it. The reasons are too many and too obvious to trouble your lordship with them. I shall only tell you, that the King promises, in the foresaid declaration, to restore the settlement; but at the same time, declare, that he will recompense all those who may suffer by it, by giving them equivalents. I mean those who have served him; and not only those here, but all who were included in the capitulation of Limerick, which will be a better security for them, than what they have by the acts of the Dublin parliament, considering the many circumstances. I do not doubt but your lordship is fully convinced of this truth; and it will be of great service to the King to convince others of it, which, I hope, will be no difficult matter. For there is no man of common sense but will think himself engaged by interest as well as duty, to contribute to his Majesty's restoration; which without the concurrence of the greatest part of his subjects, is impractable. This I have laid by the King's command.[10]

Despite James's hopes that French aid would come, there would be no restoration this time.

Mountcashel received orders for 1694. As expected, he would again serve in Germany with his troops. Before the start of the campaign period, however, Mountcashel must have been having problems with his wounds. We should not forget that Newtownbutler had been almost five years ago, and it is possible that he was troubled with infection. He had also been wounded in Italy.

The seriousness of such injury was brushed aside by French authorities but it is possible that he had been more seriously wounded. In addition, Mountcashel was no longer a young man. Now in his fifties, he had reached the 'old age' of the time and many of his contemporaries were dead. In light of the evidence therefore, it is not surprising that his first trip of the year was to the curative waters of the Barréges region in the Pyrenees in June. There seems little mystery as to what occurred here, and it is unfortunate that the curative waters did not have their desired effect. Mountcashel died on 1 July, having led his men to France and re-established the Irish army abroad. His death was announced in Paris on 31 July 1694, five years after the Battle of Newtownbutler:

> Mylord Moncassel, Lieutenant-General of the Armies of the King, Commander of three Irish Regiments, died the 1st of this month at Barrege, of the wounds that he has received on several occasions, in which he was always extremely distinguished.[11]

Mountcashel, one of the finest soldiers of the age, had requested that he be buried in Ireland. This was of course impossible and he was buried at Barréges. Andrew Lee would take over command of Mountcashel's Regiment and would go on to become a very successful officer in French service.

Irish history has been somewhat unkind in terms of Mountcashel's contribution. Despite the fact that he was recognised as a more than competent officer and general and for the most part made the correct political moves, he nevertheless is sometimes forgotten in popular histories in relation to the 'Wild Geese' with preference given to Sarsfield and those troops who travelled to France after the second siege of Limerick. Perhaps the more youthful, romantic and somewhat reckless figure of Sarsfield appeals to the modern reader. As we have seen, however, he was not the first choice of the French. Mountcashel had not only paved the way for these Wild Geese, but had proved to France both his own worth and that of his countrymen after the Newtownbutler debacle.[12]

Like so many of his Irish contemporaries, the negative aspects of Justin's career and personality are frequently highlighted; his defeat in Ireland, his escape from Enniskillen and his shrewdness with regard to his nephew and Catholic Ireland in the 1680s. He was, however, a man of his time and the manipulations of many of his contemporaries are rarely questioned in the same way. Despite being impulsive and for the most part frank with both kings and commoners, both sides in Ireland at times appreciated his efforts and his honour. He also demonstrated the qualities, unlike many officers of the time, which enabled him to understand his men and the nature of disciplined soldiery. Both his own troops and his military peers respected him for this very reason. He understood that the nature of battle, in whatever era, hinged on the reliability of the man who fought and died.

Despite having neither the material nor the support to prove this in Ireland, his French victories showed that he was persistent, enterprising and led from the front, the number of occasions on which he was wounded standing testament to this. The pioneer of the Irish brigades in France in the 1690s, Mountcashel represented the close links with France that would subsequently blossom in the eighteenth century. Despite co-existing with the multifarious factions that had ultimately proved Ireland's undoing, Lord Mountcashel had also remained a patriot, something that the French could recognise and respect, in tandem with his military experience.

The subsequent Williamite confiscation in Ireland saw the end of this branch of the MacCarthys. They had survived through much – Irish clan infighting, the 1641 war and Cromwell's subsequent invasion. Finally, however, the MacCarthys, like so many of the native Irish, had lost everything. His countrymen would not forget Justin, however. A traditional lament for him spoke of the inopportune death of a great Irishman and warrior in lands far away from home:

> Pearl of Ireland, pride of Munster
> Phoenix slaughtered by one of his own breed
> A single treasure beneath the stones beneath us
> Freedom of life from a powerful leader[13]

The Irish had lost one of their heroes. Many more Irish troops would fall before matters between Louis and William were complete. The War of the Grand Alliance or the Nine Years' War ended in 1697. In terms of battles fought, on land at least, the French had been victors. The war had resolved little, however, except to remind Louis how his efforts to increase French security, if such was his aim, could easily be misinterpreted by the rest of Europe – as a return to French plans whose intent was to dominate and thus feed Louis's lust for power. The war had exhausted all sides involved and even the massive French resources had been considerably reduced. It was thus a considerably humbled Louis who agreed to peace in 1697.

Louis's fears over Habsburg expansionism and disputed successions had started what the French believed would be a brief series of climactic battles. Instead, a gruelling and terrible war had been the result. When rapid victory remained elusive, Louis had striven to outwear his opponents, though the successive campaigns had not been decisive in nature. In the end the only significant military success had been for William in Ireland where James and the Irish were crushed. Although the fight for the British Isles had its own aims and subtexts, it was a wholly military operation without concession or compromise, something that never occurred in the European theatre of war where diplomacy and negotiation would end the affair. Louis's 'Great Miscalculation' had been to believe that he could win such a rapid and decisive war on the continent. The impending question of the Spanish succession and the subsequent war that would greet the start of the eighteenth century now occupied the minds of Louis and Europe, and would turn the Nine Years' War into an unwanted diversion that had to be terminated rapidly and gracefully.[14]

Many of those who had played a part in Mountcashel's life had their own stories to tell. The ubiquitous Earl of Clancarty would die an old man. After the war he was captured and held in the Tower for a time. Sunderland, his father in law, tried to have him released in exchange for a Dutch officer held by the French. His reputation, however, precluded his release until William pardoned him with a pension of £300 a year on condition that he should remain in exile and never again take up arms against the Protestant succession. He retired to Hamburg in Germany and lived on an island at the mouth of the Elbe, where he profited from shipwrecked goods. He died there in 1734, aged 64. He had two sons, though neither would receive his title and both remained childless.[15]

Berwick, unlike many of his contemporaries fighting in Ireland in the 1690s, would go on to have an illustrious military career. Had the somewhat older and wiser Berwick been present with Mountcashel in Fermanagh, matters would certainly have been very different. For a short time he was left in command in Ireland though his youth and inexperience meant that he was to some extent led by other parties. After the defeat there, he fought for the French until the end of the Nine Years' War. He fought under Luxembourg in Flanders and was present at Steinkirk and Neerwinden, where he was taken prisoner and where Sarsfield was killed. Exchanged for the then Duke of Ormond, he later fought under Villeroi.

By 1703 he had become a naturalised Frenchman and thus eligible to be a French marshal. In 1704 he commanded the French army in Spain during the War of the Spanish Succession. Berwick, mimicking the savage style of his French predecessors, resoundly suppressed the Protestant Camisards in the Languedoc region in 1705 and by the following year, a successful raid against Nice earned him the title of Marshal of France. 1707 would see his greatest victory, at Almanza, where he, being an erstwhile Englishman leading a French army, would defeat Ruvigny, Earl of Galway, a Frenchman commanding an English army. The battle would see Philip V established on the Spanish throne and Louis made Berwick a peer of France. The following years saw him earn a great reputation as he defended south-eastern France. Years later, he would fight against Philip, the king he had put on the throne. He would not see war again until 1733 when he advised at the siege of Phillipsburg. He was killed there by a cannon shot the following June.[16]

James II would never regain the throne that he had lost. He spent the rest of his life in exile in France until his death in 1701. The story of the Stuarts did not end there. His son James Francis Edward, known historically as the 'Old Pretender', was recognised as James III by the courts of France and Spain and proclaimed by the Jacobites who remained, including Anthony Hamilton, who would travel to Scotland with him in an abortive expedition in 1708. Each subsequent attempt would also result in failure, despite the accession of the Hanoverian George I to the English throne. His own son, James II's grandson, would attempt a similar invasion in 1745. This would meet with a modicum of success, but would ultimately prove futile after the Battle of Culloden. Charles Edward Stuart is of course more commonly known as 'Bonnie Prince Charlie'.

Mountcashel had certainly not died in vain. He had never seen Ireland again, nor had he seen his countrymen triumph. He would not be buried in the land of his birth, as had been his wish. He had, however, led Irishmen to France and to subsequent victories in French service. Irish troops had fought on the continent before, but hardly under such circumstances, where, of necessity, such actions were carried out in the hope of both garnering French support and regaining the honour of the men that had been forced into exile.

Mountcashel's (then Lee's) regiment continued to fight during the War of the Spanish Succession (1701-1714). At Fontenoy in 1745, during the War of the Austrian Succession the regiment was still made up of Irish refugees and supporters of the Catholic Stuart line. The Irish Brigade as a whole helped prevent a rout by standing fast against an English attack, and capturing English colours and guns. The regiment itself would exist in some form until the Napoleonic Wars, a remarkable legacy for a man who strove against adversity at every turn, and who had brought a disparate and defeated force to France and future glory more than a hundred years before, and who had lived and died a truly Irish general.

Lord Mountcashel, after Peter de Lily.

Appendix A

Mountcashel's Troops at Newtownbutler

The following is outlined in John D'Alton, *King James' Irish Army List 1689*. A record of Lord Mountcashel's Officers' roll.

COLONEL JUSTIN MACARTY'S, NOW LORD MOUNTCASHEL

Captains	*Lieutenants*	*Ensigns*
The Colonel.	Dominick Terry.	James Fitzgerald.
[Count Anthony Hamilton, Lieut-Col]	Francis Fitzgerald.	George --------
------ Major.	------------	------------
Garret Fitzgerald.	Edmund Sweeny.	Auliffe Callaghan.
Philip Barry Oge.	John Sullivan.	Edward Fitzgerald.
------------	Miles Carroll.	**Patrick Levallin.**
Thomas Power.	Lewis Moore.	Redmond Condon.
Ulick Browne.	Thomas Hogan.	Teiguc M'Carty.
Charles Fitzgerald.	Robert Fitzgerald.	William White.
John Hogan, Granad.	{Walter Bryan.	
	{Donogh M'Carty.	
Richard Condon.	Maurice Piers.	Patrick 'Piers.'
Kennedy O'Bryan.	John Ryan.	John Ryan.
Thady O'Connor.	John Mally.	Philip Connor.

From Gilbert's *Jacobite Narrative*;

Régiment de Montcashell.

Captaines	Lieutenants	Enseignes	Hommes effectifs
Hogan, des grenadiers	O'Brien et Macartie	-	19
My Lord Mountcashel, colonel	*vacante*	Treulee	21
Macartie	Fitzgerald	Macartie	16
Ivorie	Carol	**Lavallin**	9
vacante	Sulevan	Fitzgerald	17

Captaines	Lieutenants	Enseignes	Hommes effectifs
Brown	Hogan	Macartie	20
Duly	Macarty	Milvany	29
G. Fitzgerald, v:	Swyny	Lalesse	19
vacante	Maurice	Kouet	21
Roth	Chivers	Roth	25
Meaghir	Cusack	Comin	31
Power	*vacante*	Colgraue	20
Condon	Condon	Callaghan	61
Brien	Rayne	Rayne	60

estat major	My Lord Mountcashell
colenal	Le sieur Colgrane
lieutenant-colonel	Le sieur Panhonet
lieutenant-colonel en second	Le sieur Roth
major	Le sieur Hogan
autre-major	Le sieur Meaghir
ayde-major	Le sieur Marchand
maréchal des logis	Burk
aumosnier	Owens

Régiment de Bophin.

Captaines	Lieutenants	Enseignes	Hommes effectifs
Wich, grenadier	-	-	-
My Lord Bophin, colenal	Burk	Maddin	-
French	French	French	-
Brown	Kelin	Macdaniel	-
Kelly	Kelly	Kelly	-
Linch	Blake	Maddin	-
Burk	Flaharty	Merick	-
Linch	Ouaringh	Killin	-
Flaharty	Flaherty	Flaherty	-
Martin	Martin	Martin	-
Burk	Burk	Burk	-
Burk	Burk	Linch	-
Blake	Blake	Linche	-

estat major	My Lord Bophin
colenal	Mahony
lieutenant-colonel	Boissin

major	Maddin
ayde-major	Gilles
capitaine reformé	Lasemby
lieutenant reformé	Bahir
enseign	Dolnin
aumosnier	Sbiré
chirurgien	Higny

Régiment de Clair à Cork.

Captaines	Lieutenants	Enseignes	Hommes effectifs
Skiddy, grenadier	Skiddy, Kenedy	-	-
My Lord Clare, colenal	Courard	Fitzgerald	-
Arthur, lieut-colonel	Burk	Burk	-
Rowe	O'Brien	Mansfield	-
Callahan	Callaghan	Bourk	-
Roche	Callaghan	Stritche	-
Ryan	Ryan	Tubbes	-
Lacy	Lacy	Lacy	-
O'Brien	Egane	Barleigh	-
Barry	Lane	Bourk	-
Harrold	Creagh	Harrold	-
Rawleigh	Samson	Rawleigh	
Carol	Ryan	Macnamee	-

estat major	My Lord Clare
colenal	Arthur
lieutenant-colonel	**Marigny**
major	Walane
ayde-major	Kenedy
aumosnier	Strich

Régiment de dragons de Cotter.

Captaines	Lieutenants	Cornettes	Maréchaux des logis	Dragons
M.Cotter, colonel	Fitzgerald	O'Brien	Barry	52
Le sieur Lacy	Moore	Hagan	-	25
Le sieur Power	Burk	Kenedy	-	38
Le sieur Barry	Moore	Lacy	-	39

Captaines	Lieutenants	Cornettes	Maréchaux des logis	Dragons
Le sieur Coppinger	Coppinger	Barry	-	36
Le sieur Gallwey	Barry	Collins	Coppinger	30
Le sieur Wanelle	Lycet	Goulde	-	27
Le sieur Taylor	Keruan	Linch	Batkin	30
Le sieur Grand	Barry	Wilson	Baker	38
Le sieur Trant	Gallouay	Periman	Meskell	38
Lieut-colonel				

353

estat major	M. Cotter
colenal	M. Trant
lieutenant-colonel	Le sieur Carol
major	Le sieur O'Brien
ayde-major	Le sieur Barry
aumosnier	Le sieur Tryaden

Régiment de dragons de O'Brien.

Captaines	Lieutenants	Cornettes	Maréchaux des logis	Dragons
O'Brien, colonel	O'Brien	Fitzgerald	Kilean	-
Kilaha	Pursell	Malking	Macnamara	-
O'Brien	Ifcher	Hogan	Adea	-
Mahon	Kerly	Perry	Hehir	-
Gerard	Nayler	Lusagh	Macnamara	-
Macnamara	Hurly	Nogane	Wise	-
O'Brien	Bedford	Clancy	Leo	-
Purdon	Bedingfield	Burk	Fitzgerald	-
Daniel	Cahane	Archdeacon	Bohelly	-
Philippes, lieut-colonel	Barry	Fitzgerald	Hanford	-

estat major	O'Brien
colenal	Phillipes
lieutenant-colonel	Frayne
major	Deron
ayde-major	Daly
aumosnier	Barry
quarter-maitre	Nelan

From W.C. Trimble's *History of Enniskillen* (p.579).

Jacobite officers captured after The Battle of Newtownbutler;

COLONEL McCARTHY'S REGIMENT	
Major John Rooth	Lieut Cusack
Captain Barry Oze (dead)	Ensign McCarthy
Lieut Patrick Rivers	Ensign Patrick **Lavallin**
Lieut Thomas Hogan	Ensign Michael Mulluany
Lieut Walter O'Brian	Ensign Jo. Lawless
Lieut Daniel McCarthy	Ensign Gravalick

LORD CLARE'S REGIMENT	
Major Marany	Lieut Piercy Lacy
Captain Lawleigh	Lieut Jo. Sampson
Captain Jo. Carroll	Lieut T. Kennedy
Captain Connor	Ensign James Stretch
Captain Edward Lacy	Ensign Maur. Rawleigh
Captain Stephen Harrold	Ensign Macnamara
Lieut Darby Callaghan	

COLONEL JOHN BURKE'S REGIMENT AND LORD BOPHIN'S	
Captain Francis Bourke	Lieut John Bourke
Captain Patrick French	Lieut Chris Finch
Captain John Blake	Ensign MacDonnell
Captain Brown	Ensign Stephen Lynch
Lieut Jo. Kelly	Ensign Nicholas French
Lieut James Badkin	Ensign Peter Merrick
Lieut John Blake	Adjutant Denis Madden

COLONEL DANIEL O'BRIAN'S REGIMENT (AND CLARE'S DRAGOONS)	
Captain Macnamara	Captain Nicholas Archdeacon
Captain Murtagh O'Brien	Quarter Master Hahire

COLONEL SIR JAMES COTTER'S REGIMENT (DRAGOONS)
Lieut John Lacy

Appendix B

Le Comte d'Avaux (Ed. Hogan pp. 383–90)

The following is a full translation of d'Avaux's account of the Battle of Newtownbutler:

From M. d'Avaux to M. Louvois Dublin, 14 August 1689
(Translated from the original French document – and retaining the original spelling. 'Mountcashel' for instance is invariably referred to as 'Monkassel'. Paragraphs are inserted for clarity.)

Sir,

I have not received any of your letters since the one you did me the honour of writing on 13 June, I am quite sorry about that because I can't believe that some got lost and we are here in great need of your instructions. The last 2 packages left here on 28 July and 10th of this month, the one from 28 July went with Mylord Douvre, and contained letters from 1, 15, 23, 26 and 28 July and the triplicate of 26 June.

You will have seen through my last letter dated 10 August that the aim of the King of England was to have Enniskillen attacked by Mylord Monkassel, the Duke of Berwick and Sarsfield; His majesty had nevertheless given order to Monkassel to take beforehand the castle of Crom because it is situated beyond Enniskillen.

Mylord Monkassel marched towards it with 3 infantry battalions and approximately 16 cavalry and dragoons companies. He found this castle in a plain nearly surrounded by water controlled on the Dublin side by a small hill at the foot of which lies a lake which separates 2 sizeable encampments which Mylord Monkassel's regiment attacked on the left, and Boffin's regiment attacked on the other; they overcame it , losing very few men and the great ease with which the 2 regiments pushed back the enemy ensured that they marched on to the castle without having to go against Mylord Monkassel's orders who had asked his regiment to watch over the encampment they were to attack and who had ordered

Boffin's regiment to take the hill which was beyond and commanded the right of the castle which was to be attacked first; but Monkassel's regiment having gone too far forward and sought cover in a few huts within reach of pistol shots, forced Mylord Monkassel to place his cannon fire on the other side where having fired a few times openly, the great fire of enemy musket, which injured first 3 cannoneers of the King's troop, forced them to stop firing, hoping to be able to make an attack at that same place under cover of the night, and subsequently make a full assault; but following advice received by Mylord Monkassel that the garrison from Enniskillen was advancing to cut him off, finding this position too disadvantageous to keep it, he withdrew to Newtownbutler having lost in this fight 15-20 men and approximately 60 wounded amongst whom were his lieutenant-colonel and several of his officers.

As Mylord Monkassel after having withdrawn from Crom, wanted to protect himself from those coming from Enniskillen, he said to Antoine Hamilton to go with 13 dragoons companies to chase a group that was appearing, and then to occupy a position where 100 men could stop 10,000. Antoine Hamilton pushed 4 or 5 cavalry companies, who could not hold out, and followed them for 5 miles without stopping; and although he had no-one to support him, nor to hope anymore from this chase than to kill a few men, he went on marching until he met 2 battalions of the enemy, well ensconced, and some cavalry to the right and to the left, then he had a group of his dragoons go on foot to attack the rebels who were stronger than he, but on the first fire, all his people escaped and ran pursued by the enemy as far as Mylord Monkassel's camp.

This deed gave the rebels so much encouragement that they came to attack Mylord Monkassel the same day; as he heard that they were coming after him, he changed position and placed his cannon on the main road, guarded by dragoons; the enemy that came with 3 ramshackle battalions but very courageously, were received firmly by Mylord Monkassel's regiment, the other 2 did their duty very poorly, and the very dragoons who had cowardly ran away in the morning fled with the remainder of the cavalry without firing a pistol shot, and fled with such fright that they threw their muskets, pistols and swords, and most of them having exhausted their horses, took off their clothes to move faster on foot.

Mylord Monkassel remained at the head of his regiment and having been wounded and his horse killed, the enemy leapt on him and took him; his regiment was decimated and the rest of the army dispersed. Marigny, the captain in Champagne, major for the Claire regiment, distinguished himself in this instant, for after giving orders that were not obeyed, he led the battalion, his colonel having remained in Cork and his lieutenant-colonel having fled; but the regiment did not support him very well and he was taken prisoner and shot in the face three times almost at close range.

As the enemy are not soldiers any more than we are, they did not take advantage of their position and pursued no-one, and if we had come back after them with 4 or 500 horses, in no order, we would have defeated them. We abandoned 4 cannons and the little luggage the army had, which was not much. This deroute will do more harm to the King of England, because of the courage it has given to the enemy, the terror that has settled amongst the troops, and by the quantity of arms lost, than by the number of men killed or those who have escaped; although the loss of a dragoons regiment and 3 battalions is no small defeat, and until now only a few soldiers have been found.

I have feared greatly, Sir, that those in Enniskillen might beat the Duke of Berwick and Sarsfield, one after the other. I talked to the King about it, who said that he would let the people on the ground deal with it for fear of giving them inappropriate orders. However, as I could foresee with great displeasure, that we were risking losing a lot of time round Enniskillen and ruining the least tired troops we have here, while waiting for the Marshal of Schomberg, I felt it my duty to insist with the King that the few troops that were in Derry be sent to Dublin at once, without sending any to the Duke of Berwick, and if the Duke of Berwick was not strong enough with Sarsfield to scatter the rebels that are in the country, he should return also. We sorted out the matters thus, and named the regiments which were to return straight to Dublin. I informed M. Roze, who felt it was appropriate to send my letter to Richard Hamilton, and with this they called back the regiments that Hamilton had already organised for the Duke of Berwick. You can see, Sir, that Richard Hamilton was not written to in the way that had been decided in my presence; this is not the first time it has happened. M. Roze has been surprised 2 or 3 times to see that the letters that he was receiving from His Britannic Majesty were in disagreement with the ones that I was writing to him, and that I have often been obliged to inform him through express carriers, to avoid inconveniences similar to those caused by Mylord Melfort's negligence and carelessness. I also wrote to M. Roze, M.de Lery, and to M. de Fumeron, to come back at once. M. d'Hamilton and the other officers will come back with the troops.

You can see, Sir, through all that I have requested, that we are not capable of holding strong for Marshal de Schomberg. I had great difficulties in making the King of England agree that we should set up a camp. Boisseleau went yesterday to encamp his first battalion; the others will set up camp as they arrive. The camp is 2 miles from Dublin, where as many battalions as possible will be stationed; another one will be set up in the Cork area, but we do not think we will have enough people to set up a third one near Charlemont. I wrote to M. Roze to have his opinion; however, mine, which was to set up the camp near Dublin has been approved, and if it is true that the descent is to be done between Dublin and Drogheda, and that the army of the King is in good enough shape to march against the enemy, my feeling is to attack them; but if the army of His Britannic Majesty is not yet formed, as it seems very likely, it will be necessary to stay near Dublin as long as possible, and when it will no longer be possible, we will ransack the whole area and withdraw to Athlone with the few troops that will be there; those which will have dispersed and which will not have been able to reach the Dublin camp will be able to go to Athlone.

If you would like to consider the position of that place, Sir, you will see that it is situated on a river which flows through several lakes and forms some kind of an arc which encloses the province of Connaught, which is the one with the fewest Protestants in the whole kingdom. I have therefore proposed that we set stores in Athlone, Limerick, and Galway, three towns in this province, that we set up a garrison in Sligo and that we take a small passage which is 6 miles from it; Mylord Tirconnel assures me that it is the only passage through which we can enter the province of Connaught; this way, Sir, we could maintain our position for some time and wait for the help that his Majesty could send us. As soon as M. Roze is here I will communicate this plan to him, and we will discuss whether there is something better to do; we will examine whether we are strong enough to keep the province of Munster, the towns of Waterford and Kinsale, could be of great help to us for anything that would come from France. For Galway has no harbour, it is only an anchor point and the high seas are so strong that when the west wind blows, the ships in winter could be in danger. The King nevertheless pushes greatly for Sr. Duquesne, who arrived here 2 days ago, to go to the harbour of Innishboffin, which is on the same west coast, but Duquesne has difficulties in doing so, nobody here knows that harbour.

I do not know Sir, if the enemy is not thinking in alighting near Carrickfergus, the place is fairly clean for that and quite close to the Isle of Man. Belfast and all around Carrickfergus, is a bountiful area and the best in all Ireland; it has not been ransacked, and there are plenty of Protestants, who are protected by Maxfield, a Scotsman, the governor of C'Fergus and a good officer. This province, which is that of Ulster, is full of the best soldiers in the whole kingdom who despise greatly those of Munster. They are quite annoyed that Munster and the other provinces were chosen in preference to them for the distribution of arms and the regiments that have been kept; we will leave in that province nearly all the regiments which are from there because they would not serve if they saw that they were all withdrawn and that their province and their possessions were abandoned to the enemy. But, Sir, not even a quarter will be armed because the King of England has only 3,000 muskets beyond the 17,000 that were sent from France; among those the last 7,000 are not worth much, as you will have seen from the letters sent by M. Roze and M. de Fumeron; and what good muskets we had, have been for the most part lost or damaged through the negligence of the soldiers, and even more so through that of their officers, and unfortunately there are here very few gun makers, at least they are Protestants; thus most of the time they damage the arms more than they repair them. In spite of all that, we issued a proclamation giving permission to all colonels to reform all the regiments that had been broken.

But, Sir, as some things are depending only on the will of the King and of his ministers, and which are most necessary, we are not forcing recruitment. there are only 30 horses bought for the guard; they are only 3 years old and have never been ridden; they do not know bit or bridle; no further artillery horses have been bought apart from the 50 that we have had for some time. I have asked M. de Boisseleau to visit the Dublin arsenal and to have assembled the parts that he would consider to be good; he only found six and no matter how hard he tries, he will have great difficulty in doing all that will be necessary. No garrison has twenty shots to fire; and at the time of writing, I have not been able to obtain that an account of the troops position could be brought to the King, with a map to establish an overall plan of the places where a garrison should be left and where to abandon the position, the places where encampment will be set, how big they will be, and the officers that will be in charge.

It is very upsetting indeed that we should have so many difficulties in making decisions here, and that it can be executed so badly once it has finally been taken. We thought it advisable to dispatch 200 barrels of powder to Athlone, with fuses and bullets. I learnt, Sir, that all this only had a fifty-men escort, and that we were going to pass approx. ten miles from a castle where there were more than 200 hundred armed rebels. I immediately informed the King who told me that he would give orders. A Mylord who had come across this convoy some twenty miles from here, with only a fifty-men escort, came to warn me about it; I contacted the King again, who told me that it could not be so, and that there were hundred and fifty cavalry men to escort the powder, but they have not arrived yet. God willing that they should arrive in time.

I shall have this letter ready, and I will add another one to it when the King of England is ready to send to France. I am yours, &c.

D'Avaux

Appendix C

Irish Record Commissioner Reports

Concerning correspondence between the residents of Bandon and the compensation claim against the estate of Justin MacCarthy.

Correspondence between the provost etc. of Bandon and the Lords of the Treasury concerning the lands forfeited by Maj. Gen. McCarty in Muskerry.
(Treasury Papers Vol XXXIII, Public Record Office London)
Dublin Castle, 6th May, 1695.

Our very good Lords,

We have received (with your lordship's letter of 22 February last), the Petition of the town of Bandon to your lordship concerning a grant of certain lands late belonging to Maj. Gen. McCarty, for the repayment of 1500l, and interest to them, and likewise their petition to the late Lord Lieutenant and council of this kingdom, whereby they pray the same relief and urge their being deficient in what was set out to them, by the Acts of Parliament and Explanation after the Rebellion in the year 1641, as a further notice for his majesty's grace and favour; we cannot but upon this (as we have heretofore on the like occasion) observe to your Lordships that we conceive the only fund out of which satisfaction for such deficiencies ought to arise are the forfeited lands, which by the Acts of Settlement and Explanation are vested in his majesty to that end, and not any lands which have since that time come to the crown by any later forfeitures. As to the matter in their Petition to your Lordships, we find they were early in their appearance for his majesty's service and have suffered thereby, but how far his majesty will think himself obliged to make good the loss occasioned by the calamities of the late war, and how much that will lessen his revenue here (which is already insufficient for the necessary change of the government), and subject him to many other solicitations on the like account, we must submit to his majesty's wisdom. We have only further to observe to your

Lordships of certain lands to be made to the earl of Romney, lately transmitted by your Lordships to us.

We are, our very good Lords, your Lordships, most humble servants,
Cyrill Wich J. Buncombe

We have considered the papers you sent us relating to the Provost, Burgesses and Inhabitants of Bandon and are fully satisfied their case is deplorable and the contents of their petition true, except that part which suggests that the lands in their Petition mentioned were settled on Maj. Gen. Justin McCarty, whereas the lands of Cloghmacon and Kilbarry, in the petition mentioned, were not so settled, but descended to the Earl of Clancarthy, and are by his attainder forfeited to his Majesty, and one of them, viz Kilbarry, is enjoyed by the Countess Dowager of Clancarthy as part of her dower. So that we humbly conceive that if his Majesty be graciously pleased to gratify the Petitioners in their humble request, it may be more proper to do it entirely out of the forfeited estate of the said Justin McCarty than to do it partly out of his and partly out of the Earl's estate, and to the end his Majesty may be fully informed to choose, as in his princely wisdom he shall think fit, we have hereunto annexed a perfect list of the forfeited estate of the said Justin McCarty and the rates we have set it at upon the cost.

A List of the forfeited estates of Justin McCarty, Muskerry bar., Co. Corke.

Tenants	Denominations		Acres	Rent for yr. 1695
James Dixon,	Clashynafrin	½ pld	166.32	16li
Provost of	Knockanmore	)2 plds	527.3.8	85li
Bandon	Maghery	)		
	Clashenure	1 pld	267.1.24	
	Curryclogh, West			5li
	Castlehinchy		187	)
	Mullaghroe	)2 plds	205.1.24	)
	Lackaree	)		)
	Kilnesky	)½ pld	150.3.8	) 152 li
	Ballynemornagh	)		)
	Currybeg	)2 plds	518.0.32	)
	Currymore with two mills	)		)

Tenants	Denominations		Acres	Rent for yr. 1695
John Doe	Barnegore	½ pld	92	15li old lease
Ja. Dallycourt	Garryhisty	)2 pl	2gn.518	77li old lease
	Farranavara	)		
	Cloughda	)1 pl	258	23li 10s
	Ardrath, with a mill	)		
	Currybeagh	)2 plds	366.3.8	)66li old lease
	Powlerick	)	378	)
Do. Baldwin	Curryclough, East	-	-	24li old lease
Jn° Buyly	Cowleduff E and W	1 pl	472	15li

Dated 6 April 1695. Richard Cox, Edward Corcag, Thomas May.

To their excellencies, the Lords Justices in Gen. Gov. of Ireland.

May it please your excellencies.

In obedience to your Excellencies order of reference to me directed, dated 1 April 1695, related to the Petition of the Provost etc., of the Corporation of Bandon Bridge, referred to the Right Honourable the Lords Commissioner of the Treasury, praying, a grant of certain lands belonging to Major General Macarty, in the barony of Muskerry, Co. Cork, to the value of 230li per annum, and the Lords of the Treasuries letter thereupon to your Excellency. I have examined the matter thereby to me referred, and have also perused a report made by a Committee of the Privy Council of the Kingdom, as a reference to them from the Council Board concerning the said matters: by all which it appears that their case, as to their merits and sufferings, are by them truly set forth in their petition, 12 Nov 1692, and for better information concerning the said lands, I sent the names of the Commissioners of inspection into forfeitures of this kingdom, who have returned me a paper, under their hands, with a schedule of the names of said Major General Macartys lands and the yearly value of them.

It appears by the report of the Commissioners of forfeitures that part of the estates mentioned to be settled by the Earl of Clancarty as Justin Macarty, was not so settled and by the report of the committee of the council it also appears that there was the sum of 1000li only received by Major General Justin Macarty, the rest of the 1500li was received by others, one of which, that is the Baron of Upper Ossory, has forfeited his estate, and has a petition now depending before your excellency.

If in case the Baron of Upper Ossory be restored to his estate by his Majesty's grace, he ought, at least, to make good out of it the sum which the petitioners can prove to have been received by him, rather than that the estate of Major General Macarty should be charged therewith in the King's hands.

But the Petitioners allege that the said Baron of Upper Ossory received no more than about 60li of said money, and that the rest of the persons who received the same are insolvent, so that they rely wholly on his Majesty's goodness to relieve them out of the estate of Major General Macarty.

If the petitioners can get the residue of this debt from the other persons who received same, which does not appear very probable, then I conceive it fit and reasonable that said General Macarty's estate should be charged only with the 1000li by him received and such interest as has become due from the same with fitting abatements for the calamitous times, to which I conceive they are well entitled, though they allege that they paid the interest all along the late times and would have his Majesty make them allowance thereof.

But if it be his Majesty's pleasure to consider the petitioners as objects of grace and favour for their services, as well as of his compassion for their sufferings, he may do so by directing his royal letters to your Excellency for granting the estate of said Major General Macarty in the schedule annexed, into the petitioners and their successors (in trust and for the discharge of said debt) until said debt and all lawful interest may be satisfied, with directions that the petitioners shall account for the real profits by them received, and that they shall let the same for the best rents that can be had, and that the Petitioners may be from time to time called to an account in the court of Exchequer touching the receipts and payments, and my humble opinion is that it is a much better method for his Majesty to use his royal bounty with relation to the Petitioner's sufferings and service in his Majesty's own cause than to grant anything with relation to the deficiency pretended by the petitioner's on account of the Rebellion of 1641.

All is humbly submitted to your excellency's most prudent consideration.
12 April 1695 R.Levinge

To his Excellency the Lord Lieutenant and Council of Ireland. The humble petition of the Provost, Burgesses and Inhabitants of the town of Bandon.

Humbly Sheweth. That your Petitioners being all English Protestants, were very early and vigorous in declaring for his Majesty in opposing the Popish and arbitrary designs of the late Earl of Tyrconnel, and to that end did in February 1688, disarm one troop and two companies of Irish, which were then garrisoned in this town.

That thereupon Major General Macarthy came and besieged you Petitioners with an army, and having disarmed the Protestants of Cork and taken Castlemartyr, so that your Petitioners could have no relief of ammunition or victuals, he forced your Petitioners to a capitulation, and to pay 1500li for their ransom and pardon. That your Petitioners being mostly poor tradesmen were forced to borrow the said sum, and to be bound for one another and are now threatened to be sued for same. That your Petitioners having never suffered any Papist to lie among them, were so obnoxious to the Irish, that they omitted no opportunity to oppress your Petitioners, and at last carried them all prisoners to the mountains of Kerry, where many perished, and in their absence plundered their homes, so that your Petitioners are utterly ruined and undone, and if sued for the said debt must inevitably perish in prison and their families starve.

And your Petitioners further show to your Excellencies and Lordships that for their fidelity and valour against the Irish in 1641, there was provision made for the said town by the Acts of Settlement and Explanation, and the land of Cloghmanow, Currybehagh, Kilbarry, Polerick, West Coolduff, and East part of Currielogh, barony of Muskerry, to the value of 230li per annum, were let to your Petitioners in fee simple, but afterward Donagh, first Earl of Clancarty, being restored to his estate, recovered same lands for your Petitioners, who have hitherto had no reprisals for the same, according to the intent of said act of Parliament, only to the value of about 80li yearly.

That the said lands in Muskerry were afterwards, by the said Earl of Clancarty, settled on the said Major General Macarthy, and were by his rebellion forfeited to their Majesties.

May it therefore please your Excellencies and Lordships to recommend your Petitioners to their Majesties for grants of the said lands or such other relief as their Majesties in their princely wisdom shall think fit. And your Petitioners shall ever pray.

John Sullivan agent.

May it please your Excellencies. Pursuant to your Excellencies order of the 4th inst. Appointing a Committee to examine the Petition of the Provost, Burgesses and Inhabitants of the Town of Bandon and report to this board.

We have enquired into the truth of the allegations set forth in said Petition and do find by the oath of John Sullivan, gent. Made before us, that the sum of 1000li by said Burgesses etc. borrowed and paid to Major General Macarthy towards their ransom, and it further appears also, by the oath of Capt. Will Fortescue and May Herbert Love, made before us, that besides the said 1000li, there was at the same time paid to Capt. O'Neale and his troop, to Lt. Mesender and to the Lord Ossory and his company, the sum of 350li, as also 50li towards the taking out their pardon, and do verily believe that not only another 50li making up the 100li by the articles for their pardon was paid, but also the other sum, making up the 1500li mentioned in the petition, upon all which we are of the opinion that the Petitioners have been such eminent sufferers, upon the account of their early appearing for their Majesties as well deserves your Excellencies' favourable recommendation to their Majesties as in the petition is desired.

Council Chambers, Dublin 12 Nov 1692, Drogheda, Richard Cox

Council Court Dublin Dec 5th 1692

Our very good Lords,

The enclosed petition of the Provost, Burgesses and Inhabitants of the town of Bandon being received at this Board, praying, that in considering of their great services and sufferings, we would be pleased to recommend the same to their Majesties for a grant of the land there mentioned, and whereas we thought fir to refer the same to a Commission of this Board, to examine the allegations therein set forth and make report thereof, together with their opinion, what might be fit to be done therein, upon which reference they returned the enclosed report, both which we have thought fit to transfer to your Lordships desiring your Lordships favourable recommendations thereof to their Majesties in their behalf, from which assistance they are not out of hopes but to receive a satisfactory demonstration of their Majesties favour to them therein.

We are, our very good Lords.

Sydney, Porter C, Dublin, Meath, Anth. Meath, E. Villiers, Rob. Smythe, Drogheda, Blesinton, Will. Kildare, Nich. Coote, Wm Wolseley, Ry, Reynell, Rich. Cox.

Endorsed:
To the Rt Hon the Lords of the Majesties Treasury at Whitehall

(Note) the Commissioners of forfeitures are desired to inspect these papers, and to certify their knowledge of the matter therein mentioned, or what else they can say in his Majesty's behalf, relating thereto
5 April 1695 R. Levinge

To the Rt. Hon. The Lords Commissioners of their Majesties Treasury. The humble Petition of the Inhabitants of the Corporation of Bandon Bridge in Ireland.

Sheweth. That having petitioned his Excellency the Lord Lieutenant and Council of Ireland setting forth the miserable estate of the said Corporation for seizing upon the Irish garrison there in Feb 1688, and declaring for their Majesty. Their Lordships appointed a commission to examine your petitioners grievances, who reported how they found the same; Whereupon their Lordships were pleased to signify their desires by letter to your Lordship that your Petitioners distressed condition might be recommended to her Majesty.

Your Petitioners humbly pray that your Lordship will be pleased to take the said letter, report and petition now before you into consideration and to intercede with her majesty that your petitioners may be relieved for their losses, found by the said commission to be 1500li and also 900li interest money, due on their bond in Feb next out of the forfeited estates of Major General Macarthy and your Petitioners will pray.

Our very good Lords,

Having some time since received from the late Lord Lieutenant and Council of Ireland a petition of the Provost of Bandon, praying a grant of certain lands late belonging to Major General Mackarty in the Barony of Muskerry, to the value of 230li per annum. We here inclosed transmit to your Lordship the said petition and other papers relating thereunto, and desire you will consider the same, and let us have your opinion, what you think fit to be done therein.

We remain, our very good Lords, your Lordships most humble servants, Ste Fox, Cha. Montague, Will. Trumbull.

Whitehall, Treasury Chambers 22 Feb 1694/5
(Lords Justices of Ireland, Town of Bandon)
By the Lords Justices and general Government of Ireland
Capell, Cyrill, Wick, W, Buncombe.

Whereas the annexed petition of the Provost etc. of Bandon, praying a grant of certain lands late belonging to Major General Mackarty, barony of Muskerry, value 238li per annum, and other papers, relating thereunto, have been transmitted unto us from the Lords commissioners of His Majesty's Treasury, we think fit to refer same to you to report unto us the true state of the matter alleged by said Lord Provost, etc, of Bandon, with your opinion what may fitly be done.

Given to H.M. Castle of Dublin 1 April 1695 H.May

To Sir Richard Levinge H.M. Solicitor General

Appendix D

Mountcashel's Will

Translated from French. English version in *Journal of the Cork Historical and Archaeological Society*, Oct-Dec 1907 and originally appearing in *La France Litteraire*, Paris 1905-07.

I Justin MacCarthy, Lord Viscount Mountcashel, Baron of Castle Inchy and Blarney, Duke of Clancarthy, Lieutenant-General in the army of H.M. the King of France and Navarre, and Commander of the Regiments of the Irish Brigade, being by the grace of Go, sound in body and mind, desiring to employ what remains of my life to prepare myself for death, have resolved to make my Will; and for this purpose after having in retirement besought God for the necessary light to perform this last act of my life as I would have done for the others, I have made and written my Will as follows, without persuasion or suggestion from anyone, and of my own firm and free will. Firstly, I recommend my soul to God, beseeching Him to have mercy on me, and enter not into judgement with me, to forgive my transgressions, and grant me the grace to employ what remains of my life in expiating them by penitence, and die the death of the just, that I may love Him for ever in Heaven, which I shall beg of Him every day of my life, and is what I hope from His mercy, through the ministry of the Blood of Jesus Christ, my saviour; through the intercession of the most Blessed Virgin and of all the Saints in Paradise; and by the virtue of the Holy Souls that are in the bosom of the Catholic, Apostolic and Roman Church, in whose bosom I wish to die, as God has given me the grace to have been born and have lived in it.

I desire that my body may be buried in Ireland, if it is possible for my dear and well-beloved wife, Arabella Wentford-Strafford, to have it taken over to my family burial-ground there. I also ask her to have prayers offered up for the repose of my soul. Having no longer any wealth, since my property was confiscated by the English, I can only now dispose of my name and the titles which I hold from His Majesty King James II. Wishing to perpetuate this name and these titles, and it not having been God's will to grant me any children, I give and bequeath them, for him and all his descendants, the issue of lawful marriage, to my well-beloved cousin, Florence Callaghan MacCarthy, son of Cormac MacCarthy, son of Donal MacCarthy of Carrignavar. The said Florence MacCarthy I adopt as my son and institute him after my death heir of all my rights and my titles of Duke of Clancarthy, Lord Viscount Mountcashel, Baron of Castle Inchy, Baron of Blarney, and of all the others that may afterwards come to him as my heir and successor. I counsel Florence to bear these titles with honour, and to endeavour by all means to reconquer what the English have taken from our family; and to devote himself to the service of the Stuarts and of His Majesty the King of France and Navarre, his legitimate Sovereigns.

I therefore request all my relatives to consider my well-beloved and adopted son, Florence, as my legitimate heir, and to recognise him as such. I recommend also to my well-beloved wife these last wishes, enjoying her to communicate them as soon as possible after my death to my well-beloved cousin, so that he may benefit by them; and to bring it to the knowledge of all the members of my family so that they may obey them.

I have made the present Will, signed by my hand this day, May 8th, 1693.

End Notes

Chapter I: The Early Years

1 The history of the MacCarthys is derived from a number of sources. The best single summaries are found in: J.C.O'Callaghan, *History of the Irish Brigades in the Service of France from the Revolution in Great Britain and Ireland Under James II, to the Revolution in France under Louis XVI*, (London 1886), p.9;also see, Journal of the Cork Historical and Archaeological Society Vol XIII No.76, *Justin MacCarthy, Lord Mountcashel*, (Cork Oct-Dec 1907), pp.157-62; Dr Sean Pettit, *Blarney Castle, The Story of a Legend*, (Cork 1989), pp.9-12, Edward Maclysaght, *Irish Families, Their Names, Arms and Origins*, (Dublin 1985, 4th edn), pp.54-5.

2 Ed. C.H.Firth, *The Memoirs of Edmund Ludlow, Lieutenant General of the Horse in the Army of the Commonwealth of England 1625-1672*, Vol. I, pp. 320-21, 525.

3 The background to the war in Ireland in the 1640s, and its link to events on the mainland is superbly summarised in: Ed. J.Kenyon and J.Ohlmeyer, *The Civil Wars, A Military History of England, Scotland, and Ireland 1638-1660*, (Oxford University Press, 1998); Also see: P.Lenihan, *Confederate Catholics at War, 1641-49*, (Cork University Press, 2001); P.Beresford Ellis, *Hell or Connaught!, The Cromwellian Colonisation of Ireland 1652-1660*, (Belfast, 1975); *Nunziatra in Irlanda* (Firenze, 1844), p.350.

4 Ed. C.H.Firth, *The Memoirs of Edmund Ludlow, Lieutenant General of the Horse in the Army of the Commonwealth of England 1625-1672*, Vol. I, p.341.

5 Mary Hickson, *Ireland in the Seventeenth Century*, Vol. II pp.192-204, 235, (London, 1884); Note on Ormond's involvement is in Ed. Doubleday and De Walden, *The Complete Peerage or a History of the House of Lords and all its Members from the earliest times*, (London, 1936), Vol. III p.215.

6 Ed. C.H.Firth, *The Memoirs of Edmund Ludlow*, Vol. I, p.341.

7 *Calendar of Clarendon State Papers Vol. III*, (Oxford, 1869) p.210.

8 C.Smith, *Ancient and Present State of County and City of Cork*, (1749), Vol. II, p.172; Ed. Birch, *A Collection of the State Papers of John Thurloe esq (secretary first to the Council of State, and afterwards to the two Protectors, Oliver and Richard Cromwell)*, (London, 1742) pp. 94, 406, 693.

9 M. O'Connor, *Military History of the Irish Nation, Comprising A Memoir of the Irish Brigade in the Service of France*, (Dublin, 1845), pp.69-75.

10 O'Connor, *Military History*, pp. 76-79.

11 T.Carte, *Life of James, Duke of Ormond*, Vol. II, p.161; P.W. Sergeant; *Little Jennings and Fighting Dick Talbot, A Life of the Duke and Duchess of Tyrconnel*; (London, 1913), pp.84-6; Sir Charles Petrie, *The Great Tyrconnel, A Chapter in Anglo-Irish Relations*, (Dublin, 1972), pp.83-4.

12 O'Connor, pp. 80-86.

13 J.Macpherson, *Original Papers, Vol. I*, (London, 1775), p.32. For excellent modern interpretation of Anglo-Dutch naval wars and battle see Hainsworth & Churches, *The Anglo-Dutch Naval Wars 1652*-1674, (1998), pp 103-24; Carte, *The Life of James, Duke of Ormond Vol. V*, p.181; *Calendar State Papers Domestic 1664-5*, (London, 1863), p.407.

14 Carte, *The Life of James, Duke of Ormond Vol. V*, (Oxford, 1851), p.182.

15 *Calendar State Papers Domestic 1673-75*, p.357, Ed. Doubleday and De Walden, *The Complete Peerage or a History of the House of Lords and all its Members from the earliest times*, (London, 1936), Vol. III pp.214-16. *Calendar State Papers Ireland 1667*, (London, 1908), pp.388-9; Historical Manuscripts Commission, *Calendar of the Manuscripts of the Marquess of Ormonde K.P. Preserved at Kilkenny Castle, New Series Vol. III*, pp.300-01, (Dublin 1906).

Chapter II: French Service 1673–1678

1 M. O'Connor, *Military History of the Irish Nation, Comprising a Memoir of the Irish Brigade in the Service of France*, (Dublin 1845), pp.87-8; D.C.Boulger, *The Battle of the Boyne Together with an Account based on French and other Unpublished Records of the War in Ireland (1688-1691) and of the Formation of the Irish Brigade in the Service of France*, (London 1911), pp.67-8; J.C.O'Callaghan, *History of the Irish Brigades in the Service of France from the Revolution in Great Britain and Ireland under James II, to the Revolution in France under Louis XVI*, (London 1886), p.33; Ed. C.Dalton, *English Army Lists and Commission Registers, 1661-1714*, Vol I 1661-1685, (London 1960), p.88.

2 Ed. J.Hogan, *Négociacions de M. le Comte d'Avaux en Irlande, 1689-90*, (Irish Manuscripts Commission, 1934) pp.692-4; J.A.Lynn, *The Wars of Louis XIV 1667-1714*, (Pearson 1999), pp.105-6, 113-35, 140-4; O.Conor pp.87-95; Boulger, pp.67-9; O'Callaghan, pp.33-4.

3 Ed. C.Dalton, *English Army Lists and Commission Register 1661-1714*, (London 1960), p.207.

4 *Calendar State Papers Domestic 1676-7*, (London 1909), p.410.

5 *Calendar State Papers Domestic 1676-7*, (London 1909), pp.411-12; Boulger, p.69.

6 Lynn, pp.144-59.

7 *Historical Manuscripts Commission : Calendar of the MSS of the Marquis of Ormond*, (London 1906), Vol IV, p.21.

8 *Calendar State Papers Domestic 1677-8*, (London 1911), p.504.

Chapter III: A Return to England 1678–1685

1 S.B.Baxter, *William III*, (London 1966), pp.129-30, 148-50; Also see for an excellent treatment of the subject: Maureen Waller, *Ungrateful Daughters, The Stuart Princesses Who Stole Their Father's Crown*, pp.27, 64, 93-9.
2 *Calendar State Papers Domestic*, 1677-78, p.25.
3 *Complete Peerage*, Vol III, p.216.
4 For the best single treatment of the events see: John Kenyon, *The Popish Plot*, (London 1972).
5 *Calendar State Papers Domestic 1678*, p.444; Ed. C.Dalton, *English Army Lists and Commission Registers 1661-1714*, (London 1960), p.207;Ed. C.Dalton, *Irish Army Lists of King Charles II 1661-1685*, p.119; Kenyon, *The Popish Plot*, p.117.
6 *Calendar State Papers Domestic 1678*, p.494, 511-12, 518, 594; *HMC Ormond*Vol IV p.469.
7 Kenyon, *The Popish Plot*, p.117.
8 Historical Manuscripts Commission, *Calendar of the Manuscripts of the Marquess of Ormonde*, New Series Vol IV, (Dublin 1906), p.261. Also see Earl of Orrery's correspondence with Ormonde on subject, Vol IV pp.231-6.
9 *Calendar State Papers Domestic 1679-80*, pp.9,30; Bagwell, *Ireland Under the Stuarts and During the Interregnum*, Vol III, (London 1916) p.131; HMC Ormond IV, 230, 236, 238040, 245-6, 261, Vol V, p.104.
10 Dupuy & Dupuy, *The Collins Encyclopaedia of Military History*, (1993), p.621.
11 *Calendar State Papers Domestic 1682*, p.198.
12 *Calendar State Papers Domestic 1682*, pp.325-6, 345-7, 385-6; *Calendar State Papers Domestic 1683*; pp.13, 62-4, 98, 116.
13 HMC, *Calendar of the Manuscripts of the Marquess of Ormonde*, New Series Vol VI, (Dublin 1906), p.498.
14 HMC, *Calendar of the Manuscripts of the Marquess of Ormonde*, New Series Vol. VI, (Dublin 1906), pp.510-11, 516; *Complete Peerage*, Vol III, p.216.
15 Calendar State Papers Domestic, 1684-5, p.273; C.Smith, *Ancient and Present State of County and City of Cork*, (1749), Vol II, p.175.

Chapter IV: Ireland and the King 1685–1688

1 *Complete Peerage*, Vol. 10, p.310.
2 *Calendar State Papers Domestic* 1684-85, p.287.
3 G.Burnet, *History of His Own Time*, Vol. II, (Oxford 1900), pp.449-51; Ed. H.C.Foxcroft, *A Supplement to Burnet's History*, (Oxford 1902), pp.134-5.
4 Kenyon, *the Popish Plot*, pp.38,305.
5 Mainly Sir Charles Petrie, *The Great Tyrconnel: A Chapter in Anglo-Irish Relations*, (Dublin 1972), pp.35, 56, 81, 96-7, 103, 120. For Tyrconnell also see: P.W. Sergeant, *Little Jennings and Fighting Dick Talbot, A Life of the Duke and Duchess of Tyrconnel*; (London 1913).

6 John Childs, *The Army, James II and the Glorious* Revolution, (Manchester University Press 1980), pp.56-62.
7 *Calendar of the Manuscripts of the Marquess of Ormonde – Preserved at Kilkenny Castle,* Vol. VII, (1920) pp.454-5.
8 Richard Bagwell, *Ireland Under the Stuarts and During the Interregnum*, Vol. III 1660-1690, pp.149-50.
9 *Ormond* Vol. VII pp.360-3.
10 Bagwell p.149, *Ormond* VIII p.344.
11 *Ormond* Vol. VII p.358.
12 *Calendar State Papers Domestic* 1686-7 nos. 95 and 576.
13 *Ormond* Vol. VII p.425.
14 Ed. S.W.Singer, *The Correspondence of Henry Hyde, Earl of Clarendon and Laurence, Earl of Rochester*, Vol. I, pp.215, 219, 227, 229, 247
15 Clarendon I pp.241, 247, 248
16 Ibid., pp.248-50
17 Ibid., I p.255
18 Ibid., p.343
19 Ibid., p.360
20 Ibid., p.400
21 Ibid., pp.479, 491-2, 499-500
22 Ibid p.516-18
23 Ibid. p.537-40
24 Ibid. p.584-6, II 1
25 *Clarendon*, Vol II, pp.14-15
26 Ibid., II 32,36
27 Ibid., II 92-4, 98-9, 103-4, 116
28 Ibid., II 120-21, 148-9
29 Childs pp.65-8, 70-8, *Clarendon* I p.268, *Ormond* II p.378-84, Ed. C.Dalton, *English Army Lists and Commission Register 1661-1714*, (London 1960) p.209, *Calendar State Papers Domestic*, July 1686.
30 For main sources on *Glorious Revolution of 1688*, see: Beddard R., *The Revolutions of 1688 – The Andrew Browning Lectures*, (London 1966); Guy & Smith, *1688, Glorious Revolution, The Fall and Rise of the British Army 1660-1704* (National Army Museum 1988); Jones J.R.; *The Revolution of 1688 in England,* (Weidenfield & Nicholson 1972).

Chapter V: Munster

1 J.G.Simms, *Jacobite Ireland*, 1685-91, (London 1969), pp.48-51; *Ormond* Vol VIII, p.14
2 Simms p.51.
3 D'Avaux p.50.

4 J.S.Clarke, *The Life of James II*, Vol. II, p.322.
5 Simms p.53.
6 *Ormond* Vol. VIII, p.359.
7 *Ormond* Vol. VIII, p.354.
8 *Clarendon* Vol. I, p.584.
9 George Bennet, *The History of Bandon*, (Cork 1862), pp.191, 194-204, Bennet's work is based on local history of the Bandon Insurrection and contains some unique information with regard to the buildup to rebellion in the town. Not all of this can be taken at face value, however. Irish Record Commission Reports p.409 Plate VII, Map of Bandon from the seventeenth century showing town walls and extent of building work and gates; John T. Collins, *The O'Crowleys of Coill t-Sealbhaigh, appearing in The Cork Historical and Archeological Journal Vol LVIII*, Jan-Jun 1953, p.7; Ed. Rowland Davies, *Journal of the Very Reverend Rowland Davies, Dean of Ross, March 8th 1689-Sept 29th* 1690, (Camden Society 1857) p.6; D.J.O'Donoghue, *Droichead Na Banndan, A History of Bandon*, (Cork 1970), p.5.
10 Bagwell Volume III, p.202; Bennet, p.205.
11 Smith, p.174-5; O'Callaghan p.10
12 George Bennet, *The History of Bandon*, (Cork 1862) pp.206-13; For Bandon and surrounding Munster operations of the time also see; Bagwell pp.201-6, O'Callaghan pp.10-11, Smith II pp.192-3, d'Avaux p.138.
13 See note Smith Vol. II p.192
14 Simms 58-61
15 *Ormond* VIII, pp.360-1
16 Simms 59-60
17 F.C.Turner, *James II*, p.61
18 D'Avaux, p.1-6
19 Bagwell 206, Ed. J.T.Gilbert, *A Jacobite Narrative of the War in Ireland, 1688-1691*, (Irish University Press, 1971), pp.46-7; Simms pp.59, 62-3; MacPherson, *Original Papers*, pp.175-6.
20 O'Callaghan p.11.
21 MacPherson pp.175-7, Bagwell p.207.
22 D'Avaux p.23-4.
23 Bennet pp.214-15, Simms p.63, MacPherson p.178, Bagwell pp.207-8, *Calendar State Papers Domestic* 1689-90, p.95, William King, *The State of the Protestants of Ireland..*, (London 1693), pp.130-1, O'Donoghue, *A History of Bandon*, p.17. Although the walls were it appeared partially destroyed, the job was not completed. At the Cork Assizes in December 1690 it was ordered 'that the inhabitants within four miles of Bandon contribute their labour towards the erecting and securing of the walls of the said town, thrown down by the papists'. This was never completed, however. Boisseleau is also accused of sending £30,000 of Protestant goods to France in notes.

24 MacPherson pp.177-8, Bagwell pp.208-9
25 *Archives Nationales, Dépôt de La Guerre* A1 Vol. 894 no 15, Historical Manuscripts Commission, *Analecta Hibernica*, Vol XXI, p.27.
26 *La Guerre* A1 Vol.895
27 *Analecta Hibernica*, Vol XXI, p.36.
28 *Ormond* Vol VIII, p.362.
29 Bagwell p.208; D'Avaux, pp.52-8, 85-91
30 Simms p.64-5; D'Avaux pp.23, 36, 54, 57, 60-1, 65-70.
31 D'Avaux pp.78; 182, MacPherson p.180; *Jacobite Narrative* p.53; *Analecta Hibernica*, Vol XXI p.121.
32 Simms pp.71-2.
33 All Stevens's comments regarding the Parliament: Ed. Rev Robert H. Murray, *The Journal of John Stevens Containing a Brief Account of the War in Ireland 1689-1691*, (Oxford 1912), pp.68-70 - an excellent reference for all aspects of the war.
34 *Ormond* Vol.II p.398, Simms p.74.
35 Bagwell 236-7.
36 Complete Peerage Vol. X 309-10, Vol III 216-17.
37 MacPherson Vol.I p.176, 190; D'Avaux p.142; *La Guerre* Vol 892 de Rosen to Louvois 20 May 1689.
38 Stevens, pp.69-70.
39 For more detail on Irish parliament, its deliberations and effectiveness see Simms 74-94, Bagwell 224-36; For d'Avaux's views see pp.226, 341-2, 255, 111, 190-2, 89-90.
40 C.F.M. Rousset, *Histoire de Louvois*, Vol.IV, p.198.
41 D'Avaux p.590.
42 D'Avaux p.636.
43 *La Guerre* 892 Mountcashel to Louvois 13 June 1689
44 *La Guerre* 893 Mountcashel to Louvois 16 June 1689; also see MacPherson 319-21.
45 *La Guerre* 896 D'Avaux pp.298-9, 253-4, 250, 50
46 *La Guerre* 892 Mountcashel to Louvois 13 June 1689.

Chapter VI: Enniskillen

1 Mainly, J.G.Simms, *Jacobite Ireland 1685-91*, (London 1969), pp.95-112. Also see Witherow, *Two Diaries of Derry in 1689*, (Londonderry 1888).
2 Andrew Hamilton, *The Actions of the Enniskillen Men: from their first taking up of arms in 1688 ....*, (London 1690, Belfast 1813), pp.3-6; William MacCarmick (Ed. W.T.Latimer), *A Farther Impartial Account of the Actions of the Inniskilling Men*, (1691, Belfast 1896) pp.4-6.
3 Hamilton pp.7-19; MacCarmick pp.7-23.
4 Hamilton pp.20-6; MacCarmick pp.23-30.
5 Hamilton pp.27-49; MacCarmick pp.31-41.

6 *Dictionary of National Biography*, pp. 323-4; Ed. Charles Dalton, *English Army Lists and Commission Registers 1661-1714 (2 vols)*, (London 1960), pp.32, 37, 141, 15, 25, 125, 132.
7 Hamilton pp.50; MacCarmick pp.42.

Chapter VII: Newtownbutler 1689

1 British Library, *Mémoires du Maréchal de Berwick, écrits par lui même ....*, pp 55-7.
2 John D'Alton, *King James' Irish Army List 1689*, (Dublin 1855), p. 10; *Dictionary of National Biography*, pp. 135-7; Henry Boylan, *A Dictionary of Irish Biography*, (New York, 1988), p.143; John Childs, *Nobles, Gentlemen and the Profession of Arms in Restoration Britain 1660-1688*, (Society for Army Historical Research, 1987), p.40; J.G.Simms, *Jacobite Ireland 1685-91*, (London 1969), p. 46.
3 Ed. J.Hogan, *Negociations de M. Le Comte d'Avaux en Irlande 1689*-90, (Dublin 1935) pp.376-7, 384-6.
4 Hamilton, *The Actions of the Enniskillen Men*, (London 1690, Belfast 1813) p. 63; William MacCarmick (Ed. W.T.Latimer), *A Farther Impartial Account of the Actions of the Inniskilling Men*, (1691, Belfast 1896) p. 44; Ed. J.T.Gilbert, *A Jacobite Narrative of the War in Ireland, 1688-1691*, (Irish University Press, 1971) p. 81; G.Story, *A True and Impartial History of the Wars in Ireland*, (London 1693),p 4; Ed. J.Hogan, *Negociations de M. Le Comte d'Avaux en Irlande 1689-90*, (Dublin, 1935) p. 384; Ed. G.Plunkett & E.Hogan, *Charles O'Kelly – The Jacobite War in Ireland (1688-1691)*, (Dublin 1894) p. 7 (notes); J.C.O'Callaghan, *History of the Irish Brigades in the Service of France*, (Glasgow 1870), pp. 12-13.
5 Gilbert pp. 222-3; John D'Alton, *King James' Irish Army List 1689*, (Dublin 1855); Historical Manuscripts Commission, *Diary of Mr.Colles, Ormonde*, n.s. vol. VIII p. 367.
6 Gilbert pp. 208-9; Ed. Revd Robert H. Murray, *The Journal of John Stevens, Containing a Brief Account of the War in Ireland 1689-1691*, (Oxford 1912) p. 207.
7 Gilbert pp. 213-14.
8 Gilbert pp. 238-9, 233-4; Murray p.129, D'Avaux pp.384-5; Diary of MrColles, *H.M.C. Ormonde*, n.s. vol. VIII p. 367.
9 Plunkett & Hogan pp. 7; O'Callaghan, *History of the Irish Brigades in the Service of France*, p. 13; J.Macpherson, *Original Papers ...*, (London 1775), p. 219.
10 J.G.Simms, *Jacobite Ireland 1685-91*, (London 1969) pp. 53,71.
11 John Childs, *The Nine Years' War and the British Army 1688-1697: The Operations in the Low Countries*, (Manchester 1991) pp. 73-6; Brent Nosworthy, *The Anatomy of Victory - Battle Tactics 1689-1763* (New York 1992) pp. 26-33; John A. Lynn, *Giant of the Grand Siécle: The French Army, 1610-1715*, (Cambridge 1997) pp. 453-7.
12 David Chandler, *The Art of Warfare in the Age of Marlborough*, (Staplehurst 1976) pp.75-6; Nosworthy, *The Anatomy of Victory - Battle Tactics 1689-1763*, pp.17, 39; Lynn, *Giant of the Grand Siécle: The French Army, 1610-1715*, pp. 458-63.

13 Lynn, *Giant of the Grand Siécle: The French Army, 1610-1715*, pp. 463-4.

14 Ed. W.A.Maguire, *Kings in Conflict, The Revolutionary Wars in Ireland and its Aftermath 1689-1750,* (Belfast, 1990) p. 62.

15 Andrew Hamilton, *The Actions of the Enniskillen Men : from their first taking up of arms in 1688 ....*, (London 1690) p. 45; William MacCarmick (Ed. W.T.Latimer), *A Farther Impartial Account of the Actions of the Inniskilling Men*, (1691, Belfast 1896) p. 41; Nosworthy, *The Anatomy of Victory- Battle Tactics 1689-1763*, p. 52.

16 Childs, *The Nine Years' War and the British Army 1688-1697: The Operations in the Low Countries*, pp. 73-4, 79-80; Nosworthy, *The Anatomy of Victory - Battle Tactics 1689-1763*, pp. 15-17; Lynn, *Giant of the Grand Siécle: The French Army, 1610-1715*, pp. 469-72, 476.

17 Hamilton, *The Actions of the Enniskillen Men : from their first taking up of arms in 1688 ....*, pp. 56-7; MacCarmick, *A Farther Impartial Account of the Actions of the Inniskilling Men*, p.43; Ed. C.S.King, *Henry's Upper Lough Erne in 1739*, (Dublin 1892), pp. 27-34.

18 Ed. Revd Robert H. Murray, *The Journal of John Stevens, Containing a Brief Account of the War in Ireland 1689-1691*, (Oxford 1912) pp. 63-5.

19 Piers Wauchope, *Patrick Sarsfield and the Williamite War*, (Dublin, 1992) pp. 52-3.

20 Gilbert, *A Jacobite Narrative of the War in Ireland, 1688-1691*, p. 37. Lynn, *Giant of the Grand Siécle: The French Army, 1610-1715*, pp. 480-4.

21 Hamilton, *The Actions of the Enniskillen Men: from their first taking up of arms in 1688 ... .*, pp.5,14,24-5,27,30,34. Hogan, *Negociations de M. Le Comte d'Avaux en Irlande 1689-90*, pp. 385-6.

22 For further reference to the fighting techniques of this period, see: Childs, *The Nine Years' War and the British Army 1688-1697: The Operations in the Low Countries*, p. 85; Chandler, *The Art of Warfare in the Age of Marlborough*, p. 50; Maguire, *Kings in Conflict, The Revolutionary Wars in Ireland and its Aftermath 1689-1750,* p. 64; Hamilton, *The Actions of the Enniskillen Men: from their first taking up of arms in 1688 ...* pp. 56-7; Hogan, *Negociations de M. Le Comte d'Avaux en Irlande 1689-90*, p. 384; Chandler, *The Art of Warfare in the Age of Marlborough*, pp. 177-80; Lynn, *Giant of the Grand Siécle: The French Army, 1610-1715*, p. 506-11; Hogan, *Negociations de M. Le Comte d'Avaux en Irlande 1689-90*, p. 386 ; Nosworthy, *The Anatomy of Victory - Battle Tactics 1689-1763*, pp. 100-13; Lynn, *Giant of the Grand Siécle: The French Army, 1610-1715*, pp. 532-7.

23 Gilbert p. 81.

24 Correspondence with V.Herbert, Crom Estate Nov 98.

25 D'Avaux p. 384.

26 D'Avaux p. 384; Gilbert p. 81; Hamilton pp. 48-9; MacCarmick p. 41; Ed. C.S.King, *Henry's Upper Lough Erne in 1739*, (Dublin 1892), pp. 27-34.

27 D'Avaux p. 384; Gilbert pp. 81-2.

28 Hamilton pp. 51-2; MacCarmick p. 41; O'Callaghan, *History of the Irish Brigades in the Service of France*, pp. 14-15.
29 Hamilton pp. 52-3; MacCarmick p. 42; D'Avaux p. 385.
30 Hamilton pp. 53-4; MacCarmick p. 42; D'Avaux p. 385.
31 Hamilton pp. 54-5, MacCarmick p. 42, Gilbert p. 82; D'Avaux p. 385.
32 Hamilton pp. 55-7; MacCarmick pp. 42-3; D'Avaux p. 386; Public Record Office, *London Gazette 2481*, 1689.
33 Hamilton, *The Actions of the Enniskillen Men : from their first taking up of arms in 1688....*, pp. 58-59; Childs, *The Nine Years' War and the British Army 1688-1697 : The Operations in the Low Countries*, p. 79.
34 Hamilton pp. 57-59; MacCarmick p. 43; D'Avaux p. 386; Gilbert p. 82; O'Callaghan, p. 18.
35 MacCarmick, p. 43; Gilbert, *A Jacobite Narrative of the War in Ireland, 1688-1691*, p. 82.
36 Hamilton pp. 59-63; MacCarmick p. 44; G.Story, *A True and Impartial History of the Wars in Ireland*, (London 1693), pp. 4-5; D'Avaux p. 386; Gilbert p. 82; T.Witherow, *Derry and Enniskillen in the Year 1689*, (Belfast 1885), pp. 268-9.
37 Hamilton pp. 51-2; MacCarmick p. 41; O'Callaghan, *History of the Irish Brigades in the Service of France*, pp. 14-15.
38 Revd J.Graham, *A History of the Siege of Londonderry and Defence of Enniskillen in 1688 and 1689*, (Dublin 1829); Ed. C.S.King, *Henry's Upper Lough Erne in 1739*, (Dublin 1892), p. 29.
39 D'Avaux p. 386; Gilbert p.82.
40 Hamilton pp. 62-70; MacCarmick pp. 44-7; Macpherson, *Original Papers, ...*, p. 220; D.C.Boulger, *The Battle of the Boyne Together with an Account Based on French Records of the War in Ireland (1688-1691) ...*, (London 1911), pp. 108-10.
41 J.G.Simms, *A Letter to Sarsfield (from the Duke of Berwick, July 31 1689)*, (Irish Sword Vol II No. 6, Summer 1995), p. 109; British Library, *Mémoires du Maréchal de Berwick, écrits par lui même ...*, p. 53.
42 Correspondence with V.Herbert, Crom Estate Nov 1998, Conversation with B.Chapman, B.Lyttle, Newtownbutler, July 98-March 99, B.Chapman, *Newtownbutler, The Story of a Local Community*, (Enniskillen, 1992), p. 14.
43 Hamilton, p. 53; MacCarmick, p. 42; Revd J.Graham, *A History of the Siege of Londonderry and the Defence of Enniskillen in 1688 and 1689*, (Dublin 1829), pp. 29-30.
44 Conversation with B.Chapman, Newtownbutler, March 1999; Bagwell, p. 254.
45 Hamilton, p. 57, MacCarmick, p.43, Conversation with B.Chapman, B.Lyttle, Newtownbutler, July 1998-March 1999, Chapman, *Newtownbutler, The Story of a Local Community*, p. 14.
46 Hamilton p. 59; MacCarmick p. 43; D'Avaux p. 385.
47 David Chandler, *The Art of Warfare in the Age of Marlborough*, (Staplehurst, 1976) pp. 179-81.

48 A townland is a traditional small geographical division of land still used in Ireland as a whole. The divisions are Gaelic in origin and most pre-date even the Norman invasion. Some of the townland boundaries have been changed with subsequent plantations. In 2014, over 61,000 Irish townlands were recognised across the island.
49 All local knowledge is based on correspondence and conversation with B.Chapman and B.Lyttle of Newtownbutler, and V.Herbert of Crom Estate between July 1998 and May 1999. Kilgarret Hill is cited by Trimble as the battlefield location. Successive secondary sources are non-specific as far as possible.
50 Hamilton, p. 60.
51 Public Record Office, Lt Durnford, *Ordnance Survey Memoirs*, Gallon, Co. Fermanagh, (1835), p.37.

Chapter VIII: Escape from Enniskillen

1 D'Avaux, p.73, to Louvois 14 August 1689.
2 Hamilton pp.63-4, MacCarmick p.45 .
3 D'Avaux, p.462 to Louis 7 Sept 1689.
4 Mainly d'Avaux, *Negotiations,* pp.385, 534-5, 539, 538-9, 590, 613, 636.
5 D'Avaux, p.462.
6 D'Avaux, p.590.
7 O'Callaghan, *History of the Irish Brigades in the Service of France*, pp.23-4.
8 D'Avaux, p.636
9 D'Avaux, p.636
10 Boylan, *Dictionary of National Biography*, pp. 135-7, 323-4; Ed. Charles Dalton, *English Army Lists and Commission Registers 1661-1714 (2 vols)*, (London 1960), pp.32,37,141,15, 25,125,132. John D'Alton, *King James' Irish Army List 1689*, (Dublin 1855), p. 10; John Childs, *Nobles, Gentlemen and the Profession of Arms in Restoration Britain 1660-1688*, (Society for Army Historical Research, 1987).

Chapter IX: A Return to France

1 Fumeron laid most of the blame on Hamilton, but also raised issues over Mountcashel's handling of the affair. See: *La Guerre*, A1 Vol 893, Fumeron to Louvois; *La Guerre*, A1 Vol 894 no.15, Mountcashel to Louvois Feb 1689; *La Guerre* 960, Louvois to MacCarthy, Feb 1689; *Analecta Hibernica*, Vol XXI p.27.
2 *La Guerre*, A1 Vol 1066, Sarsfield to Mountcashel February 1691; *La Guerre*, A1 Vol 1066, Sarsfield to Mountcashel March 1691; *La Guerre*, A1 Vol 1109, Mountcashel to Louis August 1691.
3 *La Guerre*, A1 Vol 892, de Rosen to Louvois May 1689; MacPherson Vol I pp.176,190; d'Avaux p.142
4 D'Avaux, p.531.
5 D'Avaux, p.519; Also see d'Avaux pp.287, 300, 515, 520, 584
6 D'Avaux, p.635.

7 D'Avaux p.590.
8 Lynn, *Giant of the Grand Siecle*, pp. 331, 366; Lynn, *The Wars of Louis XIV*, pp. 49,178.
9 O'Conor, pp.98-9.
10 D'Avaux, p.688.
11 D'Avaux, p.689.
12 Boulger, pp.208-12; O.Conor, p.98.
13 Boulger, p.215.
14 O'Conor, pp.98-9.
15 Boulger, p.215.
16 D'Avaux, p.658. Letters in *La Guerre* also outline the dispositions of the Irish troops at Brest. See: A1 Vol 961 May 1690, Seignelay to Louvois April 1690, ans Vol 1082 *Etats des Soldats des Regiments Irlandoise*, May 1690.
17 Boulger, p.216; Hamilton, pp.31-8, MacCarmick, pp.35-41, Trimble, pp.408-9; Ed. Maguire, *Kings in Conflict*, (Belfast 1990), p.62.
18 For best references to 'War of Grand Alliance' or 'Nine Years War' see: Lynn, *The Wars of Louis XIV*, (1999); Lynn, *Giant of the Grand Siècle, The French Army, 1610-1715*, (1997); John Childs, *Warfare in the Seventeenth Century*, (2001).

Chapter X: The Wild Geese

1 Rousset Vol. IV pp.6, 24, 28; Lynn pp.179-81, O'Conor p.209, Childs p.184, Boulger p.218.
2 *La Guerre*, Vol. 1066 Sarsfield to Mountcashel Feb & Mar 1691; *La Guerre*, Vol 1080 Mountcashel to Louis Aug 1691; *La Guerre*, Vol 1080 Mountcashel to Louis Aug 1691;Macpherson p.233; Simms p.158-73; Petrie, *The Great Tyrconnel*, pp.215-29.
3 This quote is taken from O'Conor pp.100-1. More detailed information regarding the general history of this period can be obtained in Lynn pp.210-14; O'Callaghan pp.54-5; Boulger pp.217-20; Childs, *Warfare in the Seventeenth Century*, p.18; De Quincy Vol. II p.292; O'Callaghan, O'Conor and Boulger, their work stemming from the nineteenth century, do not give clear references, though their work seems for the most part to stem from de Quincy and letters from *de la Guerre*. O'Callaghan in particular gives additional details which do not appear in the remaining French archives – although his style does not use direct quotes, his dramatic descriptions of the terrain are excellent.
4 O'Conor pp.102-3, Boulger p.219, O'Callaghan p.55, de Quincy Vol. II p.304. Although Mountcashel's wound may have been slight, the nature of warfare and medicine needs to be taken into account.
5 *La Guerre*, Vol 1065 Louvois to Tyrconnel, Mar 1691.
6 Boulger p.219, O'Callaghan p.55-8; Lynn pp.214, 221; de Quincy Vol. II 437, 444; Also see in *La Guerre*, Louvois's letter to Tyrconnell in spring 1691 re. Requirement for 1,200 additional Irish recruits.

7 Lynn pp.236-8; O'Callaghan pp.32-3, 39; O'Conor pp.221, 224

8 *Calendar State Papers Domestic*, 1694-5, p.464 7 1697 p.354; Irish Record Commissioner's Reports, pp.373, 384-89.

9 Taken from *La France Littéraire (Paris 1905-07)* and reported in *The Journal of the Cork Historical and Archaeological Society* 1907 in the article, 'Justin MacCarthy Lord Mountcashel'.

10 MacPherson, pp.445-6.

11 O'Callaghan, p.39; O'Conor, p.224.

12 One example of this is cited in Patrick Bishop's *The Irish Empire* (1999) where Sarsfield is hailed as the leader of the Wild Geese and Mountcashel does not receive a mention. Otherwise this is an excellent work.

13 Dineen and O'Donoghue, *Dánta Aodhagáin Ui Rathaille*, (London 1911).

14 Lynn pp.263-5. John A.Lynn refers to this war as Louis's 'Great Miscalculation'.

15 Smith, pp.174-5; Complete Peerage, pp.216-17.

16 Sir Charles Petrie, The Marshal Duke of Berwick, The Picture of an Age (London 1953). Petrie's work is an excellent record of Berwick's life.

Index